LIFT Leadership is a must read for new and seasoned leaders alike. Randy Dewey does a remarkable job mixing his vast personal experiences as a CEO with fascinating up to date research, relatable case studies, interesting historical anecdotes and easy to understand and apply practical exercises. You will learn how to implement the LIFT principles and put them in action right away. If you are on a journey to becoming a better and more effective leader then I would highly recommend this book.

Stephen Clements
Currently- Business Advisor/Retail Coach- The Pace Network
Formerly- SVP/GM National Sports/Pro Hockey Life

WHEN THE UNTHINKABLE HAPPENS

How to Lead Your Team and Pivot Your Business for
GROWTH AND OPPORTUNITY

Randy L. Dewey

Published by Best Seller Publishing®, St. Augustine, FL

Best Seller Publishing® is a registered trademark

Printed in the United States of America.

ISBN: 978-1-956649-08-6

This publication is designed to provide accurate and authoritative information with regard to the subject matter covered. It is sold with the understanding that the publisher is not engaged in rendering legal, accounting, or other professional advice. If legal advice or other expert assistance is required, the services of a competent professional should be sought. The opinions expressed by the authors in this book are not endorsed by Best Seller Publishing® and are the sole responsibility of the author rendering the opinion.

For more information, please write:

Best Seller Publishing®

53 Marine Street

St. Augustine, FL 32084

or call 1 (626) 765-9750

Visit us online at: www.BestSellerPublishing.org

TABLE OF CONTENTS

ACKNOWLEDGMENTS

Alexander the Great once said, "My treasure lies in my friends." I would modify the quote to be "My treasure lies in my God, my family, and my friends" because they contributed to my life immensely—from top to bottom.

God, first and foremost, without any exception. Then, always, my family, starting with my amazing wife Christine, the countless times she gave me incredible and timely advice, unwavering support, years of managing the kids while I traveled the world, and worked endless hours. My eleven children, in so many ways, created an incredible home filled with love and support. They gave me so much to look forward to when I came home from so many long journeys. Thanks to Caleb, Rebecca, Chad, Victoria, Anna, Joshua, Jessica, Judah (2007), Chava, Mahalia, and Mathew. Kids are the true fountain of youth, and they gave me a lot to be thankful for and kept me young at heart. As well, to my inspiring Grandfather, Arie Vanderjagt, and my great parents, Lawrence and Ellen Dewey.

My friends and colleagues are many—I wish I had enough pages to list them all—but I'd like to name a few:

JCR provided immense opportunities for which I'll be forever grateful. Thanks for all the years of growth and the chance to contribute.

Dennis Sheptika and Ted Priddle took a chance on the long-haired college guy and supported me when I probably didn't deserve it. The commitment to helping me fuelled my rocket in the early days of my career. Thanks for your friendship and for cheering me on for 30 years.

Ida Goodreau, CEO of Fletcher Challenge, accepted a meeting request, back in the early nineties, from a total stranger—me, a young, eager HR fellow with a question on how to become a CEO—then, gracefully took the time to sit for hours and teach me. It made a deep imprint on my career.

Doug Hahn, RIP, was a gentle giant of a man, known for his talents as a leader and his tenacious spirit. He left us early but left a legacy and a significant impact on my life.

Harry Todd, in so many ways, taught me so much about life and business and mostly about how the two intersect. His ability to prioritize personal integrity while leading a business was an amazing testimony. I'll cherish our years together.

Tom Cochrane, RIP, you were an amazingly talented guy, unbelievable witty humor, and our friendship was special in so many ways. I will always appreciate his support and never letting me go until you were called home.

Derek Armstrong, we met many years ago, and I've appreciated your vision in marketing, and your contributions have made a big difference to me and the companies I've led. It's great to see your creative talents transcend industries and your abilities are exceptional.

Many others that helped me along the way: Ryan Robinson (2018), Mario Serratore, Gilles Vachon, Brian Hannan, Dan McNamara, Steve Foster, Tanya Dickson, John Garlick, Andre Heroux, Jim Hall, Dave Crowe, Tracey Prymmer, Doug Kelly….and so many more.

DISCLAIMER

After 15 years of corporate turnarounds, I came home and told my wife that our PE friends had another assignment for me. She turned lovingly and with a smile on her face said, "Wow, did you know that in 15 years of marriage, this is going to be the 15th move". Since that moment, another 15 years has also passed and though the moves slowed to a mere 5 it is interesting to remember and many of those years and moments in business and life are crystal clear and some fuzzy. As I've led literally a few dozen leadership teams in those 30 years we'll all have our own recollection of events. The work contains many wonderful and difficult memories and I've represented people and these events in the best possible way that I can remember. I have changed a few things to protect some people's privacy but please don't take any offense as I've not meant to hurt anyone in the things that I've written. The goal of this book is to take a unique career, full of incredible learnings, which has literally spanned the globe and to provide this generation of leader's insight and advice to better the business world. Using a term from the world of business, we are all WIP, and may my experiences and insights bring answers to some of your burning leadership questions. Please feel free to visit me at www.randydewey.com and leave me a note or comment.

REVIEWS FOR RANDY DEWEY

"Very few people could write a book like this one. It is rich with decades of successful turnaround stories about what made the difference between bankruptcy to sustainable success. Every executive and leader should read this book. Randy Dewey's examples of integrity-based leadership are admirable and inspiring."

Amanda Holmes, President and CEO, Chet Holmes International

"This is the most important business book of the year. Randy Dewey has taken the complexity out of navigating the unthinkable business crisis with his 100-day pivot so you can transform the crisis into strategic growth. If you are a C-suite executive, you must read this book!"

Kimjera Whittington, President and CEO, Evolve Marketing

"Randy brings together religious truths, juxtaposed against brutal conquerors and game winning sports tactics to deliver a message through his very diverse lens of experiences, shared insights, vision, extraordinary life and tough business decisions. Written in prose that is easy to consume, this is an invaluable "conversation" that was difficult to put down.

Having lived through many of Randy's experiences but only seeing the end result, this book was a revelation which explained the inner workings of the decisions made, problems solved and the critical thinking behind the decisions."

Daniel Kim, President, Satichi Consulting Inc.

"Randy's revealed #1 rule on successfully pivoting a company of "Never surrender to time … momentum cannot be underestimated", wonderfully underscores the urgency in which any aspiring or maturing C-Suite leader should embark on the extraordinary learning and mentorship journey provided by Randy in this book."

D'Arcy Newcomer – President, Dealer Source Inc.

"Randy addresses the real-life issues of change management, leadership and accountability. He inspires the reader to seek opportunity in adversity and find the path to success in the fog of corporate battle. In insisting on accountability, Randy forces leaders to look inside for strength, creativity, resolve and persistence in order to transform and shape circumstances. Leadership demands clarity, consistency and drive. Randy does not abide blame; leaders lead.

Having known Randy for over a decade, I can attest that he practices what he preaches and demands of himself before asking others. This book is genuine and the product of his hands-on experience and approach to life. Randy's style, of real-life examples and practicable suggestions as a means of illuminating his principles, makes the book an easy read as both a personal strategic plan and a handbook for dealing with difficult situations.

I recommend it to anyone who prefers to learn from the experience of a successful, thoughtful business leader."

Sagiv Shiv, M&A Investment Banker New York

"In my experience with turnarounds, I always thought about the challenge at hand being the shortage of 3 elements - time, talent and financial capital. Randy's LIFT leadership concept takes this idea to a new level for me, by providing a playbook for leaders to embrace the "what" and to get their heads around the "how."

Randy draws on his unique experiences as a hands-on operator – and proud family man - across a multitude of situations in multiple industries, to tease out the simple yet often hard to implement fundamentals and tactics that will unpack the complexity of The Turnaround.

The principles of this values-driven, people centric approach should be taught in business schools, and its handy models and checklists kept close by turnaround practitioners and business leaders alike."

Ian Brenner, Partner, A. Farber & Partners Inc.

"In "When the Unthinkable Happens", Randy Dewey provides a roadmap to success for any situation you find yourself in as a leader. Applying the L.I.F.T principles to all facets of business, Randy explains how this approach has been an integral part of his success as a CEO. This is a book that you first read as a novel, then you place it within arm's reach as a resource guide. When you have a situation to manage, you will find practical tools to assist you. If you are in any position of leadership in life, this book is for you."

Alan Dick, Principal, Impactful.ly

PRECURSOR

Ten company turnarounds taught me how to pivot the "unthinkable" into opportunities

---

After leading ten company turnarounds—adding over $1.8 billion in corporate value collectively—I learned one unequivocal fact: the "unthinkable" crisis is a cycle of "when" not "if." Embrace the resulting business pivots as an opportunity, or it will crush you in its grip. The secret of success is the fast pivot—no more than 100 days. To help ready you to manage the 100-day pivot, I distill my leadership success secret down to four critical methods, which I call "L.I.F.T."

"Unthinkable" crisis is an opportunity—stop the blame game

Over a decade ago, the "unthinkable" happened in my career. Government officials entered our building and ousted our C.E.O. from his position in a dramatic moment worthy of a movie. This crisis propelled me to "defacto bank president" of a newly chartered Canadian bank during the 2008 sub-prime financial crisis—a "battlefield promotion" with appalling potential consequences. One mistake, the government banking officials would shut us down. Fortunately, lessons learned over my decades of experience allowed me to steer the bank away from a meltdown.

At the time, the fear was palpable in the bank. Would we lose our bank license? Will the government shut us down? It is no exaggeration that this was the pinnacle high-pressure moment in my career. They don't teach these real-life scenarios in books or business school. The fire

1

of the crisis either tempers you or you are consumed by it. For myself and my team at the bank, there would be many sleepless nights ahead, many round-the-clock sessions in the meeting rooms, but we emerged a stronger institution at the end of the crisis.

This would not be my first crisis or my last.

What I've learned after ten corporate turnarounds is that "crisis is just opportunity."

Failure comes down to poor leadership. Period.

If you study failure case studies in business, the post-mortems usually reveal four recurring causes:

- lack of capital

- poor leadership

- unrealistic business plans

- weak marketing and publicity. [1]

You can add a dozen more reasons for business failure—but, in my experience, they all boil down to "poor leadership."

Even in the face of outside disasters—such as COVID-19, economic downturns, wars, pivotal technologies, and other disasters—failure still distills down to poor leadership. Why? Because good leaders should pro-actively anticipate the risks, build contingencies for those moments, amass stakeholder support, and execute well when facing a big crisis. The inability to manage a crisis is just poor leadership.

Ten Turnarounds taught me four methods I call L.I.F.T.

My history of ten business turnarounds taught me one inescapable truth—and four key methods.

The unavoidable truth is that in a crisis, the "enemy is time," regardless of the scenario. This is where the four methods—together with my practical map to your own Pivot in 100 Days (Chapter 15)—will weaponize you for your inevitable pivotal battles.

Faced with crisis, where the enemy is "time," the opportunity-oriented leader—the one who will lift the company to new heights—embraces the resulting business pivot as an opportunity for stunning, positive, and rapid change.

I call the four key methods I teach in this book—and their detailed methods and tactical maps—L.I.F.T., which stands for:

Lead with passion.

Inspire your people.

Focus on what makes lasting change.

Transform obstacles into opportunities.

These aren't just concepts. I teach, in these 15 chapters, practical methods to "LIFT" your own leadership and manage your own crisis. L.I.F.T. leadership methods are also the secret to avoiding preventable "unthinkable" situations. Embracing the spirit of leading with passion, inspiring your team, focusing on lasting change, and transforming obstacles will make you ready to face crisis and fast-pivot when needed.

L.I.F.T.: Looking for Opportunity

The L.I.F.T.-oriented leader looks for opportunities, not only when there is a crisis. An underlying principle of Lead, Inspire, Focus, Transform is adeptness. The one thing you can count on is momentum. Either you create it—or you are tossed around in a metaphorical storm, not of your making.

In the "Covid-19 Crisis" we saw companies converting production lines to masks and ventilators and other health and personal protection products. Content and technology companies such as Alphabet, Facebook, and Zoom exploited the "stay at home" orders, streamlining operations and tapping new markets. Investors steered their money in emerging markets, tapping into sudden opportunities. Clearly, in these dire circumstances—and, I would argue, in any business pivot situation—the fast pivot was a matter of necessity. Companies with cumbersome, slow-moving leadership were unable to maneuver their ungainly "ships" in these stormy waters.

What I've learned in three decades of business turnarounds is that any crisis is an opportunity—and that transformation is only the beginning of the story.

Leading with passion, **I**nspiring the team, and laser-tight **F**ocus are the facilitators of crucial **T**ransformation. Leaders never throw up their hands and give up. In a crisis, real leaders are already working on inspiring the team to focus on a solution.

L.I.F.T. your Leadership—all or nothing?

This book shows you how I do it. It's up to you to adapt these methods to your situation and leadership style. The one thing I can assure you is that top growth leaders always **L**ead with passion, **I**nspire their people, **F**ocus on what makes lasting change, and **T**ransform obstacles into opportunities for growth.

All four of these leadership characteristics are vital. Not three. Four. **I**nspiration—the great "patented idea" or business concept—by itself can still fail if you don't **F**ocus on your stakeholders. Even if you're **F**ocused, are you ready to **T**ransform the inevitable obstacles from competitors and markets?

The bottom line is this. You need all four—**L**eadership, **I**nspiration, **F**ocus, **T**ransformation—to see rapid and sustained growth. The key to success in the opportunity pivot—in addition to these leadership methods—is adeptness. Planning around timelines of less than 100 days ensures you can meet any target or overcome any crisis. You, the captain of your ship, need to drill your crew and build an efficient, insightful, and motivated team. The key to surviving any storm is not your ship. It is your crew, led by an inspired and focused captain. Thirty years of experience in the corporate turnaround world has taught me this and more.

The formula of Leadership—no luck needed

Even though I talk the language of "inspiration" and "transformation," the L.I.F.T. method is more formula and method than luck and creativity. I can show you how I have successfully repeated these proven methods with ten separate companies over the last thirty years. In the final chapter, I even share my 100-day secret—precisely how to map your rapid business pivot. First, though, lay the foundation for a motivated crew with L.I.F.T. leadership.

You can easily exploit my techniques, assuming you always remember that all four areas of this method are necessary—the four pillars that support your success. I will explain in more detail, topic by topic, with variations by application and situation, but these four principles can be summarized this way:

Lead with passion.

Inspire your people.

Focus on what makes lasting change.

Transform obstacles into opportunities.

Why do I say, "no luck needed?" Because we make our own luck. I am typically brought into companies only when there is a significant need for a turning point. In other words, to deal with a crisis. Historically, in most of the ten turnarounds I've faced, we started in a "negative" position, or at least where we expected a substantial turnaround. Luck is not a factor.

Hard work is not even the primary factor. In most turnaround situations, time is critical. Smart work—following the four fundamental principles of L.I.F.T.—will predictably bring success.

The leader—you—must be the smart, inspirational coach for your team. As a coach, you can inspire the team to make great plays. To do this, one more thing is needed. Ethical Leadership is a centerpiece of L.I.F.T. I start and end this book with methods anchored in Ethical Leadership and Compassion. Why? Because no team wants to play for a coach who isn't genuinely on their side and who doesn't embody what they believe.

Above all—Ethical "Principled" Leadership

As much as my passion is creating great companies that last—I am, above all, driven by the guidelines of principled and ethical leadership and good business practices.

How can you **L**ead with Passion, without a clear conscience? How do you **I**nspire the team to face any crisis without principled leadership? How can you **F**ocus on sustained change without standards, virtues, and values? **T**ransformation depends on the credo of moral values.

It is for this reason that I begin and end this book with the theme of Principled Leadership. The term Ethical Leadership is a little "tired" and often misinterpreted. It implies an imposed societal ethic. While society's ethics are essential, what I mean by Principled Leadership is a company that has stated values and published values. It is up to your team and your stakeholders, including customers, to buy into the stated values. The closer your Principle Values are to the ethical standards of society, the wider your audience. (You'll also sleep better at night.) However, as you'll see from my "Reflections from the Conqueror" feature in each chapter, even Conquerors have their principles.

Your obligation is to fulfill these principles without exception. L.I.F.T. is a "success" leadership method inextricably bound up in the ideal of Principled Leadership. To "**L**ead with passion," you must believe in the stated principles. To "**I**nspire the team" requires they feel enthusiastic about these same principles. To "**F**ocus on lasting change" requires collective goals and principles. To "**T**ransform obstacles into opportunities" requires these goals.

L.I.F.T. Leadership is an implementation method for Principled Leaders.

What's in each chapter

Busy business leaders need to tap into information quickly. I've organized each of the fifteen chapters for quick access. In most chapters, you'll find these features:

In this chapter

- A summary of the top five points in each chapter

Important Take-away

- If you only take away one thing, remember this.

Reflections from The Conqueror

- *Insights from the ruthless Conqueror Mehmed (More on Mehmed in a moment.)*

Real-life L.I.F.T. Values Case Study

- One real-life case study to illustrate the guidance.

L.I.F.T. exercises, forms, and formulas

- Most chapters have multiple interactive forms or exercises that summarize, illustrate, or concisely map the chapter's key points. Don't miss the "one-page" plan and the "Are you Crisis Ready?" exercises.

Chapter 15—the all-important tactical chapter with my 100-Day how-to—breaks this pattern, focusing instead on a step-by-step, day-by-day guide or tactical map. This serves the important mission of accomplishing needed transformation rapidly, mindful of the real enemy—Time.

Why listen to Randy Dewey's advice?

A little about myself may help you decide how much weight to give my advice. Not all of my leadership adventures are as dramatic as the bank crisis I mentioned, but all were exciting and challenging. I don't deserve the credit—that goes to my teams—but I do know how to "bring out their best."

Nine of the ten companies I "pivoted" to the next level of success are still growing today. Collectively, we've added nearly two billion dollars in value to these companies.

I have been a part of many companies over the past 30 years, worked in over 32 countries, and flown over a million miles to keep inspiring my teams and driving change and transforming companies through some of the most interesting business pivots. [For more on my life and career, see the About Randy Dewey page at www.randydewey.com.]

Lessons from the Conqueror?

You might wonder why each chapter has a small section titled "Reflections from the Conqueror"?

Why use the example of Mehmed the Conqueror—a brutal leader who impaled his enemies—to illustrate exemplary leadership? While Mehmed can be thought of as a mass killer, who brought the Roman Empire to its knees, he was, to his people, an inspiring leader who rose from the status as "son of a **slave**" to become the Conqueror of much of the world of his time.

Mehmed transformed all his obstacles into opportunities for victory.

To his own "team" he was a leader they would die for, but he was a ruthless monster to his enemies. He inspired trust in his team. He was famous for "walking the line" before a battle, greeting each of his thousands of soldiers. His example *L.I.F.T.*ed up his team, inspired them to such fervor they achieved the impossible. And the rest is history. Constantinople fell. The Roman Empire died.

War has long been a favorite metaphor in business. *The Art of War*, by Sun Tzu, is an enduring classic. If you put aside the killing, torture, and fanaticism, there are lessons to be learned from the conquerors of history, especially Alexander the Great and his posthumous student Mehmed the Conqueror.

How did Mehmed—and Alexander before him—achieve this? I'll cover the history of Mehmed in more detail in an appendix, but his principles could distill down to what I call L.I.F.T.:

"Lead with Passion. Inspire your people. Focus on what makes lasting change. Transform obstacles into opportunities."

Conquering hearts and minds

I'm going to deliberately use the word "Conqueror" as a persistent reminder that business leaders need to focus on leading not only in their industry; they must "lead the troops"—your team—in an inspirational way. They don't just conquer the unwilling and "enemies—in our metaphor, competitors or prospective customers—but they also conquer the hearts and minds of their own team. In history, conquerors were brutal, yet, almost universally—including the likes of Mehmed and Genghis Khan—they were heroes and champions to their own people.

While business does entail some moments of ruthlessness, great leaders also have compassion. Conqueror leadership, in our context, refers to inspiring leadership, strategies, and inspiration, not brutality. The "Conqueror" style of leadership brings with it eight critical principles. And, the greatest among them is "conduct" and values. Alexander the Great said that his greatest treasure was his friends and that above all —

"Remember upon the conduct of each depends the fate of all."

Alexander the Great was clear that victory came at any cost while doing the right thing and that your enemy's behavior didn't dictate yours.

Mehmed and Alexander's "principles" can be summed up in four essential methods. Taken together, I call this L.I.F.T. leadership: Lead, Inspire, Focus, then Transform. These management methods can work for any company or brand.

In Brief: the Brutal Story

How a Brutal Dictator Used *L.I.F.T.* to Conquer Much of the Known World

In 1452, 21-year old King Mehmed II brought the Roman Empire under Constantine XI to its knees. He was the son of a slave in the royal harem of the Ottoman royal family. He was second in line for the throne—but a long-shot for an emperor. To make his mark as the son of a slave, he embraced excellence—the example of the long-deceased Alexander the Great. Though he was quasi-exiled by his father, the King, he used this time to sharpen his leadership skills and prepare himself to be King. He studied every battle of Alexander. He learned all there was to know of Alexander.

As any business leader would today, he set a goal—in his case, the nearly impossible: the fall of Constantinople. The great city had resisted twelve major attacks to the shame of the Ottomans. With this lofty goal in mind, he studied every past failure, learning from their mistakes. And, he learned how to **Lead**—with undeniable passion. He **Inspired** loyalty and motivated his followers. He **Focused** on his one goal, the fall of the iconic walled-city of Constantinople, with a vision for long-lasting change—in his case, the growth of his empire. He **Transformed** countless obstacles into opportunities. He applied all of these principles not only to his overall vision—but to each battle and situation.

On April 6th, 1453, King Mehmed II led the Ottoman Army to attack the 1100-year-old City of Constantinople. After a harrowing 53-day siege, the upstart Mehmed, against all odds, delivered the final blow to the 1500-year Roman Empire.

Like any great conqueror—the likes of Alexander and Genghis Khan—he Led with passion, Inspired his troops, Focused on a goal, and Transformed the world. In his mind, he was true to his values.

Today's transformative business leaders follow a similar pattern—Lead, Inspire, Focus, and Transform. In this book, I'll show you how.

I would strongly encourage you to read Mehmed's fascinating story and how he used L.I.F.T. methods to power his conquest. See the Appendix – Mehmed II, The Conqueror.

1

LEAD: "PRINCIPLED LEADERSHIP" —VISION AND VALUES

"Winners never cheat"—principle values that drive business

"The purpose of business is not to make profit. The purpose of business is to produce profitable solutions for the problems of people."
—Jay Jakub, Mars[2]

L.I.F.T. Fact

Would you be surprised to discover that publicly-traded companies with strong principle values perform ten times better than the overall S&P 500 index—according to the Harvard Business Review? These companies are characterized as "Conscious Capitalist" companies—a new wave of businesses, led by principled leaders, shaking up many sectors.

Whether you view principle values as a meaningful ethical guidepost in business or as a "strategy" to dominate the market, companies who ignore ethics underperform the average substantially.

In this chapter

- Principle values are critical—and why companies that ignore their values underperform: "Companies that Practice "Conscious Capitalism" Perform 10x Better."[3]

- Why "principled leaders" who embody "principle values" win, especially in times of crisis.

- How the principled leader bonds with the team over values—game-changing moments that can define and empower your company's course.

- How you can use values to create a "Conscious Capitalism" culture and brand, ready to face any crisis.

Important Take-away

- **"Principle values have tangible power in business."**

Reflections from the Conqueror

- *"Remember upon the conduct of each depends the fate of all."—Alexander the Great*

The Principle Values of L.I.F.T.

Principle values and vision go to the heart of all aspects of L.I.F.T.
Lead: Vision and principle values define the entire brand and company.
Inspire: Ethics and principle values inspire team-members and customers.
Focus: The top-level objective of focus is a mission—driven by principled values.
Transform: To transform a company requires the entire team to act as one, united by mission and principle values.

Even brutal and bloody historical conquerors can unite armies under common values. Mehmed, the Conqueror, didn't miraculously raise an enthusiastic army, ready to take on the remnants of the once-great Roman Empire. He very precisely weighed the strengths and weaknesses of his followers. He embodied the words of his mentor Alexander the Great: "Remember upon the conduct of each depends the fate of all." He might have been a conqueror, but he was no petty, unloved dictator. His followers adored him. Why? Because he inspired them with principle values and a mission.

In business—where our armies are salespeople, logistics people, accountants, engineers, designers, and executives—we face the same challenge. To transform our people into an enthusiastic team requires common "principle values."

Principle values naturally align with our broader ethics—shared ideals such as honesty and loyalty, and trust—but the key to principles is that they are truthfully stated. If your stated values align with your audiences and your team members, you will inspire loyalty and develop leadership in your segment. Even if your values are very narrow and uncommon—such as "super luxury for the one percent"—that's still a "principle value" as long as you, your customers, and your team believe it…highly unlikely you'll get to consensus on that one. Still, nevertheless, by definition, it could be stated. Principle values require brutal honesty and must be defined.

Once you discover and state your principle values, they are cardinal. Your leadership must embody these core principles.

Actual L.I.F.T. values case study—
"Winners never cheat."

Transforming "I don't want to cheat" into "Winners never cheat."

What do I mean by "discover and state your principle values?" As a specialist in "turnarounds," I am always challenged and confronted with obstacles. I am usually brought in because there are problems. In many cases, they boil down to a lack of transparent principle values. In other words, the team itself doesn't know exactly how to answer, "What are our principle values?"

In one of my earlier company take-overs, it was critical to bring together the new team to discover their principle values. We needed a simple and actionable values statement—crafted as a team and not dictated by one leader.

I took the first step in L.I.F.T.—*Leading* with passion—by pulling together my group in a town hall meeting format. Although my goal was to *Inspire* the team, we immediately became stuck on the third step, *Focus*. We knew the problem—but not the why. There was a literal elephant in the room—but it remained hidden. Without *Focus*, we couldn't move forward to the final step, *Transform*.

I knew right away that the management group became uncomfortable with the brainstorming exercise. The tension was evident on every face in the room. They were hiding the issue—because they were ashamed of it.

Everyone knows the problem

Finally, during a break, an executive pulled me aside at the coffee table and whispered, "Everyone here knows the problem. The bottom line is that we buy our sales. Nobody wants to say it with the V.P. of Sales in the room."

I faced a difficult decision at that moment. Do I deal with the elephant now, with the group, or take my time and handle it more discretely? Charging the elephant head-on might offend or embarrass the V.P. of Sales. Since time was of the essence, I decided to face the issue now in the group.

I called the meeting to order and told the interesting story of a company who "bought" their sales with under-the-table incentives. I didn't confront anyone. In the town hall, I asked the group, "Hypothetically, do you think this practice is sustainable?"

For a long while, there was only silence—and the shifting of people in their seats. Finally, I said, "Anyone? Don't hold back. What do you think?"

Finally, the V.P. of Sales jumped in, "It's complicated in our market. I've worked in this segment for a while, so I look at it a bit differently." He tried to explain what was going on, attempting to justify past practices, especially in light of immense sales target pressures.

No one criticized him directly. But, for the next hour, I unpacked the problem with everyone watching—trying not to embarrass our V.P. I asked, "So, we know this is an issue. What other options do we have?" With the problem stated clearly, the team came together, inspired to find solutions.

I don't want to cheat

At one point, one team member said, "I don't want to cheat." The implication was clear. No one wants to cheat, but it seemed to be "expected" in the industry.

As a team, we Focused, working through this moral dilemma.

Were there other ways to close the business? Does it matter that all our competitors do it? I was surprised and beyond happy when it became clear the team had decided together to exemplify the value:

"Winners never cheat."

At the end of it all, it seemed so obvious; payoffs in any form are unethical and not consistent with good business practice. There were other ways to close the deals. No need for blame. Just—what do we do to fix it?

The real work started at that moment. We now had a shared "principle value" to uphold as a team. We had agreed to it together. We now stood for it together. It made us a team, an enthusiastic team, but the stakes were high. To uphold our principle value—"winners never cheat"—we had to withdraw a previously-promised lavish gift for a Procurement Manager. The situation was awkward, not only because the gift had been promised but also because these incentives and gifts were customary in that industry.

To uphold our agreed new principle value, we had to stop the practice immediately—not at some future date.

We arranged to meet the Procurement Manager. I explained the situation and asked him to offer us a solution to our ethical dilemma.

Suffice to say, we endured several hours of threats and a staggering display of furious venting. We listened, but we didn't back down. We just kept repeating, to ourselves, the new principle value, "Winners never cheat."

Finally, when it was clear there was no solution, I politely withdrew from the bid process. I let him know we'd like to continue serving them as a supplier, but we needed to reset the ground rules.

Sales dropped 15 percent

We lost the bid. We lost all other bids for the next three months. Our sales dropped fifteen percent. It was a difficult time—but I knew it was the right thing to do.

In the fourth month, I received a call from the C.E.O. of that company. He invited me to Detroit for a meeting. The Procurement Manager's frantic efforts internally to de-source us and pull us off the approved supplier list was noticed by the C.E.O., who requested my presence in Detroit for clarification—although, at the time, I assumed it was a post-mortem exit meeting.

At our meeting, he asked me to explain what has happened to the relationship. Although I assumed the worst, I felt I should abandon diplomacy and directly explain why we withdrew. I didn't accuse anyone of misdeeds. I simply explained our team's principle value in business and how our team collectively decided on transparency and honesty, and that we would not be offering gifts or incentives. I prepared to go home, empty-handed but satisfied I did the right thing.

"I'm glad you told me," the C.E.O. said. "I find your team's enthusiasm for ethics inspiring." He explained that our stance with the Procurement Manager—and his subsequent aggressive actions to de-source us—triggered a whistleblower to come forward. The complaint led to the discovery of several unacceptable practices. The day before I met with this C.E.O., the Procurement Manager had been terminated.

The C.E.O. also gave me the good news that they removed us from the de-source list, and, for our "pain and suffering," he gave us extra business for the next several months to make up for what we lost in the previous ninety days. I was in awe and over-the-top grateful.

Talk of the town

Even though we tried to keep the situation quiet, our company was the "talk of the town"—how we, as a team, painfully took a stand for what is right, didn't look to embarrass our customer, and bowed out politely. The painful loss and lesson turned into a humble victory for our team, even though it sparked a cascading of issues and unlocked many other behavioral problems within our own company.

Now, team-members came forward with other issues, one after another. As we worked together to **T**ransform obstacles, they began to feel empowered and **I**nspired as a team. They knew we stood by our collective principle values—and that we were willing to face the difficulties and **T**ransform any obstacle together.

In less than a year, we unraveled and corrected many issues—with an eighty percent positive outcome on each issue we tackled together. In the end, our business grew 25 percent in the first year—and our reputation in the industry climbed substantially.

The lesson learned: principle values in action result in growth. Aspiring to grow is never enough. It is only when the team collectively stands on principles that they act to accomplish and sustain growth goals with inspiring enthusiasm.

Why values are critical: the "Principled Leader"

All four aspects of the L.I.F.T. Leadership System rely on principle values. You can't **L**ead with passion if *you* don't believe. You can't **I**nspire the team if *they* don't believe. You can't **F**ocus on a crisis if your core principles do not guide you.

Andrew Hewitt of Game Changers 500 explained, "With this huge gap between societal values and corporate values, it's no wonder that purpose-driven organizations are far outperforming the pack. Doing good has become good business, not only because of changing consumer values but also because good companies attract the top talent..." In other words, Principled Leadership is not just the right thing to do—it's equally the profitable thing to do.[4]

Conscious Capitalism is about profit, not just ethics

Conscious Capitalism goes to the heart of Principle Values. As R. Michael Anderson explains in *The Four Principles of 'Conscious Capitalism'*:

> *"If you had a chance to implement a system that would bring in 10 times more profit than similar firms in your market, would your first thought be... What part of your soul you'd have to sell?... The truth is that by doing business the right way—being truly authentic, sticking wholeheartedly to your ethics and morals, and caring more*

about your customers and employees than your shareholders—you can achieve that gain without losing your soul."[5]

The concept of "principle values" is not new—although many leaders and companies give it no better than "lip-service." All companies have, or should have, a "values statement" and a "mission statement." Yet, in real life, especially when a leader or a company hits a crisis, it's the last thing the team embraces. Economic crisis or disaster tend to trigger panic decisions and tactics that "temporarily" ignore essential values.

Why leaders who embody core values win

According to Gallup, "only one in 10 people possess the unique combination of talents needed to effectively manage."[6] Probably less than 10 percent of those, or one in 100, can rise to executive leadership. That same report, which covers data from 2.5 million manager-led teams, summarizes the qualities of great leaders this way:

"Great managers possess a rare combination of five talents. They motivate their employees, assert themselves to overcome obstacles, create a culture of accountability, build trusting relationships and make informed, unbiased decisions for the good of their team and company."

Interesting language, isn't it? "Culture of accountability" and "building trusting relationships," and "for the good of their team and the company." In other words: Principled Leadership and Core Values.

While you could say that a company without a unified set of core values is like a metaphorical ship without a compass, it is equally important that the ship has a principled leader at the helm. Well-articulated core values—stated on the website and plaques on the wall—aren't enough. The entire team, and especially the leader, must embody those core values.

In my opening case study, "Winners Never Cheat," my team and I developed our principle values, then backed it by withdrawing our lucrative supplier contract when it didn't meet that standard. Although we hemorrhaged sales for a short time, we grew exponentially once our client understood our principles.

The key is consistency. Yes, you must sleep at night—but it's also important to be open, transparent, and consistent with all your stake-holders. Once you decide on your guiding principle values, you, as the leader, need to make it part of the real culture—not just fancy words on the website.

Do you believe in corporate conscience? You and the team are the company's conscience—and it is that sense of right and wrong that attracts like-minded ethical customers, suppliers and investors, and future employ-ees. It's not only about accountability; core values *are* the culture of your corporation and brand.

Live it, not only at work

The values-based corporate culture guides by intention, action, and performance. Good intentions are not enough. It starts, of course, with the principled leader—the best kind of L.I.F.T. executive. The leader should guide by example first, not by rules and police-state rigidity. Do you remember our military subject, the brutal conqueror Mehmed? He was famous for chatting with his troops, walking the line before a battle, asking about their families. He valued his team.

Yes, the principled L.I.F.T. leader has to be willing to enforce core values. But you also have to have a bond with your team. Like Mehmed, you have to "walk the line." As I demonstrated in my chapter case study, you start with a team-process, team debate, and many questions. Let your team solve it if possible—bonding with them.

The best tip I can give principled leaders of "conscious capitalist" eth-ical companies is—live your core values. If you genuinely believe in your values, you'll tend to embody them in all you do. You'll attract clients who respect your values.

Values and ethics have been influential in business for decades. Do you remember the 1990's, when corporations went through the values, mission, and vision statement process? I remember well those high-sounding meetings and the fancy wall plaques. I also remember it was almost always an academic exercise, quickly forgotten in the pressures of "real world" business. The secret to a "working" principled values process that is actually used in your business is to base it on the team's consensus, state it clearly, make it realistic, then enforce it—as we did in my first case study, by being willing to resign our agreement.

A word of caution—Principles have Power

If a business has either not established their values or abandoned their values, then be aware of these important facts:

1. The conduct of your employees will only be guided by their own personal values. Expecting any other standard would be unreasonable.

2. Chaos is inevitable when you haven't set out corporate principles. It's irrational in this case to expect organized, systematic and consistent results.

3. Don't assume unified responses between departments or divisions or affiliated companies if you have no standards and values. Leaders in one department may drive one standard, and leaders in another take a different direction.

4. To make matters worse, if serious value compromising actions become tolerated or encouraged by one group over another— then there can be tensions, animosity, and conflict between these groups.

5. Competing values and cultures between groups or departments may not only be challenging to manage—they will almost certainly impact the bottom line.

Even if your company is not overly socially conscious—although I'd argue it should be—you still can thrive if you at least have common, stated, transparent principle values. I'm not espousing a lack of ethics in favor of consistent values, but I am saying that it is vital everyone is working to the same principles.

What about social ethics? Yes!

Let's be practical. Principle values are about consistency and productivity. But, regardless of your personal beliefs, corporations should also embrace societal values and ethics. Consistently, in survey after survey, consumers expect companies to "act on social and environmental issues." I mentioned the revenue upside earlier in this chapter, with the Harvard article that demonstrated ten times revenue potential for "conscious capitalist" companies—or, what we used to call "socially responsible corporations." On the consumer side, most studies demonstrate consumer preferences for "Corporate Social Responsibility" or C.S.R.:

- 2017 Cone C.S.R. Study: 86 percent of U.S. consumers expect companies to act on social and environmental issues.[7] More importantly, 76 percent in the same survey would refuse to do business with a company that held views that conflicted with their own beliefs.

- In a three-year study, organizations with a commitment to C.S.R. enjoyed up to 19 times higher returns.[8]

- Many studies support the notion that companies who embrace C.S.R. are superior recruiters. Susan Cooney of Symantec (quoted in Forbes) said, "The next generation of employees is seeking out employers that are focused on the triple bottom line: people, planet and revenue."

L.I.F.T. Fives: Five ways to bond with your team over Principles

We cannot expect everyone to have the same principles, but a company with a clearly stated "Core Principle Values" Statement will attract people who embrace those values. For this reason, "Core Principle Values" should not be about enforcement, punishment, and criticism. Instead, use values to build a bond with your team. We tend to embrace like-minded friends. This isn't about being narrow-minded. It's about sharing common values.

Later in this chapter, I offer a L.I.F.T. Exercise to help you bond with your team over Principles. Aside from this specific exercise, the five ways to bond over Principles are:

1. Transparency and communication

In the previously mentioned Gallup study, 12 percent of employees strongly agree that their manager helps them "set work priorities," and only 13 percent agree their manager helps them perform. In the same study, it's worth noting, 50 percent left a job to "get away from their manager."[9] That's fairly pathetic, isn't it? To **L**ead, **I**nspire, **F**ocus, **T**ransform your team, you need to work closely with your people, communicate your plans, guide them, and, above all, meet with them regularly. You don't need to be friends—but you do need to communicate and embrace transparency. Does it work out that way in corporations? Most emphatically, no! Based on a July 2020 survey of 1000 full-time employees[10]:

- only 15 percent of employees are satisfied with the quality of communications in their companies

- only 15 percent believe their managers give them "highly valuable" feedback.

2. Opportunities and incentives

Your team is motivated by the same things: your opportunities to advance or be recognized and incentives to perform. Incentives to perform aren't always financial. People feel rewarded when their managers listen to them (see point 1), when they are praised, and when they are proud of their employer. Many team members are motivated by opportunities to develop professionally.

3. Life outside of work

I'll focus on this a little more in a future chapter, but I'm a keen believer in taking the time to get to know your team outside of work. Who do they care about? Employees are people with families, friends, interests, hobbies, favorite sports teams, and passions outside of work. Ask yourself:

- What do I know about my team members?

- What are my team member's professional goals?

- What sports and activities do my team members enjoy?

- What do you know about their family?

- What do they do when their workday finishes?

- When was the last time you socialized with your team members outside of work?

This isn't about personal-intrusion or stripping away your team member's privacy. It's about showing interest and engaging without being invasive.

4. Support and help

Yes, your team is there to help the company. You, the leader, are also there to offer direction (not commands), support, help, and guidance. Teaching moments fill every day. In that Gallup Poll, we cited (under 1 above), only 12 percent of employees "strongly agree" that their manager helped them set quarterly goals and priorities. Every company and every manager should strive for 100 percent. If you aren't helping them set quarterly goals and priorities, what are you doing with your time?

Setting goals and priorities—then achieving them—is how your team feels truly rewarded in their career. They can do it on their own, but if you're not offering support and help as a leader, you're not setting a good example as a leader.

5. Appreciation—say thanks!

We all want appreciation and gratitude, not only from family, friends, and significant others—but from our managers. As a society, we expect it, thanks in no small measure to our schools and our passion for sports. Sports teaches children not only respect and achievement but also the value of appreciation and praise. In a feature in *Entrepreneur Magazine*[11], they cited a report that indicated 86 percent of employees rated hearing "thank-you" at work as a significant factor in happiness with their employer. Such a simple thing. It costs nothing to say thank-you.

Values are the "Rules of Engagement" in the "Battle" for business

Even though the "battle for business" is possibly an overused metaphor, it is never-the-less precise. In line with this metaphor, I think of business core values or principles as "Rules of Engagement" in the business "war."

The US Marines defines Rules of Engagement (R.O.E.) as: "those directives that delineate the circumstances and limitations under which United States (U.S.) forces will initiate and/or continue combat **engagement**."[12]

In our case, the combat engagement is about the "fight" for business, for the deal, for our employee's well-being, for the investor-return. The Business Dictionary defines them as "practices or behavior displayed by participants in situations of opposing interests, such as negotiations." Like the marines, we cannot engage in this business combat without our own form of R.O.E. In the case of the Marines, the stakes are the country. In the case of the manager in business, it might be the company.

The company's brand is bound up in its values. To erode those values will have a corrosive effect on the brand, and ultimately, the company.

In other words, the company's principles, once defined, are not just guidelines—and not only a page on the website—they stand for the brand itself.

I call it —

The Power of Principles.

As I illustrated in the first case study, when you discover one of your team-members has breached the Rules of Engagement, you can remedy the situation.

How to turn your Principles into a tangible, marketable culture and brand

Principle Values are not intangible aspirations. They are powerful—the Power of Principles. Expressed as words, they manifest tangibly. They are bound up in the very brand and culture of your company. To manifest principle values, I suggest:

- **Value is a soft word**. Use something more concrete, like "Principle Values," or just "Principles," or even "Rules of Engagement."

- **Put your "Principles" in writing**. It should be the first thing a new employee reads when they join. It should be reinforced everywhere—in proposals, on the website, on the team intranet, on the boardroom wall.

- **Principles bring clarity and comfort**. In business, where goals are often numeric and competitive, it's easy to fall into a "win-at-all-costs ruthlessness" that can create adverse outcomes to both company culture and the bottom line. Make numbers and competition a part of the goals—but not its only focus. Remember, in the first case study, we gave up significant business to stand on Principle.

- **Principles start at the top**. You set the example. There is no better training than a leader who exemplifies the principles of the company.

- **Principle values are about accountability**. Formal training, tough decisions, re-affirmation, and calling out sub-standard behaviors will be necessary. Principle values need accountability, or else they become words on the wall.

- **Principle values, stated as words, have power.** They express who we are, who we want to be, and how we want our company to act with every stakeholder. It's like the ten commandments of company culture.

- **Principle values are equity positions, not mutable standards**. Values are not an exercise we repeat every year when we do the budget. In the first case study, you read how we changed our values—but this was a required change triggered by past abuse. Once you state the Principles, they are sacrosanct.

- **Principle Values should be everywhere**: print them on the wall, on your budget, on your strategic plan, on your email footers, on your employee handbooks, on your lobby wall. Equally, incorporate Principle Values into your hiring protocols and your internal performance appraisal process.

L.I.F.T. exercise: The Power of Principles

Venting without fear is the first step to common values.

If you find yourself in a situation where the company's principle values are not stated, or incorrectly stated, or worse—simply ignored—I suggest you adapt this L.I.F.T. exercise on "The Power of Principles."

The first step in a principle values exercise is to put everyone's mind at ease. No one will offer constructive feedback if they feel criticized. Make your process an open one—a chance to vent without being a "whistleblower." In other words, ask your team not to mention names. Let them know that even if you feel singled out, the process is not about blame but about fixing. Explain this is their chance to express concerns, helpful stories of how things worked well—or not so well.

Most importantly, be explicit that you're inviting them to aspire, to be the idealist, to dream about how things should be in the company in a perfect world.

I typically set aside a whole morning with my c-suite group to work through this exercise with the cellphones turned off. I do everything I can to create a relaxing open dialogue.

Explain the power of Principles

Even if this isn't the first time you've undertaken this exercise, it's worthwhile re-iterating the power of principles. Many people have gone through this exercise, but for various reasons—such as the pressures of goals or deadlines—they never truly adopted the company's principle values framework. Explain how principle values should inform all their decision making, the mentorship of their people, and guide their actions and behavior as a leader. Give examples that clarify expectations.

If you handle this exercise in a positive, noncritical way, you will find issues will churn to the surface. Treat this as a discovery process. Let the team tell you what they think is holding the company back, or creating a working environment that may be toxic, or driving a lack of loyalty within the people.

I start with two open-ended questions and then ask—and wait for—an inevitable dump of ideas. I simply facilitate by writing them on the whiteboard without commenting.

Step #1

Ask the question: ***In the mind of an outsider—or our customers— what words you think they would use to express our values as a brand or company. In other words, we are best known as what?***

Instruction: Write all the keywords that describe value points made by the team, even if the word doesn't truly explain a value. For example, "cheapest supplier" may not sound like a value, but it may be what your customers think of your brand. Collect your team's feedback. You are a facilitator, not a critic. The most common words that people throw out are integrity, honesty, trust, boldness, accountability, customer minded, passionate, or humble. List them all.

Step #1: In the mind of an outsider—or our customers—what words do you think they would use to express our values as a brand or company. ***In other words, we are best known as what?***

Step #2: Categorize the above download of value words and ideas into five logical categories.

1)

2)

3)

4)

5)

Step #2: Organize

After listing all the keywords, organize them, and distill them into categories or buckets that make the most sense. For example, you could place integrity and honesty in one bucket because you believe you cannot have one without the other. Attempt to categorize all the words into five buckets. Force your team to take every word and put it in one of the five buckets. If you find you have too many categories, start merging them until you have just five.

Step #3: Bucket groups

Once you have finished the bucket exercise, split your group into five teams (at least two people per bucket) and give them each the mission to express their bucket with three real-life stories or examples of how the company exemplified that value. Then, ask for three stories or examples of how the company did not uphold the value—and its consequences. There's no need to ask them to write out the stories; they can discuss them, then give them each a name. Later, when you come back together as a group, they can explain the stories more fully in their own words.

Give the group 30 minutes to work through their stories and develop three "good" stories and three "bad" stories.

Step #4: Presenting the Good and the Bad

When your sessions finish, ask them to select a spokesperson to come forward and summarize the three good anecdotes and the three damaging scenarios. As the facilitator, your primary job is to summarize the key takeaways and distill them down to core concepts and keywords. For example, when we engaged in this exercise in one of my past companies, the stories revolved around ugly anecdotes about competitors cheating—and how it "forced" some salespeople to take the same low road—and others who held to the high road. In both scenarios, it was clear everyone came away feeling bad and uncertain how to handle these situations. In this group, the keywords used were "winning at all costs" (negative value) and "winning the right way" (positive value) or "cheating is for losers."

Oddly, this was the same conversation from one of my earlier stories. I took the theme of this group's stories and the words from my previous experience years before, and we crystalized all the concepts down to the same words:

"Winners never cheat."

The group locked in on that statement, like the team I led years before. That became the rallying mission and led us to our "big five" key phrases.

THE BIG FIVE

In getting to that point, many suppressed emotions rose in the group session—but the session also rallied everyone in the room to identify our value, "Winners never cheat." As I mentioned, we came up with five key phrases—they don't have to be lofty concepts, the more practical, the better. In this case, we came up with:

1. Winners never cheat.

2. Protect the team.

3. Be prepared and on time.

4. Be better, not cheaper.

5. No excuses/complaining/whining.

Doing it this way, as a group, makes the principle values mutually owned statements.

The entire team invests in ownership of the statement—and that, by itself, instills a sense of responsibility to act in fulfillment.

Be sure to complete this exercise for all five value buckets, no matter how long it takes. By engaging the team in this way, you, the Senior Leader, draw out both the positive and negatives stories. You paint a valuable picture. You'll soon discover whether your issues center around sales issues, operational problems, logistics/supply chain, direct labor force, supervisory staff, or corporate structure.

Clarity of the Big Five

Imagine the clarity my team enjoyed after this exercise. Now, when we hired new team members, we knew how to guide them. When we hit a sales obstacle, we could ask ourselves, can we "win without cheating" by being "better, not cheaper?" For regular staff reviews, we could bring up these talking points; we can ask questions like, "how did you protect the team this month?"

This exercise is just one way to invest your team in your shared principle values. Now, the key is to act on your discoveries as a "Principled Leader" of a "Principled Company."

Reflections from the Conqueror

History portrays King Mehmed II as a brutal conqueror who impaled his enemies. Yet, to his own people, and especially to his armies, he was the upholder of their values that they admired. If we view Mehmed's conduct through the lens of his times—rather than with our 21st-century ideals—we can appreciate that he treasured his people.

Mehmed was a student of Alexander the Great—who was well known to uphold values and a grand vision. Famously, Alexander said, "Remember upon the conduct of each depends the fate of all."

Mehmed II took that lesson instilled this principle value in his troops. Unlike other brutal war leaders before him, he offered a truce to Emperor Constantine—who was the target of his early campaigns. Ultimately, he even offered the people of Constantinople the opportunity to surrender with safe passage to another Byzantine city. Unprecedented, he offered the inhabitants the right to keep their belongings—and even to stay or leave their homes as they wished. From our 21st-century perspective, we may view Mehmed's offers of truce as a harsh compromise—albeit to avoid bloodshed and pillaging—but in that society, an invader typically offered no mercy or compromise, and certainly not the opportunity to keep their possessions of life.

Mehmed II's principle value vision was to build the Ottoman Empire into a world power. The vision led to the first step in his campaign: to take Constantinople, a city that had resisted all invasions for centuries.

Mehmed II stirred his people's passions with the promise of fulfillment of the destiny inspired by their forefathers Osman, Bayzeid, Murad, and others. He passionately spoke of the sacrifices of those before them and how their blood cannot be wasted. He talked the language of Empire. He set forth a principle value and vision—even if we ethically disagree with his methods. It was a principle his people could embrace.

Mehmed II was guided by Alexander the Great, who said, "Who does not desire such a victory by which we shall join places in our Kingdom, so far divided by nature, and for which we shall set up trophies in another conquered world?"

How these lessons apply to 21st-century business

I realize that correlating the life example of a brutal dictator may seem odd in the context of 21st-century business. I use these historical snippets only as a "punctuation mark" to demonstrate that these concepts have endured through history and that leadership is about having values—not about judging them. Yes, I believe in ethics and Judeo-Christian values above all, but the bottom line is practical values the entire team can embody. In most cases today, those will be a high standard of ethics and morality. Indeed, in any company I've led, this has been mandatory. But the critical point is principle values drive that leadership—and it is up to the leaders, and the leadership team, to establish those principles. Once established, they are the law.

It's important to remember that principle values are also practical. Don't let anyone tell you that your values or mission statement costs you business. I led this chapter with statistics that showed that Principled Companies earn up to ten times as much as the overall average. From my own experience, I have helped guide multiple companies to turnarounds— turnarounds that almost always started and ended with principle values.

Ask yourself—and ask your team—what kind of company are we? What kind of company do we want to be? How do we make it happen? Now, act on your Principles. In the remaining chapters, I'll show you how.

2

INSPIRE: RELATIONSHIPS AND PILLARS OF STRENGTH

Bonding and building your team – growing pillars of strength from within and shamelessly "poaching" your competitors A performers

---

L.I.F.T. Facts

Disturbing fact one—"About 75 percent of employers rate teamwork and collaboration as "very important," yet only 18 percent of employees get communication evaluations at their performance reviews," according to a breakthrough study by Queens University of Charlotte.[13]

Disturbing fact two—"86% percent of employees and executives cite lack of collaboration or ineffective communication for workplace failures," according to a poll by Salesforce.[14]

Interesting fact—"54 percent of employees say a strong sense of community—great coworkers, celebrating milestones, a common mission—kept them at their company longer and was in their best interest."[15]

In this chapter

- Why relationships are your pillars of strength—and transforming weaknesses into strength.

- Learning to be shameless—"poaching" the industry's A performers

- The team comes first—but all relationships are important.

- How to deal with incompetent performers.

Important Take-away

- **"It can be important to rattle the company in a positive way."**

Reflections from the Conqueror

- *In 1452 Mehmed II brought the Roman Empire under Constantine XI to its knees. He didn't have superior numbers. He had the "A-team" and he took nothing for granted.*

Building the A-team through inspiration and relationships is essential to L.I.F.T.

Lead: A Leader's first duty is to build relationships with his "soldiers" and to make his entire team an "A-Team."

Inspire: Inspiring teams to excel is not about skills—even though skills are vital. Inspiration to perform comes from common goals, visions, values—and rewards.

Focus: The leader should focus on the relationships within the team. What drives them? What motivates them? What "brings them down?"

Transform: Commit to turning every single member of your team into an "A" player.

The disturbing L.I.F.T. Facts I cited at the beginning of this chapter speak volumes. I believe relationships with *all* stakeholders, past and present, are essential—perhaps the most important aspect of L.I.F.T. Leadership. The first and second fact so clearly delineates the importance in the mind of all the employees that relationships, communications, teamwork, and collaboration are vital and directly linked to their sense of loyalty and devotion to the company. How come this deep need for personal relationships and camaraderie is not magnified by leadership? In fact, many leaders believe there is a conflict of interest if they have too close a relationship with their people, and it makes them less effective. The opposite is true.

In my own career and life, the relationships with the people around me must be authentic and real. I view every new relationship as an opportunity to learn and grow. My interaction with stakeholders must be two-way to be fruitful.

As a father of 11 kids—yes, you read that correctly—the one thing you quickly learn is that the load is best managed when the family carries it together. I apply that to my leadership style as well. In business, the shared load is critical. Authentic relationships and real two-way interactions are essential.

In every business, there are many interconnected stakeholders; employees, managers, customers, suppliers, service providers, competitors, former employees, owners, board members, regulators, governments, auditors, investors, industry voices, developers—and countless others. I view every stakeholder as important to the success of a Principled L.I.F.T. Leader and a Principled Business.

The *Empathetic Leader* is vital, as I'll demonstrate in this chapter. A recent Gallup poll cited in *Forbes* indicated that 96 percent of employees believe showing empathy is important in a leader—to advance "employee retention." I'm surprised it isn't 100 percent.[16]

Empathy does not mean sympathy. Sympathy can be superficial. Empathy is taking an authentic interest in your team. In the L.I.F.T. Leadership Method, we teach this as "Bonding with the Team." Both this chapter case study and the chapter exercise demonstrate how you can easily adapt these methods to your stakeholder relationships.

Actual L.I.F.T relationship case study—"Bonding with the team"

Transforming a "B team" into an "A-team"—without top guns

I actually enjoy the challenge of transforming a team of "under-performers" into solid A-players. Since I am often brought in to underperforming team situations —parachuted to a new environment with the expectation of the "turn-around"—the first thing I remind myself is:

Everyone starts with a fresh slate and a full reset.

The reset begins with the L.I.F.T. values process. You'll remember how I did this from the case study in chapter 1, "Winners Never Cheat." You work as a team, bonding with the team as you go, building consensus through the all-important process of: Lead, Inspire, Focus, Transform. It's easy to say, "everyone gets a fresh slate, a full reset"—but what if they don't want to start fresh? In my experience, there is one type of personality that resists the full reset. I call them the self-proclaimed "top guns."

A number of years ago, I took over a company with two executives who clearly possessed extensive institutional knowledge—yet, who appeared to be intransigent to the point of incompetence in their positions. They thought of themselves as the "top guns" in the company. This was exacerbated by caustic behavior and a lack of respect for the other team members. The previous CEOs (plural) were willing to accept their misdeeds due to their invaluable expertise and important business relationships.

Within hours of arriving in my new company, these "top guns" became evident—even to me, a newly parachuted-in CEO. I can only describe the attitude as "palpable arrogance" because they weren't even trying to disguise it.

The two tried to tag-team me into the same corner as previous CEOs; basically, in a nutshell: "we're indispensable, so we'll tell you how it's going to be"—basic "top gun" prima donna behavior. The entire c-suite watched, probably expecting me to "cave" to the inevitable.

There are times when you just know that termination is the only option for change. *(See point 5 in L.I.F.T. Out-Take: How to handle the prima donna.)* Usually, even the most habitual "offender" will at least put up a mask—pretending to go along with the "naive new boss." Rarely do I see in-your-face arrogance at that level. It was even more shocking coming from two separate people. The two would have to go to make a meaningful reboot feasible. I felt like everyone in the c-suite knew it.

L.I.F.T. out-take: How to take out the "top guns"

Here are five ways to "work with" a so-called "top gun" or prima donna successfully:

1. Since they think they know everything, give them the benefit of the doubt and listen to them first. They might actually know something important. Give them credit, then gently remind them the "team comes first." Remember, they are a product of past leaders that encouraged or facilitated this type of behavior.

2. In extreme cases—where they really appear to prefer "going it alone," there may be a role for them as a solo flyer. Just remember to bring them back down to earth everyone now and then. Again, reinforce that the "team comes first." (The rest of the team will appreciate this "space" as well.)

3. If they are truly indispensable, give them a crisis to handle. Let them be the "hero." As long as the team's morale is not damaged, there's no harm in having a hero in the group.

4. Since they believe they are the "A-Team," give them A-Team goals and hold them accountable—assuming you can give them a solo mission. Prima Donnas don't work well in teams they can't dominate. In the absence of a solo mission, you may have only one choice left.

5. Conduct an immediate performance (relationship) review—it is critical you discern if there is any way they are willing and able to change into a team player over time or is the situation truly untenable—if so, then move towards as gentle a separation as possible.

When "top guns" leave

One reason "top guns"—prima donnas and narcissists—thrive in companies is that many of them genuinely have talents, hidden know-how, or relationships that keep the cards on their side of the table. This enables their rise, and it feeds their condition. If you can make them better team-players—working for the good of the team—you have a major asset. If they insist on solo flights—it's a problem.

It was clear that if I just let these two "top guns" go—let's call them Maverick and Goose (from *Top Gun*, the movie)—it would leave a substantial hole. There was no doubt the financial impact on the company would be profound—and based on our balance sheet, at that time, we didn't have the ability to endure for very long.

On the other hand, these two alone couldn't grow the company. I needed every single member of my team to become an A-player on the team. I had only two options: to mold and mentor the two top guns into better team-players; or to let these two executives take flight from the company, find a new opportunity, hopefully with my competitor. We'd lose their expertise, but I knew we could build an A-Team that would dominate our space, and the pace of change would grow.

I sat with a core group of trusted people within the company, and we conducted a preliminary post-mortem on the exit of our two executives. What do I mean by preliminary post-mortem? I don't believe in waiting until disaster strikes to analyze what went wrong. L.I.F.T. Principled Leaders always engage in preventative disaster planning. (Or, hypothetical post-mortem.)

We were collectively appalled by the depth of their hold on the company. Yes, the list of what we'd lose was long. But there was an upside, too. The rest of the team, who resented our two top guns, would evolve into a bonded, stronger team. Ultimately, we could potentially mentor them into A-listers. But, I wasn't satisfied with that upside. I asked my advisors for a list of people within our industry who held similar experiences, relationships, and credibility—without the ego issues. I was surprised and delighted to find that the list of people we could recruit was not as limited as I once thought.

My mission shifted to finding two replacements as quickly as possible. A-listers, but not prima donnas. Team players. Over the next eight weeks, I focused on the issue full-time, interviewing dozens of candidates.

What did we ask in these interviews? Our questions focused on team-bonding. On Lead, Inspire, Focus, Transform. On behavior. We barely even touched on their skills or experiences. Our priority was the team. The series of interviews and face-to-face discussions were all about fit, relationships, and culture. We needed to get this right.

We landed on two executives, closed the deals, timed their entry to be the same day—and pulled the trigger. We knew it would rattle the company, and it certainly did. It shook up the team in many positive ways.

The key thing to remember is —

The team comes first.

The goal is an A-Team, not a team with some narcissistic top guns.

Lessons learned: a "clean slate"

Whether you're new to the team or working on a team-reboot, I cannot emphasize enough the need to prioritize the team relationships above all else.

When you reboot—everyone gets a clean start.

Analyze the past and the issues, but don't judge the past management decisions, or the history these leaders have had, nor the things they had to do in the context of a crisis or situation. Tell them you're giving them a clean start—and mean it. Although history is important to understanding issues, the goal now is "bonding with the team" and engineering a "reboot." Even if you're not working on anything so grandiose as a complete turn-around, never forget the importance of just bonding with the team.

Human nature: defend

It is human nature to defend. Defensive arguments quickly poison team dynamics. Blame-games go nowhere. If you're really serious about change, start fresh. Even if the team is resisting, defending, whining, and resorting to leverage and politics, the high road is the new road. Walk up to the metaphorical whiteboard, and erase everything, making a point of saying to the team—"okay, we're starting fresh."

You will immediately see who truly wants to step up and adapt to the new way forward. You'll notice who wants to play games. There will also be the "watch and see" team-members. They all have a chance to start again. Make it clear you'll hold everyone accountable—going forward— but the past is gone, left behind.

Testing your commitment

As you saw in my case study, the rogues will start to challenge your commitment to change. This is the real test of a Principled L.I.F.T. Leader. You have to tolerate—to understand that these rebels are a product of their history. The L.I.F.T. Leader is able to categorize those who are willing to change—but don't know how—versus those who will never change, like my two "top guns" in the case study.

The Four L.I.F.T. Relationship Pillars

In business school, the relationship pillars are sometimes called "teaming." Basically, whether you're working with your internal teams, as I demonstrated in my chapter case study, or with other important stakeholders—such as investors, client groups, or suppliers—the *L.I.F.T. Relationship Pillars* are the secret to leadership success.

Principled L.I.F.T. Leaders always encourage these four "teaming pillars" from all stakeholders. Ask every team member to think about the four pillars in everything they do.

The Four L.I.F.T. Relationship Pillars are stated in our familiar L.I.F.T. matrix for easy recall, but you can call them whatever you prefer:

L: Learning

I: Ideas

F: Feedback

T: Teaming

Turn every team experience into four questions. What did we learn? What new ideas could solve the problem? Do we need more feedback to solve this? How can the team collaborate on this solution? Make the questions more specific, of course, to the situation. The "sales team" will ask different questions to the "development team." The point is to make sure the team dynamically interacts with learning experiences, ideas, feedback, and networking.

L: Learning

No problem is unsolvable. Adopt the approach of an investigative law-enforcement team. Assign specialists to research different solutions. If you don't have the needed information, the team should be empowered to find them. Questions, investigations, forensic analysis, and research are anchors of investigation.

In Harvard Business School, Harvard Business Professor Dr. Amy Edmondson describes this as "reflection":

"Reflection: Teaming relies on the use of explicit observations, questions, and discussions of processes and outcomes. This must happen on a constant basis that reflects the rhythm of the work, whether that calls for daily, weekly, or other project-specific timing."

The dynamic of the team is special. The chaotic interaction is the crucible of learning, adapting, and growing. In L.I.F.T. teams, mistakes are not criticized; they become learning experiences.

I: Ideas

Learning is in the service of ideas to solve our problems. Turn every project into a problem to be solved, then turn every team into collaborative brainstorm maniacs. No idea is a bad idea. Every idea goes on the whiteboard.

Depending on the goals and issues, your team may take an "iterative" approach to creative solutions. It is often worthwhile to take small steps, test, another step, test. For new launches or for "big" issues, a major brainstorm may be needed. Either way, the power of the team quickly becomes evident.

In this chapter's case study, I described the two "top guns"—and why we collectively decided we were better off with collaborative teams. The power of the team—over the top gun—is the collaborative brainstorm. Ideas flow from the dynamics of relationships. The ultimate power of the team is its foundational nature. Nothing brings you back down to earth—from the realm of lofty ideas—faster than the reality of your market. Your team will keep the creative process grounded.

F: Feedback

Ideas don't grow in isolation. They are inspired by an issue or problem to be solved. Then, they grow in the cheerful light of creative minds: ideas. But, they must stand the test of feedback. Does the great idea really resonate with the target audience? Is it credible? Is it affordable? In the case study in chapter one, you'll remember how we listed all the ideas on the whiteboard, the good and the bad. Feedback and deconstruction are how you hone the list down to workable solutions. Again, this is something best implemented in a team. The solo "top gun" often cannot appraise their own ideas in the light of the reality of the market.

T: Teaming

Finally, Teaming. Collaboration. The team mindset. This is what it's all about. As I described it earlier, "the Team Bond." This is why "top guns" are not always assets in the company—unless they are also team-players. What is Teaming? Harvard Business Professor Dr. Amy Edmondson[17] describes Teaming as:

1. Speaking up: honest, direct conversation between individuals in a team.

2. Collaboration: a collaborative mindset and behavior.

3. Experimentation: an interactive group approach to iteration.

4. Reflection: discussions, reflections, and observations as a team.

Learning to be shameless—the art of the poach

Now I'm going to be a little bit controversial. So far, all this rosy, cozy talk of teams, relationships, and teaming sounds really uplifting.

Who wouldn't want to work for a company with a tightly bonded team? Everyone knows your name. People care about you. Of course, you want to work with that group.

Let me flip this around now. There are times when a leader has to be somewhat shameless. I'm not talking about within your team. Never shame your team. Here, I'm talking about—wait for it—"poaching" from other teams.

I know—your jaw just hit the ground. Randy Dewey, the ethics guy, is a poacher. Okay, so I'm going to come clean and admit it. I'll gladly poach the top players on other teams. That's what any great team does. The 1959 Green Bay Packers stole Vince Lombardi from the New York Giants to coach their embarrassing team that had never won anything and were the laughingstock of the NFL. Vince went on to win five NFL Championships in Green Bay, became a hall of famer, and the league trophy was renamed after him. He took this team from obscurity to dominance that forged a reputation in the league they still enjoy to this day. Green Bay shamelessly poached an A-player from the Giants that turned their franchise around. You are hired to take your team to the top of your league, and your industry has great A-players that can help you catapult to the top.

I often use the sports analogy in my workshops and sessions. It works on a number of levels. Team sports are about "teaming." You may have "A players," but you try to avoid the overt "top guns" who can't team-play. You, the leader, are the coach. And, you, the coach, have to draft the best players and even "poach" players from other teams.

Let me be clear. As long as you're not dishonest in the process, there is nothing unethical about poaching a top performer from another company. You offer, they decide. The other team can counter-offer. It's all very fair.

I call it poaching, not because it's "stealing" but because you're trying to benefit from someone else's work. You'll pay for it. The salary and the signing bonus, it's inevitable, will not be inexpensive. From the point of view of the company you "poached," it might be seen as stealing—but there's not even a whiff of bad ethics here. It's just business. It swings the other way as well. Your competitors will try to poach your new A-List team as well.

The team comes first

The reason you do all of these things—including the hard decisions on removing "negative" players and poaching "better" players—is because the team comes first. A Principled Company and a Principled Leader can't progress to goals without the team's enthusiasm, insight, hard work, and productivity. This is where you, the Principled Leader, engages the team, considers the wellness of the team, and inspires the team.

There are two core things your team needs—and they're not what you think:

- inspiration through engagement

- wellness.

Wait, don't close the book, despairing that I've lost it. My rather strong statement is backed up with statistics. This is according to the pre-eminent research group Gallup[18]: "Highly engaged teams show 21percent greater profitability." That should be enough said.

Inspiration and wellness of the team are really in the hands of you, the Principled L.I.F.T. Leader. Your constructive feedback and frequent check-ins will engage and inspire. Eighty-nine percent of HR Leaders, according to SHRM, indicate that frequent and regular check-ins are vital.[19] (We cover this extensively in chapter 5: *L.I.F.T Trajectory: Dynamic Feedback and Recognition.*) Great leaders listen more than they speak, backed by another study, this time from Forbes, indicating "Employees who feel their voice is heard are 4.6 times more likely to feel empowered and perform their best work."[20]

One thing that is fundamental to a Principled Leader is perceived empathy. I stated it as "perceived" only because it doesn't come naturally to some leaders. If not, you should coach yourself on this important leadership trait. Like a father—remember, father of 11 children, here—you need empathy. Don't believe me? The numbers are overwhelming in a study cited in Forbes[21]: "96 percent of employees believe showing empathy is an important way to advance employee retention." Think about that employee you just "poached," which costed the company a small fortune. Imagine now the reason they leave is because they found their new leader lacked empathy.

Do you need a number to inspire you to think about Employee wellness and engagement? "In an exhaustive report by The Engagement Institute… disengaged employees cost U.S. companies up to $550 billion a year."[22]

As a true Principled Leader, it is vital you learn empathy and how to inspire your troops, if only for the sake of the bottom line. Empathy only develops as you get to know your team—and this is where chapter 5 in this book will be vital to your Leader-Team relationship.

Better relationships: the three L.I.F.T. Leader requirements

What specific skills and attitudes does the Principled L.I.F.T. leader need? You need at least three things in any relationship: time, boundaries, and appreciation.

Time is essential.

You need time with your team. You need to actually "schedule" weekly time with each team member you actively work with. If they never see you, you're not part of the team. Be visible. Schedule times, and not just reviews, but just to get to know them better. Even if you're very limited in your time, ask yourself these questions:

- When was the last time I just dropped in on a team-member for a chat?

- Do I even know what my team members write on Twitter or LinkedIn?

- Do I know the names of each of my team members—and the names of their families?

- What are my team members specifically working on?

- Did I ask them if they need any help?

I'm not suggesting you, as a C-Suite leader, should drop-in or engage daily. That would just be annoying and unproductive. But, at least engage often enough they keep you top of mind—and vice versa.

Boundaries.

On the flip side, you need to have some boundaries. If it's none of your business, don't intrude. Learn to distinguish the difference between empathy and interest—and being overly nosey. Be interested, not intrusive. Companies, for example, that expect and demand teams to attend all company events, dinners, and parties are intrusive. Taking an interest in something is not the same as forcing an engagement.

As the Principled Leader, you may also have to help manage the relationship between your team members and their boundaries. Peer pressure can be as difficult to deal with as manager intrusiveness. It's nice to have friends at work but being friendly is just as good. Encourage boundaries on personal matters to ensure your team feels safe and valued. Discourage gossip. Listen.

Appreciation

You would expect that appreciation goes without saying. You'd be wrong. Statistically, most team members feel underappreciated. Don't wait for the 90-day review to offer appreciation. Make sure you balance every criticism with a counter-balancing positive reinforcement: "I know you worked hard, but..."

When someone does something beneficial to the group, make sure you announce it to the team—don't let them be "unsung heroes..."

One of the main ways you can show you appreciate someone is to "listen" to them. Principled Leaders always listen.

I suggest you use what I call the *L.I.F.T. Personal 90-Day Dashboard*. I can't over-state its effectiveness in a team-environment.

90 Days to L.I.F.T.-off

Whether you're working with your team on individual performance or team-on-team performance, or with your executives on company performance—I can't stress enough the 90-Day Rule. The cycle for L.I.F.T. is conveniently a 90-day cycle. For each stakeholder, ask them to set their own 90-day goals and the tactics they propose for achieving those 90-day goals—stated in a one-page plan.

Important: it must be a one-page 90-day plan. It must be in writing. It must be realistic. It must have trackable goals.

To state the overall L.I.F.T. cycle in an over-arching formula, think of it this way:

- **L: Lead** by setting goals for all stakeholders. Do this separately for each group: team-members, the employee teams, the leadership, the company, the investors. You do this by creating "goals" for each 90-day cycle. Invest the stakeholders in the process by allowing them to set their own goals—realistically moderated by you, the leader, of course—and then hold them to their own goals. By making it theirs, they become invested in the goal.

- **I: Inspire** achievement of the goals by asking them to set their own goals for each 90-day cycle. By empowering them to plan, you inspire them to achieve.

- **F: Focus**—ask them to list the tactical steps needed to achieve each 90-day goal cycle. How are you going to achieve your goals in those 90-days? What help do you need? What resources do you need? What dependencies do you have to achieve your goal? What is your contingency plan? What is the cost?

- **T: Transform**—when they get to the end of each 90-day cycle, we can, together as a team, see what goals were achieved, what obstacles were transformed, what goals have to be modified or pushed back, and what it will take to achieve the revised goals. Everyone is accountable—because it is their personal plan.

Adapt the 90-day pattern to all management touchpoints

This pattern is repeatable and adaptable to every scenario. Each person on your team can have a personal 90-day dashboard. You can separately have a team plan you worked on with the whole team—also one page. Another "dashboard" might be your cash flow plan. Your investor plans. Your publicity plans. Think in terms of manageable 90-day bites: one page only, goals, tactics, timeline.

90-day personal plan

Sitting with your teammates every 90 days to do formal performance reviews is the L.I.F.T. secret to creating an interactive, inspired, focused, goal-oriented team. Every 90 days, you can reflect on the things your team, your executives—and you—did well in the past 90 days and inspire agreement on the things that are a priority for the next 90 days.

In my experience, no tool in management works better than this simple adaptation. I call it an adaption because the plan idea is not a new one. I'm adapting it to this pattern, which works for me (change it in whatever way works for you):

- Every stakeholder group has a one-page plan in writing.

- Each plan is a 90-day cycle.

- Each plan is no more than one page.

- Use the 90-day plans at any time in the cycle—and certainly at the end of 90 days in a formal review—to Lead, Inspire, Focus, and Transform their performance. Nothing is more motivating than saying, "how are you doing with *your* goal for this period?" (The word "your" being highly empowering.)

This way, you have a "formal" enough process to be trackable and useful, yet a "simple" enough template that people don't mind doing it. That, in a nutshell, is management secret number 1: simplify, clarify, and make it accountable.

Specifically applied to team members on an individual basis, the *L.I.F.T. Personal Dashboard* gives you ample opportunity to share views on problems, substandard performance, behavioral problems and to dig into areas that are uncomfortable before they become major problems.

If you have a good relationship with your people, then you can easily have those discussions without intimidating anyone, and you get ahead of any problems before they become serious.

At all levels of a team, this is important, but even more so at the c-suite level. In high-level leadership teams, you cannot let anything hide and fester. You have to **L**ead, **I**nspire, **F**ocus, **T**ransform, even at the level of personal performance.

Accountability and rewards—90 days also

I am not a believer in annual performance reviews. Today's world moves too quickly for annual reviews to be anything but a quaint notion. Information that's six months old is already stale.

Accountability should also be tied to 90-day cycles. If someone achieves, give praise every 90 days or sooner. If someone exceeds the goal—offer a reward, and don't wait for an annual salary review. If someone falls behind—help them.

L.I.F.T. Personal 90-Day Dashboard

Here's how you do it. Give each team-member you personally lead a "dashboard." Think of this as their "at-a-glance" panel. In L.I.F.T. Leadership, we use the *L.I.F.T. Personal Dashboard*. (See the *L.I.F.T. Personal Dashboard exercise* later in this chapter.)

You work together with your team members, coaching them on developing their own dashboard. You, the coach, the empathetic Principled Leader, will work with them on their dashboard and help them self-monitor their own engagement.

This, in my experience, is the most empowering way to manage a team. Let them set their own 90-day goals with your help.

In L.I.F.T., these 90-Day dashboards are important. It encourages collaboration with your team while also inspiring them to self-improve. By setting their own goals—with you as their coach—they feel inspired. When they fail, they feel more invested in fixing the problem. When they succeed, they feel empowered.

I suggest you have this simple one-page dashboard plan for each and every team member. Then, follow through with a 90-day "how did we do" session.

L.I.F.T. Personal Dashboard exercise

Every 90 days you review their specific L.I.F.T. dashboard with their specific deliverables. this form helps to keep track of things that occur during that 90 day period that should be mentioned. keep these forms and the 90-day l.i.f.t. dashboard for that period in a file to help keep track of individual performance.

Employee's Name: **Next review date:**

5 top goals for   1.
the 90 day period
on their L.I.F.T.   2.
dashboard

                             3.

                             4.

                             5.

Accomplishments noticed in this period to be mentioned at next review date:

Areas of improvement or concern to be mentioned at next review date:

Core value re-enforcecments during the 90 day review is important. What is your theme to mention to each direct report this quarter?

Notes from the review:

90-Day performance reviews—minimum

The reason I encourage the 90-Day Personal Dashboard is to feed the most important team-management technique in L.I.F.T.: setting 90-day goals. The onus is on you to review every 90 days. You will find yourself doing this more often, assuming you're a Mindful Leader—checking in weekly or monthly: "How are we doing against your dashboard?" Call these informal reviews or chats. It doesn't matter. The key is to engage frequently, not occasionally.

Formally, though, at least every 90 days. Without exception. Part of this review, too, will be to review their next 90-day dashboard. You review their performance for the last 90 days and set their goals—with them as a team—for the next 90 days. Never vary from this minimum.

Anything your team-members did not accomplish in the previous 90 days you must deal with. How did it happen? What changed? Is it still relevant? What circumstances prevented it? Were other members or groups causing a hindrance? How can I help you achieve it? Should we move this to your next 90-day plan? How can we make sure it happens?

What's the format of the review? At the least, you'll be reviewing their dashboard and goals for the previous 90 days and setting goals for the next 90 days. The flow of information and level of engagement at this frequency does wonders for both parties. It's all about alignment.

Team Member reviews the leader?

As part of the review, I suggest an interesting L.I.F.T. twist. Ask them to review you, the leader? Ask these flip-around questions:

1. How did I do in those 90 days?

2. How could I have helped you more in the last 90 days?

3. How can I help you in the next 90 days?

The bottom line is you're all part of a team. As a team leader, you're part of that team. Let them have a little "payback" and review you as well. You might learn something important. At the least, you'll know how you can help them improve.

The Mindful Leader, and how to deal with incompetent performers

As important as empathy and inspiration are, you, the Principled L.I.F.T. Leader, will still be faced with the "tough decisions." It is for this reason; I deliberately use the example of Mehmed the Conqueror throughout this book. That very peculiar dichotomy—between being loved by your stakeholders (army) and being ready to deal ruthlessly with anything that doesn't advance the march—is what will make a truly great leader.

You know you have an incompetent performer only if you are a Mindful Leader. If you don't engage in empathy—in business terms, characterized by frequent reviews and regular feedback—how can you spot the incompetent performers? If you're not a Mindful Leader, how can you act in a timely way to prevent damage to the team? Especially if you have successfully rebuilt the team into an "A" team, you have to remain mindful of every person on the team to be ready to prevent devolution into another "B" team.

Mindful leaders also inspire trust. If you only engage in the annual review, and at that late point, you suddenly start criticizing everyone, you'll lose the trust of the team. Mindful, present-minded leaders watch for issues before criticism is needed. Frequent feedback is more positive than infrequent reviews.

For this reason, I strongly endorse the 90-day review at a minimum. (See the *L.I.F.T. Personal Dashboard exercise above*. Also, see chapter 5.)

What to do with incompetent performers?

You have empathy. You listen. You engage in frequent performance reviews. You make time. Your team is becoming a solid, energizing force in the company. But—what do you do with the incompetent performers?

Spot them first

You can't deal with incompetent performers—especially the ones who could be molded into strong performers—if you are not engaging in the L.I.F.T. Leader requirements: time, boundaries, and appreciation. Part of this, of course, is the *L.I.F.T. 90-day Personal Dashboard*, which helps you, as their leader, to accomplish all three of these requirements.

Time includes taking the time to communicate. Are you communicating frequently enough to spot the under-performers?

Boundaries require documentation. You'll need this anyway if the only resolution to the incompetent performer becomes the worst-case scenario of dismissal. Documentation, in the form of reviews and documented meetings, will also help you spot the team-members who need help.

Appreciation: if you've always appreciated their work in the past, there's a reason. Find out what changed? If you haven't appreciated their work previously, there's also a reason? Have you missed the obvious signs of an under-performer?

The Mindful L.I.F.T. Leader never misses the under-performer. The big question now is—what do you do about them?

The Signs of Incompetence

The signs of incompetence—and this applies to you, the leader, as well—are:

1. Arrogance or over-confidence.

2. Preoccupation—does the team-member always seem unnecessarily pre-occupied?

3. Impulsiveness or temperamental behavior.

4. Lack of communication – does the team-member always seem too absent and they never tell you what you need to know, and you're always surprised by something.

5. Goal and milestone failure.

These are just the signs you should move forward in your review with a team-member. There can be many causes of all of these, including temporary issues at home. But, the engaged, Mindful Leader is ready to engage and review.

Fixing the Incompetent Performer

The Mindful Leader uses the *L.I.F.T. Leader Requirements*—time, boundaries, and appreciation—as a base from which to "fix" the incompetent performer. You'll need to spend time listening, guiding, and teaching. Take the model of the sports coach. You have a talented team-member but now need to discover what is making them underperform. You'll still need boundaries, but make sure you also appreciate their positive assets: training, skills, contributions, attitude—whatever it is you saw in them your company hired them for. Work with that. Be Mindful that their incompetence could be a result of the incompetence underneath them and that part of the problem is a weak team or player that creates the failures, misses, or perception problems. Be careful you don't target the wrong person. It is a costly choice to terminate people, and though the leader is ultimately responsible for their people, you may want to address the fundamental problems of weak performers first within the organization before you remove the leader.

If, after a thorough review, the incompetent performer is that leader, and they are either not leading their team well, cannot manage the incompetence underneath them, and/or you have practically determined that they are the problem. You are faced with—tough choices.

The Tough Choices

You, the Mindful Principled Leader, did everything right. You did all of the necessary things to mitigate the underperformer:

1. You communicated explicitly and regularly. You offered help.

2. You documented everything. You discussed the highs and lows.

3. You stayed calm and measured and analyzed—including giving them opportunities to improve.

In the end, there is either an unwillingness to change on their part, an inability to improve, or a lack of desire. Either way, you've hit the clichéd fork in the road. Now, what's left, is the "tough choice" for the betterment of the team. Remembering, the "team comes first," you prepare for the tough choice.

It might be tempting to wait until the next review. Or to let it slide. Always keep in mind, "the team comes first." If the team is content with some backsliding, and as a result, is working harder to make up for it, the Mindful Leader may wait and see. If the under-performer is impacting team performance, that's a different situation. Remember the old rule of thumb, a bad under-performing employee usually costs you 10x their salary in poor decisions, pulling down others performance, and negatively impacting the business.

The key thing, once a decision is made—and assuming you've communicated, documented, and stayed calm—is to do what's best for the team. If a person must be dismissed, transferred, demoted, or retrained, just do it. Never forget, though, team-members are people first. Remember to be:

1. Compassionate and empathetic, above all.

2. Honor all your agreements, verbal and written, with them.

3. Measured and calm in your approach.

4. Decisive to avoid ambiguity once that decision is made.

5. Direct and do not tip-toe around the truth, everyone knows.

Reflections from the Conqueror

Mehmed II knew from a young age that relationships were critical. Growing up with disadvantages had taught him the importance of a team. By himself, without an inspired team, he could never have conquered Constantinople.

Mehmed's Stepmother Mara was a trusted advisor and one of his biggest supporters. She was instrumental in taming the young King. Early on in his leadership, immediately after he rose to the throne, Mehmed decided to remove all his Father's court advisors. The court advisors begged his Father, the retired King, to come back and lead the Empire. They convinced Murad II to return, and he humiliatingly dethroned his son and told him that he needed to grow up and wait several more years before he is ready.

This "lesson" was a thorn in his side for years—and it was his first "obstacle" in his leadership career. Fortunately, he was able to learn from his experience with the help of his Stepmother, who knew the importance of all relationships—and the importance of transforming these obstacles into opportunities. Young Mehmed didn't allow the bitterness of that early defeat to eat away at him. Though he was angry with this father— and shamed in front of the court—he turned to his most trust advisor, Stepmother Mara, and, like a good leader, he listened to her advice. She reminded Mehmed to emulate his idol, Alexander the Great. She coached him to learn from Alexander's passion. She showed him how Alexander also faced personal adversity but then "transformed" them into opportunities.

Mehmed II learned from Alexander the Great lessons such as: "Whatever possession we gain by our sword cannot be sure or lasting, but the love gained by kindness and moderation is certain and durable."

Tolerance and winning the respect of people became an important key ingredient to his ultimate success. By dealing early on with a reversal, the rogue leadership, he learned how to tackle the obstacles and "transform" them into opportunities.

Why This is Important

Mehmed the Conqueror and Alexander the Great led by example. They had a vision. True, they were bloody conquerors, leading bloody warriors—but to their followers, they were great leaders. How does that happen? The leader's vision has to be clear. They have to be willing to learn—as Mehmed did from his stepmother.

Mehmed inspired his troops with the goal of conquering Constantinople and building the Ottoman Empire into a dynasty. They were like-minded warriors—with the same values. The people that followed him felt inspired by his strength and lack of fear—despite an enemy of overwhelming supe- riority and incredible historical might.

What does all that mean in the modern context of today's "business warfare?" To our troops, we must lead with values, empathy, and strength. In our case, our mission target is conquering our competition, generating a profit, and winning new business. We aspire to build formidable companies that set an example in our respective industries, creating a company people want to be a part of and that builds value for all our stakeholders.

3

FOCUS: LEAN-WITHOUT-MEAN LEADERSHIP

L.I.F.T. Lean Leadership is a Focus method—enabling dexterity and Transformation of obstacles into opportunities. Don't lose sight of who you are trying to help when you engage in enhancing efficiencies and processes. L.I.F.T. Lean Management can help you Focus your resources and equip your teams for success. They are not the ultimate goal—only a method.

In this chapter

- L.I.F.T.'s nuanced version of "Lean Six Sigma"—"Lean-Without-Mean Leadership."

- Learning to be "extra" lean—turn on a dime to seize the opportunities.

- Going even leaner does not have to be "mean"—involving the entire team in solutions invests them in your success.

- Process Improvement is like pruning the tree—vital to growth.

Important Take-away

- **"Lean thinking brings versatility on the battlefield."**

- **Lean is a mentality, not a process per se!**

Reflections from the Conqueror

- *Mehmed's management style was lean. Instead of relying on layers of commanders—he got off his horse and talked to his foot soldiers. He understood the lessons of history: that battles can be lost when armies are slow to mobilize.*

Values of L.I.F.T.

Lean thinking is a driving force of L.I.F.T.

Lead: Lead by example, without layers—for instant feedback and the ability to exploit opportunities.

Inspire: Inspiring the teams to act by empowering them. There is a time for debate, but lean teams are always ready to act.

Focus: Lean thinking drives sharp single-pointed focus on goals. Empower action-focus in your teams.

Transform: Transform a sudden apparent weakness into a new opportunity. Lean thinkers are always ready to dynamically exploit problems—rather than worrying about them.

L.I.F.T.'s contribution to Process Improvement, Lean, Total Quality Control, and Six Sigma—or various blends thereof—is not one of propriety or originality. It's about emphasis. We all know we have to engage in "process improvement" and real-life lean thinking. What is often forgotten is the people factor. Performance and efficiency are more about people than they are about process. You can improve, go lean, earn your black belt in Six Sigma—but at the end of the day, you are a team leader. Your improvements are in the service of your stakeholders, including your board, team, employees, suppliers, investors, shareholders, and customers.

In L.I.F.T. Leadership, the key differentiator is *"lean-not-mean."* It is easy to let process or efficiency take priority over people—who are the very reason we engage in the process. In this book, we're focused on leadership. I'll refer you, in my bibliography, to many sources of wonderful, authoritative information on Lean, Six Sigma—or, for simplicity, its combined version, Lean Six Sigma. Here, in this chapter, I want to emphasize the importance of how we blend lean processes with ethics, morality, and compassion—without losing sight of efficiency. In other words, "Lean-not-mean."

Why you ask? Isn't a leader's role to be fearless, and sometimes callous, even ruthless? It's true your role is to drive into the company lean and efficient financial performance for the benefit of all stakeholders. That likely will involve ruthless precision. It equally should include compassion, ethics, and the greater good. There are ways to be lean without being mean, as I hope to illustrate in my case study.

Real-life L.I.F.T Inspiration Case Study—"Going lean, not mean"

"No problem, we're going ahead with or without you."

Lean Management Culture

In the 90's Edwards Deming and the Toyota way inspired me so deeply that I pursued my Master Black Belt Six Sigma designation through a great educational institution in Montreal. I had just taken over leadership of an automotive company—one with deep operational inefficiencies with a hard-nosed union. At the time, my Vice President of Human Resources, trying to be funny and helpful at the same time, described the company as "standing with one foot in the grave and the other on a banana peel." His joke proved prophetic.

I came into a company where the Union President wouldn't even discuss the concept of Lean Management. Irritated, he said, "leanness just means jobs will be lost." The Union, he said, was not interested in participating.

Of course, I heard him out and showed my compelling logic for Lean, but when we came to a full impasse, I said, "The decision was already made. We are going ahead, with or without you. Why not participate in the process and help your members—with the much-needed changes? Help us understand what is in your member's best interest."

Six Sigma

And so, we pushed ahead with these desperately needed changes, beginning with "lean training." We brought in consultants, created working teams—and developed a plan covering all the areas in the company. The first project team got busy with the Six Sigma process, and within two weeks, they implemented a major vital change to our axle line.

At the beginning of the next shift, the union asked all 400 members in that area to sign a pre-written grievance. With a dramatic flourish, they carried in the massive stack of papers and put all 400 grievances on my desk. My office was open to the factory, with glass windows. That morning, when I walked into my office, I saw this mountainous stack of papers on my desk. I realized everyone on the floor was watching me through that glass for my reaction.

Calmly, I read the first grievance. After I confirmed that all 400 were that same grievance copied and signed, I put the first one in my desk drawer—making sure everyone saw my action—then proceeded to shove the entire remaining stack to the edge of my desk and into my garbage can, which was conveniently placed at that edge. Who says only the Union can be dramatic? Of course, there's a fine line between toughness and arrogance, but I had made my point. Clearly, the stakes were high.

I know I began this chapter by writing "Lean-Without-Mean" thinking, but I hoped everyone involved could forgive me for my theatrical flourish.

We continued our relentless pursuit of Lean-Without-Mean to save this company from itself. The Union, over the past 80 years, had created a virtual "choke hold" over the company through onerous rules, processes, lines of jurisdiction, and confining contract language. Needless to say, it is difficult to be "lean" when the mechanisms for waste are built-in to all the daily processes.

The rules in place at the time gave the union stewards a tool to debate every reasonable change. In my view, this union contract was a book of restrictions, obstacles, and barriers—but, by now, you know how I view obstacles. It was time for some **T**ransformation.

To manage the needed **T**ransformation, I exploited the "Management Rights Clause," as I call it: if it's not written in the contract—and if it's not illegal—then management has the right to do it.

Not every aspect of production and production flow is mandated in union contacts. Slowly, over time, I managed to push for lean efficiency changes on those things not specifically covered by the collective bargaining agreement. Little details mattered. Each little nuance of "leanness" mattered. If I couldn't orchestrate the bigger changes needed for Lean-Without-Mean Six Sigma, then I could at least incrementally move us to a better position.

Making it "Lean-Without-Mean"

My approach is what I call "Lean-Without-Mean" Leadership. By making change incremental and thoughtful, allowing all stakeholders to participate, you can "show" instead of "tell." All the arguments you can possibly construct are never going to convince your team—especially entrenched Union members—the way results can. Start with the small tactics.

Communication is the one way you can ensure that there is no spite involved in lean management. The goal is to make everything efficient, high quality, and profitable for everyone's benefit, including all stakeholders, from Union to Shareholders.

In this case, over time, as our "Lean-Without-Mean" changes created no immediate hardships—and we started to see some amazing little gains in productivity—I think the Union realized I was not going to stop, and that maybe I had the right idea. Some members pressured their union officials to get involved because they wanted a say in the process. Patience is a big virtue when it comes to dealing with Unions.

How did I communicate? I held back nothing. I was open about the company's financial position, which was dire. Without wagging my metaphorical finger, I let them see for themselves that the 1200 jobs depended on productive leanness. I persisted. Work with us as a team. Here's what we have to gain. Here's what we've already gained with our little steps so far.

Over time, our union president himself became an honorary black belt in leanness, the shop stewards became green belts, and team leaders became project leaders.

Happily, over the next 24 months, we restructured the business, the bargaining agreement, and the company went from tens of millions of losses to tens of millions of profits. The company just celebrated its 100th year in business, and it remains a major employer in that community.

L.I.F.T. and "Lean-Without-Mean" Dexterity

Regardless of labels, there can be no question that "Lean Thinking" is vital in today's market. Today, markets and customers are volatile. To be able to handle a crisis—and to Transform—you need to minimize delays, layers, and processes that add nothing to deliverables.

There are plenty of books on Six Sigma and its earlier cousin Total Quality Management. I'll only summarize a few points here and refer you to in-depth books on those topics. What is different in the L.I.F.T. approach is a matter of emphasis. I label it "Lean-Without-Mean" dexterity. This doesn't mean to imply that Lean Six Sigma or other methods are without compassion or are mean. It's just a matter of emphasis. You'll need a tenacious spirit. Ultimately, you need everyone on the team to join in with enthusiasm to maximize the impact and results. Just because it looks good on paper, and should work because the models say so, doesn't mean it's practical. Your people are what makes it work, and listening to them—and engaging their wisdom—can make a good idea great.

Here's a hard fact. Master Black Belts in Six Sigma can sometimes over-emphasize the "lean" aspects to the point it subsumes other interests. In the first two chapters, I think I've made it clear that ethics and compassion are just as important in business as leanness. They can go together, hand-in-hand.

This is why in L.I.F.T., we emphasize "Lean-Without Mean." It's not enough to be lean enough to make critical decisions in a timely way. It's also not enough to run a lean company with plenty of reserves and cash—if that reserve isn't in service of better quality. More critically, if you want to really elevate your L.I.F.T. Leadership beyond words on a page, you need an enthusiastic team. Leaders don't work in isolation. To be lean, you don't have to be mean. In fact, I'd argue, for business dexterity, you need an eager and empowered team. Lean, yes, but super motivated.

Lean-Without-Mean Leadership standard

Although I'm a big advocate of Six Sigma, I believe one of the "holes" in Six Sigma thinking is evaluation. Engineer Dr. Jody Meulaner agrees:

"What's missing from current quality engineering standards, including Six-Sigma, is a way to quantitatively evaluate what's most appropriate for a particular application."

The reason why this doesn't matter too often is that "what's most appropriate tends to be what's most profitable." However, if the inputs reduce quality, how does that affect profit? Dr. Meulaner advocates Cost Optimized Quality.[23]

I don't plan to cover this in this book. But, the key to "Lean-Without-Mean" Leadership is flexibility. Standards and systems are in service of the goal—which in the case of Leanness, boils down to "dexterity." Remember, lean thinking is a mentality, not necessarily a process.

Dexterity is about building what's needed for the future

Why dexterity? Because running a profitable business isn't just about what's needed now. It's about what's needed in the future. We may not always be able to anticipate—or in some cases, to create—the future, but we can be ready for it.

Lean Management, ultimately, after you get past quality, profitability, and issues of survival, comes down to the leanness to "turn on a dime." To flex. To be supple in the market. To out-compete the competitors. To deliver higher returns to investors.

Learning to be lean—turn on a dime to seize the opportunities

The entire L.I.F.T. Leadership system is in service of several missions—but it is always going to land on one important fact. Businesses, and leaders, who can **T**ransform (the T. in L.I.F.T.) obstacles into opportunities will lead the market. To that, you need to Focus now. Lean-Not-Mean Leadership is about that **F**ocus for the future.

For a lean company, with minimal team layers, to be able to innovate and grow requires an energized, optimistic, engaged team—which is why relationships are so important in L.I.F.T. You really do need that "A" team we discussed in the second chapter.

Difference between TQM and Lean Six Sigma

The key point in L.I.F.T. is to embrace leanness without meanness. For this reason, Total Quality Management (TQM) is certainly critical to L.I.F.T. leanness—because as important as numbers are, so are the stakeholders: board, suppliers, customers, employees, investors. Lean Six Sigma differs slightly in focus, with a more incremental approach (TQM tends to be long-term.)

If you're not familiar with Total Quality Management and Lean Six Sigma, I strongly suggest you change that. I'll only summarize the key points and differences here, very quickly, to encourage you to learn more (if you aren't already a Master Black Belt.) Layer in my "without mean-ness" description, and you're equipped for lean the L.I.F.T. leadership way.

Total Quality Management (TQM)

Total Quality Management, developed largely by William Edwards Deming, inspired the so-called "Japanese post-war economic miracle." In an extremely abbreviated synopsis form, TQM is based on six principles:

1. Customer-focus: the successful company focuses on the customer and their needs/wants first. In other words, *Quality is Job 1* (the old Ford slogan.)

2. Long-term: TQM is a standard, a long-term program, and even a commitment.

3. Continuous improvement encourages the active and pro-active search for better ways.

4. By the numbers: TQM is above-all by the numbers. All changes and plans are based on data.

5. Eliminates waste: hence, leanness, with a special focus on produc-tivity and efficiency, without compromise to quality standards.

6. Total employee involvement: the secret to achieving TQM is cer-tainly an empowered team, stripped of layers of inefficiency that hampers innovation.

Today, we think of TQM as "common sense." It has become "job one" for many companies.

Six Sigma differences?

How does Six Sigma differ from TQM? They're certainly cousins, but in some ways, they're dramatically different. Sometimes it's a matter of context—just as my emphasis in L.I.F.T. for "Lean-Without-Mean" provides its own unique context.

The main three ways TQM and Lean Sigma differ are:

TQM	Lean Six Sigma
High emphasis on quality.	Same high emphasis on quality, but in context of business goals and process optimization—and with heavy emphasis on collaborating as a team.
Quality and expertise tend to be focused in one department (i.e. Quality Dept.)	Quality disciplines, empowerment and expertise are distributed to every area of the company.
Main focus for improvements processes is on products, tools and services.	In addition to these, Lean Six Sigma seeks improvements in all areas of the business, including cycle times, organizational improvements, business goals and development.

There are other ways they differ—especially in emphasis on waste reduction and efficiency —but Lean Six Sigma is perhaps the most practical and comprehensive, taking into account all areas of a company.

In terms of streamlining and waste-reduction, Lean Six Sigma remains laser-focused on every inefficiency. Fuji Cho of Toyota famously wrote that "anything other than the minimum amount of equipment, materials, parts, space, and workers time, which are absolutely essential to add value to the product" is wasted.[24]

L.I.F.T. Enhanced Leanness?

"Lean-without-mean" is not an invention—just an important emphasis. Total Quality Management and Six Sigma and Lean Six Sigma certainly take ethics and empathy into account tactically—as a driver for quality. *The L.I.F.T. emphasis makes it indispensable*: your stakeholders—clients, suppliers, investors, team-members, unions, and many others—are all part of the focus. In other words—being lean without being mean.

This is why we use the language of "Principled Leader" and "Principled Company." Our "Lean" emphasis is in service of reducing layers of decision and bureaucracy and doubt to allow teams to flourish and innovate and "Transform the obstacles into opportunities."

It may seem like a fine distinction, but it's an important one. Lean Six Sigma and other methods must remain in service to the Transformative nature of all businesses.

What do I mean? Imagine a company so focused on Lean management that they pump up their bottom line. Investors are happy, right? Short term, certainly. But, what happens in a year or two when a competitor starts to innovate you out of the market because they were less "harsh" with their teams—a team eager and ready to innovate? How happy are investors when the quest for the bottom line leaves the company without a future?

The real secret to sustained L.I.F.T. is empowered enthusiastic teams, which makes "without mean" an indispensable part of the lean equation.

Lean L.I.F.T. Leaders listen— the team has the answers

It seems easy to talk the "lean game." All of us can learn the techniques. A Master Black Belt in Six Sigma will give you solid training, methods, and knowledge.

Yet, at the end of the day, the real people with the answers are your team. I already discussed how to empower them. There's one more thing you need to do. To really empower your team, you have to actively listen and not talk. That's why in chapter 2, we emphasized real communication, strength in relationships, and the importance of the team.

Stop telling your team how great *your* ideas are—and listen for their great ideas. Make sure they get the credit, too.

Most great L.I.F.T. Leaders plant the seeds—the goals, the aspiration, the idea—then watch your team turn it into a solution. They are the gardeners. Watch and listen. Your team has the answers.

If you want to be lean, without being mean, you need to turn to your team—that team you nurtured through deft L.I.F.T. Leadership. They are valued assets of the company for a reason.

L.I.F.T. Lean Cycle

Six Sigma uses the standard framework DMAIC—Define, Measure, Analyze, Improve, Control—ideally charted and tracked constantly. It's important to remember this is a dependency cycle, though. You define, then measure, then analyze, then improve, then control—then, to continue growing you DMAIC all over again in a loop. The language changes—sometimes these are labeled: define, measure, analyze/design, verify. The basic idea of the dependency cycle remains, regardless of labels. Continuous improvement is a never-ending story.

L.I.F.T. enhances the cycle in two ways. We've already discussed the people aspect—and the importance of implementing without "meanness." The other way we enhance the basic Six Sigma DMAIC is by breaking the analysis into two discrete steps.

Analyze becomes two discrete stages

In terms of L.I.F.T. Leadership, we add a step with six instead of five discrete cycle stages. (See the diagram.) "Control"—the final step in the cycle—for me is too broad a term to be meaningful. In real life, the "control" stage consumes more of your resources, and it can make a major difference in the sustainability of a change. It might seem like semantics, but in real life, this is what we do. Instead of control we:

- Implement (including Training)

- Maintain

Am I splitting hairs? If I am, it's in the interest of clarity and long-term sustainability. "Control" is a broad term. In real life, implementing and training—the actual process of becoming productive—is not the same as "maintaining and producing." It is just labeling, but because Maintaining is a big task in the cycle, it deserves its own consideration in terms of planning.

We also re-label "Measure" in DMAIC as "Collect." We state it this way to encourage the unbiased "collection" of information. Measuring can be both collected data and analyzed metrics—it seems a little vague. The goal is to collect—then, in the next step to "Examine." We use the language "Examine" as distinct from the analysis in the context of a "forensic examiner." Examiners analyze, but they also strive to be unbiased and generate every possible conclusion to ensure they are not missing anything and not making biased conclusions.

In L.I.F.T., we modify the DMAIC cycle this way —

- Define

- Collect (which is "Measure" in DMAIC): collect more correctly defines the process here. The goal is to collect all the data, and in the next step, to examine it.

- Examine (which is "Analyze" in DMAIC): because in L.I.F.T., we both analyze the data and make conclusions from our examination of the data. Examine mirrors "investigative" modeling methods, such as in law enforcement.

- Enhance: ("which is "Improve in DMAIC): because in L.I.F.T., we prefer the term Enhance to suggest the purpose of this step.

- Implement (this would be part of "Control" in DMAIC and will include training.)

- Maintain (this would also be part of "Control" in DMAIC)—discretely separating the function of Control from the Implementation aspect.

I'm the first to admit it doesn't make for a catchy anagram—it becomes DCEEIM —but it does more precisely reflect the L.I.F.T. version of DMAIC.

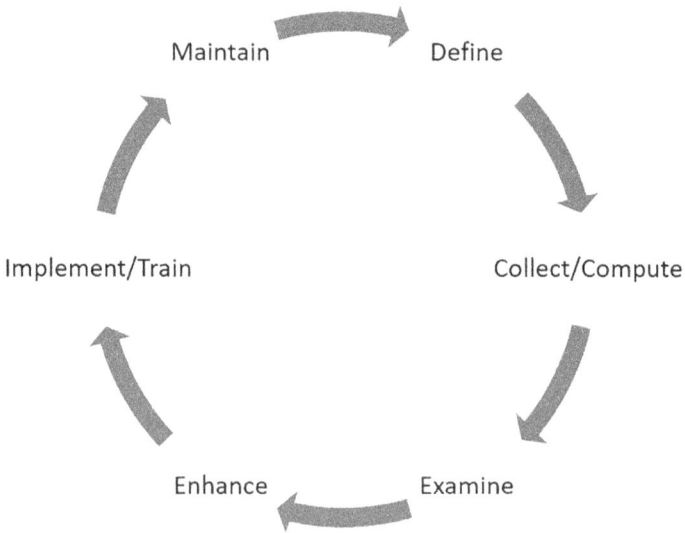

Caption: L.I.F.T. Lean-Not-Mean Cycle

Lift exercise: What can you do without?

As a parent, one thing I learned early on is that you can "coach" your children to perform better—or, using reverse psychology, to accept less of something—if you incent their sacrifice with a much better reward. Incentives work, and they often start early in our life—and they are also part of our professional life. We do reward our teams with incentives.

In a large company, I find the fastest way to implement lean thinking is to dangle an incentive. Everyone loves to celebrate a victory or accomplishment with a reward.

For example, you're trying to convince your sales manager to give up the idea of hiring an assistant because it's an unnecessary expense. So, you say, "You're right, I could budget an assistant for you right now, but wouldn't you rather spend that money on marketing and increased sales incentives?" Who wouldn't rather take an incentive over an assistant? The benefit for the company is the reward comes from the gain, not incurring an expense in the hope of a reward.

Putting bribery aside, one exercise you can implement organizationally is what I call the "What can you do without?" exercise. You can even add this to your 90-day dashboard if you want to add "lean" thinking to your reviews.

Run through this exercise for yourself, or adapt a variant of this exercise for your team members. It's a simplified version of L.I.F.T. Lean Planning. Keep this at a "micro" level, with just a small milestone you want to achieve. For instance, you want to convince everyone to chip in to get a Nespresso Coffee machine for the lunchroom. (Of course, feel free to make your milestones bigger—this is just practice for now.)

Answer these questions in writing. Print it, and review it as the month progresses:

1. My number one milestone—the one thing I must achieve—for the next month is:

2. Study the "Lift Lean-Not-Mean Cycle diagram. Now work through that cycle for your milestone. In step 1 (above), you already DEFINED. Now, List what you know about your scenario (This is COLLECT, on the diagram):

a

b

c

d

Now list what you don't know and must research:

a

b

c

d

3. Based on your list above, what are the OPPORTUNITIES contained in that list? What will help you succeed in your milestone? (In other words, EXAMINE on the cycle.)

a

b

c

d

4. Are there any innovative solutions to my problem or enhancements I can consider? (**ENHANCE** on the cycle)

5. How do I implement this? (**IMPLEMENT / TRAIN** on the cycle.)

6. Does this require maintenance? What is the realistic life cycle? (**MAINTAIN** on the cycle.)

7. What resources do I absolutely need to succeed in my milestone? (Time, money, help, data, list them all)

8. What will these resources cost?

9. What five things am I willing to sacrifice (give up) to attain my goal:

    i

ii

iii

iv

v

10. What are the repercussions if I fail?

11. What is my reward if I succeed?

Reflections from the Conqueror

Lean management wasn't a concept in Mehmed II's time, but the concept of efficiency and prioritizing was definitely critical in war-planning. Lean thinking was actually a matter of life and death, especially for things such as long and expensive as city sieges. In the siege of Constantinople, every day spent containing the enemy inside their walls would cost

Mehmed in terms of the goodwill of his soldiers, suffering at the front, and his resources—feeding a hungry war machine.

In that era, the ability to contain—then to breach—the great walls of Constantinople was a seemingly insurmountable obstacle to victory. Many armies before Mehmed had failed.

Mehmed and his army "engineers" would have gone through a L.I.F.T. Lean Cycle exercise of their own, examining all the options, feasibility costs in lives and money. As in our L.I.F.T. exercise, "What can you do without?" Mehmed would have gone through his own list of what he was willing to "give up" to achieve the goal. To analyze the options, he turned to an ambitious and talented engineer named Urban.

The engineer Urban developed a nearly impossible cannon concept—an innovation (Enhance in our L.I.F.T. cycle)—a weapon that had never been developed previously. It would be the "biggest" and "baddest" canon of all time.

Mehmed II understood the enormity of the challenge—but also the incredible opportunity to succeed. If they succeeded, they would have a tremendous advantage. Of course, he would fund the impossible canon—the risks and costs were high, but the reward would be immeasurable in terms of the goal if Urban succeeded.

In true L.I.F.T. Lean Management style, Mehmed agreed to fund the project but gave Urban a deadline—90 days to finish the project and to produce not just one but dozens of these massive cannons.

In business, we often say if you want something done, give the project to the busiest person. Limited time can often create an environment that squeezes out waste and excess time. Inevitably, that "busy person" is likely your best, lean thinking person.

Urban was a lean management expert. He ended up creating the world's largest cannon with 20-centimeter walls and an eight-meter-long barrel, robust enough to hurl a half-ton cannonball over the staggering distance of one full mile. Imagine that in the context of history.

Urban then replicated his feat dozens of times within his 90-day deadline. Urban is the perfect example of the "lean" leader. It was nothing short of miraculous. Except, it was no miracle—it was well planned and executed.

How these lessons apply to 21st-century business

Mehmed's miraculous engineer Urban was his period's version of a genuine L.I.F.T. Lean Leader. His story demonstrates that with the right motivation—in his case, the war depended on it!—a strict deadline (90 days!) and, no doubt, sufficient reward, even the near-impossible can be achieved. He did not have a vast team of helpers.

Would Urban have pulled off this amazing feat if he had not been amply rewarded? Mehmed did not threaten to "chop off his head." Urban's incentive was nothing less than the monetary gains and financial rewards for him and his assistants if they could pull off the greatest feat in military history of that time. Urban was of Greek descent and the Ottoman's hiring him to build these cannons was not about the protection of people or heritage but a job and an opportunity to do something truly amazing and historical.

In a modern context, in your own company, you likely have your own version of the engineer Urban. He is motivated to change things in the company, self-motivated to accomplish difficult or impossible things, a natural desire to help his company win the competitive war, surely, he views his salary as recognition for his daily contribution, but he's truly motivated by the impossible and pushing excellence within his craft. Of course, he enjoys the bonus he is given, which did act as an incentive for the truly amazing accomplishment.

4

TRANSFORM: THE FOUR PILLARS OF ACTIONABLE DECISIONS

Transformation relies on actionable decisions, which in turn relies on all four of the Transformative Pillars: Means, Motive, Evidence, Context. Great L.I.F.T. Leaders weigh all four, then decide with relentless tenacity. Meaningful Transformation starts with the Leader's final decision.

L.I.F.T. Facts

- Almost 66 percent of leaders lack sufficient understanding of what is expected of them and are "unprepared for what they will face."

- Sixty-seven percent of executives struggle to let go of their previous roles.

- Fifty percent of new leaders/executives fail within eighteen months.[25]

Allll of these facts are cited from a wide longitudinal study of 2700 executives. This shouldn't surprise anyone reading this book. What differentiates a leader who will succeed from one destined to fail is almost always the ability to embrace what I call the "Four Pillars of Actionable Decisions."

In this chapter

- Transformative decisions require four pillars of Transformation: Means, Motive, Evidence, Context.

- Means—Is it feasible?

- Motive—What's at stake?

- Evidence—What are the hard facts? Hard evidence and forensic analysis are the basis under which leaders make critical decisions.

- Context—How does this impact our stakeholders: clients and customers, investors, team members. How does it impact our competitors?

Important Take-away

- **"No transformative decision should be undertaken without the four pillars of support."**

Reflections from the Conqueror

- *Mehmed walked the line and spoke with his foot soldiers. He sent out spies. He brought in engineers. He undertook his "impossible mission" to conquer the unconquerable only after ensuring he had the four pillars of support: Means (money, taxes, and soldiers), Motive (his people were passionate about the goal of conquering Constantinople), evidence (he examined all the logistics of battle), and context (the honor of his family and his people mattered more than their lives.)*

L.I.F.T. When was the last time you walked the line—got off your horse and talked with the troops? Transformative leaders are there with their team.

Lead: Your decisions impact everyone in the company. Your team deserves decisions based on all four pillars.

Inspire: Your team will rally to solutions that make sense. Explain your decisions and the rationale. You are a leader, not a dictator. You are not seeking approval at this stage but rather full adoption and unequivocal support.

Focus: You listened to your team. Now, give them concise clarity by making it a proclaimed resolution—and allow them to focus on the solution and the means to the end.

Transform: Transformation is a team effort. Make the team the enforcers of transformation. If you've built your own "A-Team," trust them to succeed.

Strategic decision-making, based on critical thinking with provable facts, is absolutely vital. There's no room for "fake news" in the corporate arena—you're not running for office; you're running a corporation that depends on you. Don't underestimate the cost of a bad strategic decision in business. In my experience, bad decisions are a result of poor research, jaded information, missing data, prejudiced assumptions, and/or biased analysis.

A great strategic decision, on the other hand, can save the company, rejuvenate the brand, or bring new life to a struggling team. That doesn't mean you should make decisions for the sake of looking decisive. Your decisions have consequences, which is why every aspect of L.I.F.T.—Lead, Inspire, Focus, Transform—are aspects of effective leaders. In the case of decisions that can change the entire trajectory of a business or brand, the Lead, Inspire, Focus, Transform takes on new layers and nuances:

- **L**ead: bring together the resources you'll need for a critical decision.

- **I**nspire: Inspire action on your final decision by collaborating with your team on your direction. Once you make the decision, that's final. But, prior to that, listen, learn and bond with your action team.

- **F**ocus: You cannot know too much. Research and extensive reconnaissance are not optional. Do you know everything you can know about the situation and your competitors' positions? No decision should be made without **F**ocus and real **F**acts. (Today, you have to differentiate real, substantial facts from "fake facts.") Also important is to Focus on what your audiences want. Just because you have made something better doesn't mean anyone wants it. Your audiences are central to Focus.

- **T**ransform: Transformation begins with your decision. The **L**eader's decision (**L**ead) is the action itself if it is based on your team's insights (**I**nspire), research and facts, and analysis (**F**ocus).

Not every decision you make will succeed, but it may still Transform. Transformation can be negative as well as positive. With high stakes, the need for quality information, team insight (and buy-in), and good analysis are vital. Even if your decision seems sound, but it doesn't resonate with the audience.

I can show you how to make Transformative decisions. However, transformation is entirely up to you and your team.

Real-life L.I.F.T. inspiration case study—nine months of anarchy

One of my early Leadership projects involved a media company in Europe that had recently received a broadcast license. Prior to me coming in as the new leader, they were already an amazing organization. Their list of accomplishments was a long one: they developed their own studios, recruited cast, staff writers, script editors, audio engineers, video editors, cast directors, production coordinators, data wranglers, mobile field crews, and cameras to bring live-action; they had veteran weather reporters and advanced systems, enhanced post-production editing systems; they even built a public relations and a legal compliance group to manage all licensing and content. They had made stunning development and were the talk of that country's media industry with their bold actions and exciting progress.

In my initial inventory and review, over the first 100 days of my leadership, I discovered that their inventory of production assets was long. Unfortunately—and this is where I came in—the fundamental economics were completely unbalanced. They had a staggering productivity engine—but didn't know how to sell, exploit, market, or achieve a return on their substantial investments. Additionally, the market and total available advertising opportunities didn't support the revenue/profit expectations for a relatively new player with limited exposure due to channel placement.

The financial demands of the impressive team and infrastructure far outstripped the advertising revenue, key content distribution sponsorships, or any potential content redistribution revenue. And worse, there was no momentum behind the revenue generation efforts. In one way, the built infrastructure was a delight for a newly landed leader. Unfortunately, that infrastructure had to be paid for—and make a return on its hefty price tag.

As any leader would, now that I understood the issues, I began the process of Transformation: options had to be analyzed, and decisions had to be made fairly quick. The "burn rate" of that costly infrastructure was appallingly fast.

I soon discovered one practical aspect of channel placement in this particular country was not optimal. In those days, and in that region of the world, channel placement mattered if you wanted to capture the casual browsers for information and entertainment. It was like having a posh hotel in a run-down neighborhood. We would have to develop strategies to promote and market our channel.

As **L**eader, I pulled together my action teams, **I**nspired them to **F**ocus on all the problems—including analyzing all the options—then, it would be time to decide on which passage we'd take to **T**ransformation. Although it became clear to us and me, as we worked through these stages of L.I.F.T. that we did not have enough advertising dollars to initially support the business, we would only be able to sustain one key transformative strategy, and time was of the essence. Compounding our issues, we were competing with well-established state-funded channels that were well equipped to squeeze out the young entrepreneurial broadcasters.

Analyzing and churning

My teams and I went through an extensive but rapid audit of data. We remained objective regardless of what we found, spoke to all stakeholders, considered all opinions—as a team in a Focus environment—then it was time for the leader to make the big-stakes transformative decisions.

The pending decision weighed heavily on me. This amazing team had built this stunning broadcast infrastructure—quite expensive to remain. At the time, I think I must have thought of it as a ravenously hungry beast. We didn't have the endless food to feed this dragon.

As I weighed the options—keeping in mind all stakeholders, including the team, investors, advertisers, viewers—I came to a shocking conclusion. Despite all the hard work and investment, my analysis of all options determined that the business could never support the "hoped for" broadcasting model, especially with the gorilla-sized state broadcasters. The clock was ticking, and we only had seconds left.

We would have to narrow our focus to something we could definitely win. I determined—and not without some angst, emotion, and hesitation—that our path to success was to reposition as a content re-distributor. This would be contingent on the crucial pivot down to a single-digit channel placement. To say this was a bold decision would be an understatement. I could control the massive transformation to a content re-distributor but doing this in concert with convincing a Minister of Communications to wave a wand without the gorillas in the way was beyond highly audacious. This was an upheaval of cosmic proportions coupled with shewd maneuvering, but the future of the company was at stake.

Don't misunderstand chapter 3, "Lean without mean," to suggest a leader does not have to do what's needed for the overall team. In times like this, the Utilitarian theory has to be the overarching philosophy, "The greatest good for the greatest number….sometimes a few have to suffer for the whole." In cases of poor cost control, people are often the casualty of cost reduction. Don't misread compassion for weakness. When a leader has to make tough choices, it's based on hard analysis and fact. It's not personal; it's business. If it must be done, the strong leader acts to Transform.

Massive course changes are not for the faint of heart. You'll have to sleep on it and get comfortable with the facts. Make sure the changes are really necessary. If they are, don't look back. Act compassionately with those you cannot afford to keep but act decisively.

My decision meant an enormous restructuring of the company. It meant selling off, closing, or disposing of five studios in two locations. It meant a reduction of staff by 80 percent. For any leader, this is devastating, no matter how ruthless. The greatest good is to keep the company alive for all stakeholders, but the number that had to suffer to survive was beyond painful.

The anarchy of transformation begins

The decision had been made, and now would begin the transformation. As sympathetically as possible, we implemented our changes. Meanwhile,

I made the application to the government for a new channel placement, and I initiated efforts through my network to get to her and find a means to leverage my request.

It was anarchy for nine months as we reversed millions of dollars of investment, sold assets at a discount, and paid severances to the people we were forced to usher out the door.

Within this anarchy, a miracle occurred. It was a miracle born on the wings of sacrifice, but never-the-less a huge win. After a series of quick off-the-record meetings, an application prepared in haste, and a meeting on the outside stairs of the ministry—and just before an emergency meeting before the summer break—the Ministry of Communications granted us the license to a lower channel, single-digit placement. It was over before the National Public Broadcaster even realized. I won't run through the several months of activities that we went through to ensure that alloca-tion—but suffice to say, our hard actions had paved the way.

Within a year, the business went from a loss to a small profit, from a broadcaster to a content re-distributor. Importantly, advertising dol-lars went up by 290 percent, and ratings quadrupled. The business was eventually sold to a major broadcaster in Europe, and the station lives on today. So, although this case study makes clear the need for strategic decision-making—it can make or break a company—it also illustrates that, when needed, leaders must be decisive and strong. They should not be made lightly because the transformation could be positive or negative, depending on the quality of your decision-making—but once you commit, it's not for the faint-of-heart.

The best metaphor: being a Judge

Why am I discussing "being a Judge" in a chapter titled "Transform: The Four Pillars of Actionable Decisions"? Because a business leader, especially C-Suite leaders, must make decisions that affect lives, just like honorable judges in a court of law. Like judicial judgments, C-Suite-level decisions are not a game. They impact lives in a very profound way.

For this reason, I use the model of the law-enforcement as my metaphor for "actionable decisions"—especially judge and police detective examples. The ideal detective is relentless in the pursuit of answers, requiring multiple pieces of evidence that cannot be refuted. The Judge makes a final decision that will impact lives forever.

Bear with me as I explain my metaphor and why it works. Before the detective makes a life-changing decision—to charge someone with a crime—he has to be convinced by the evidence beyond a reasonable doubt (or, at least, she/he should be.) The Judge and Jury (think of the Jury as your leadership team) ultimately decide the fate of the person charged. This decision will be based on evidence compiled by various law-enforcement professionals (your team and consultants), although the detective (your project leader) carries the heaviest weight of conscience for any decisions.

You can even have fun with the analogy. In a bigger corporate action team, you can have one of your project managers act as the advocate (defense) and another act as the challenger (prosecutor) prosecutor. Don't forget your forensic examiners (research team, in your case.) This entire metaphor works well because the judicial profession is a confrontational arena—much like corporations and marketplaces.

I use this metaphor because of the "weight" of responsibility the judicial professionals carry. C-Suite decisions are no less weighty than those of a Judge—arguably weightier since many lives can be affected, many unknowing lives. Your leadership team, your Jury, carry that weight as well.

The stakes are as high or higher. The reliability of your facts and analysis, therefore, are life-impacting. Don't settle for internet research, and "he said, she said." You need facts to make decisions. You need to ask the five whys in your iterative interrogative drill down to get to the root cause. You need backup to your sources. You need reliable citations and research. You need the opposing view. You can never assume.

Once you make these decisions, only the weight of an appeal (to finish my metaphor) can change the course of a leader's decision. Appeals are expensive, and by then, lives have changed. In other words, you carry the weight of making the right **T**ransformative decisions.

The Four Pillars of Judgement

To make the "right" judgments—decisions in the corporate world—four supports are needed:

- Means

- Motive

- Evidence

- Context (for example, in a judicial trial, guilt is put aside in the context of certain disabilities)

In a serious judicial trial, no one or two of these would be enough. Without evidence, the motive is not enough. Without evidence, means and motives aren't sufficient.

As a leader who has helped steer numerous corporate turnarounds, I believe all four of these are also needed to bring meaningful decisions—and the resultant tangible transformations. The great equalizer is time. How much and how fast can you gain the insights needed to define the means, motive, evidence, and context versus the opportunity window to make the decision. Time is always of the essence, but too quick or too slow can be disastrous. You need to be mindful and discerning on the moment you have to act.

Analyzing the Case Study: The Four Pillars of Judgment

Although my example in this chapter's case study is a harsh one, we had to make tough judgments based on the weight of the four pillars. Even if we had other options—we clearly did—without all four pillars in place, there's no certainty you can succeed. When stakes are high, decisions should take into account all four. In my broadcaster scenario:

- **Means**: We did not have the means to support and pay for the studio broadcaster aspiration: the studios, recruited cast, staff writers, script editors, audio engineers, video editors, cast directors, production coordinators, data wranglers, mobile field crews, and cameras.

- **Motive**: Our motivation was nothing less than a complete turnaround. Without means, we either would have had to fund the extensive infrastructure in place or modify the goal to fit our means (see above.)

- **Evidence**: I came in fresh to the company, impressed by all their assets, but the evidence clearly indicated we had no prospect of paying for the existing infrastructure out of the foreseeable revenues.

- **Context**: I had to consider the context of the greater good for the investors, the company, the team, and our viewers. I had to also weigh the competitive context of "state broad-casters" with unlimited funds. By streamlining operations to a new model of content re-distributor (versus original content creator broadcaster.)

Would I have made the same decisions in the absence of one of these? Obviously not. If we had the "means," we would probably have kept our already-built infrastructure. But, even if we had the means, if the evidence demonstrated that there was not enough demand for original content, that would also change the decision—and ultimately, the needed Transformation.

All four pillars are critical in decisions and in Transformation.

Means—Great ideas alone are not enough

It is unlikely an investigator will bring charges against a suspect where they didn't have the means to commit the crime. In corporate decisions, the leader likewise has to take "means" into account. Does the corporation have the means to implement the great ideas that the team is proposing? The difference between brainstorming great ideas, and implementing them, often comes down to "do we have the means to pay for this idea?" Ideas transform only with resources (means).

If the Leader determines one of the options or pathways presented is the right path, but the corporation lacks the means, that's not necessarily the end of the story. If lack of funds hampers planning, the Leader can look at various sources of investment or funding: investments, partnering, financing, sponsorships, or even non-traditional resources. Lack of means alone need not disqualify an option in decision making—but only if there is enough support from the other three pillars of decision: motive, evidence, context. If you have a *motive*—a compelling need or goal—and you have *evidence* and analysis suggesting the best path to that goal, then you can certainly pursue *means*. The L.I.F.T. Leader thinks through all the options, including innovative ways you can pay or sponsor your tactics.

In my experience, the more innovative and original the tactics, the more likely you'll have to be similarly ground-breaking in pursuing alternative means.

Motive—What's at Stake?

It may sometimes seem like motive is the most important element of the "crime"—in our case, our project. If there's no reason for the project, why go further? (Likewise, if there's no reason for the crime, why suspect them?)

Often, we start with motive. Other times we create the need. We may have to dig deeper to find out what's really motivating us. In the studio case study, I asked myself, "what motivated this team to build out this incredible infrastructure of studios without any demand?" They made the mistake of assuming, "If you build it, they will come." This line from Field of Dreams is pure fantasy. In the context of business (or baseball), building it is usually feeding a dream. Dreams are not goals or motives. A motive is an irresistible force.

In a crime, the more compelling the motive, the stronger the suspect. In business, the more compelling the motive, the more likely you'll achieve it. Lukewarm goals and motivations mean nothing in business.

If my team at the studio had given me compelling motivations— proven to me that we had to have studios for content creation because, without them, we would fail—that would have been a different scenario. It was obvious to me, after analyzing the data, there was no compelling motivation to keep what had been a costly mistake.

In your planning, as a L.I.F.T. leader, start with motive and end with motive. If there isn't a strong motive, move on—no need to spend time on evidence and context if no one is motivated by the mission.

Evidence—Prove it or Forget it

You can have the greatest idea in the world. You can be strongly motivated to trademark it, patent it, own it, promote it—but if there's no evidence you can find an audience for your great idea, it's worthless. Write a novel if you're motivated just by ideas. In business, everything needs evidence.

What's my feeding metaphor for evidence? In law enforcement, the prosecutor might be 90 percent convinced a suspect is guilty. Without evidence, she or he would never consider bringing it to trial. There might be a basis for investigation, but not for "charges."

Likewise, if you have that great idea, and you believe you can find an audience, then investigate. Is it just wishful thinking if you can't prove it?

Context—Competitors, Regulations and...

Context is often overlooked. You have a great idea. You can prove it's unique. Your lawyer says it's patentable. You found an untapped audience. So, what's the problem? The context matters. Here's a shortlist—the long list you can develop on your own, depending on your industry:

- Your key competitors are much bigger and better-financed: they might steal your idea knowing you can't afford to defend it.

- In your area, various regulations might inhibit your project.

- Liability—did you analyze any potential hidden liabilities? Whether you produce food, entertainment, or auto parts, there is always a liability to analyze.

- Your brand is too weak to credibly market the idea.

- You don't have the infrastructure, and it will be too costly to build.

- Unstable politics in your area.

- International trade barriers...

I'll end with ellipses since every industry has literally hundreds of contextual factors to consider. The issue for leaders is it's often the last thing you, or your teams, consider. It might even be forgotten until it is too late.

Relentless Decisions—Making Tough Choices

Here, the judicial analogy still works—judges make life and death decisions. Depending on your industry, so will you. If you can't cope with that idea, get out of the C-Suite.

I deliberately used the most haunting scenario case study from my own career in this chapter on Transformative decisions. In this case study, I was compelled to let go 80 percent of my team. Trust me; it's not enjoyable. What gets you through the process, and helps you sleep at night, is the people that will remain, their families depend on us, and the future success. You turn around a company, and hundreds of employees and investors and customers benefit.

L.I.F.T. leaders do have to be "big picture" planners. If you focus too narrowly, it might be because you're afraid of tough choices.

You wouldn't be alone. In a Harvard Business Review ten-year longitudinal study of 2,700 business leaders, a whopping 57% of executives said that their decisions were more difficult than they expected.[26]

The most commonly given reason in that study was "I'm being considerate of others." Another common reason was "Morale is already low."

Excuse me? Morale is low because there are problems and a proverbial train coming down the tracks. Problems don't disappear on their own. Abdicating the tough decision because "it might hurt someone's feelings" is nothing less than the ineffective leader who helps no one and allows the company and all of its people to careen towards the end quicker.

Here is your watch list of thoughts (excuses) that might occur to you when you hesitate in making the tough choices. Treat them as warning signs you are not making the needed decisions:

- "I want to be fair."

- "I'm being considerate."

- "Everyone is hurting already."

- "Stress in the workplace is too high right now for this."

- "My best people will leave in the throes of the changes."

You get the idea. We all have these thoughts, even the toughest of relentless decision-makers, but leaders are responsible for the many, not the few.

Three types of decisions

There are three distinct types of decisions in the L.I.F.T. Leadership system: Cardinal, Strategic, and Battlefield:

1) **Cardinal decisions** – High stakes, fundamental decisions that impact everyone in the organization. This doesn't have to be about business or financial fundamentals. In my view, among the most cardinal of decisions are those involving values. Frankly, any breach of core company values is a cardinal compromise, not a "little thing." You saw how I dealt with a "cardinal" issue in the first chapter case study, "Winners never cheat." I was willing to let go of substantial financial deals to protect my teams' values. Anything that involves the entire team is "cardinal" by definition.

2) **Strategic / Tactical decisions** – These are the decisions most leaders face daily, weekly, or monthly. They are vital, important decisions related to markets, M&A, product roadmaps, a board of directors' matter, budgeting, banking/financing, corporate structuring, investments, and important executive team direction. This is likely where you'll spend most of your time as a leader—this is your main space. The leader, above all, is a master of strategy and tactics.

3) **Battlefield decisions** – Leaders face these time-sensitive decisions often, not on a schedule like Strategic / Tactical decisions, but with appalling frequency. Battlefield decisions are just what they sound like. You've taken the field with your team (army), with your strategy and tactics mapped out (2 above)—only to be faced with real-world circumstances. Inputs and outputs in Battlefield scenarios are fast and furious. The truly adept leader manages the chaotic churn of information. It may seem like

a battlefield decision requires a lot of instinct, grit—to make the quick call in battle—with a nimble attitude to make things happen. But, like Mehmed, we only seem that way because we prepared ahead. We didn't come to the battlefield unarmed. We planned for contingencies.

Regardless of the type of decision, you still need to engage in the form of analyzing means, evidence, motive, and context. What might change is the urgency and timing.

L.I.F.T. Fives: Five Keys to Great Decisions

In L.I.F.T. we outline five keys to making great decisions in business:

Key 1—Layered Thinking

Collecting evidence, we've touched on it in my "legal analogy." Layered thinking means digging deep into that evidence and viewing that collected data from all perspectives. But, before digging too deep, remind yourself that in all stages of critical thinking and decision making, that you and your team will remain neutral. You are fact-gathering, not judging. Even when you start your "layered thinking"—viewing all perspectives—remain unbiased.

We are all people, and, let's face it—people spin things from their own personal perspective and with their own personal bias. Recognize that. Become the master compiler, the master listener. Don't make conclusions yet. If you do, you may miss an opportunity buried in those facts.

In my chapter case study, I described how I inventoried the company—very impressed with their assets, built over months of hard work. The important nugget of information lay in two areas—which I could have missed if I didn't finish my full inventory. Those two pieces of critical, actionable information were: government broadcasters compete unfairly, and we were stuck on a channel range no one visited. If I had made my decision too quickly, I might have missed those two key facts. After all, I was literally buried in lists of facts.

In other words, avoid forming opinions until all the facts are in. (To use my metaphor, the trial hasn't begun yet. You're still investigating.) The problem with forming an opinion too quickly is you may not be able to shake yourself from that belief later. (You've read stories of prosecutors who were so convinced the "family member" did it, they missed the real suspect who lived around the corner.)

Just be the unbiased gatherer of the facts at this first stage. You must dig deeper and remain committed to getting everything on the table to assist you in making a proper decision.

Layered Thinking—Now, part two of this is—analyze in layers. You have all the facts. Now you have to sit with those facts and see the issue from a variety of perspectives—all perspectives if possible.

There are always different points of view. In my case study, if I only saw the point-of-view of the content creator, I might have missed the fact there is no market for another content creator.

Try to make connections between parallel events that possibly create a pattern or a meaningful connection.

Key 2—The Right Data for the Right Decisions

As a C-suite leader (or aspiring leader), you already know the difference between information and data. Data guides decisions. Information can obscure decisions. This is why we state key 2 as "the Right Data for the Right Decisions."

How do we differentiate? Cited, numerical data is the most reliable. Even so, numbers can be factual without being helpful. Don't assume that you understand your numbers. Challenge yourself. Does this data really indicate what I think? Am I imputing a spin on the data? Did my researchers leave out data? Should I consult an expert?

Data is vital, and numbers run businesses, but it's important to have the right data and metrics. I devote an entire chapter to metrics—that's how critical it is. (*Chapter 6. Your Insight: Five Essential Metrics.*) Not all numbers are equal. Some widely accepted business metrics are actually misleading. Some forms of analysis are dated in terms of today's businesses.

Data collection, analysis, and its use in planning is an effort that never stops. It requires vigilance and frequency. The dynamic of modern business is fast: margins change, prices change, contracts expire, contracts are signed, spending patterns change, new technology arrives, people are hired/fired/promoted, and your financial picture is in a constant state of change. You cannot assume you know the current numbers. This a continuous cycle of information/decisions. The more time you spend with data that matters, the sharper your instincts will become.

Key #3 Parallel Thinking

Only the most skilled of L.I.F.T. Leaders tend to develop this nuanced skill. Parallel thinking, as we developed it, involves compartmentalization. If you can visualize six monitors on your desk, each running different scenarios, you get the idea. If you are able to concentrate on all six at once, thinking in parallel, you may have what it takes to be that top one percent of leaders—the L.I.F.T. Leader. Or, to use my law-enforcement metaphor, you could be an investigator who has six suspects. You need to keep them all in mind, investigate all of them, collect all the evidence—means, motive, evidence, context—from all six.

To manage this skill—mentally, not on individual monitors on your desk—the key is to remain open, seek the input of many, listen to all the involved stakeholders, ask questions from all angles of the situation and gather the information. There's a reason, only ten percent of team-members are suited to be leaders, and only ten percent of them (or 1 percent in total) are suited to be C-Suite leaders. This is not an easy skill to develop.

Once all the critical inputs and facts are gathered, they can then be put into the crucible, and then the arguments should be considered. Your six suspects are still suspects until they're not.

I like to use convergent and divergent thinking at this stage.

Argue all the possible options from every side. Remain unbiased and argue each side with equal enthusiasm. I believe the most creative thinking comes out of these unconventional approaches to generating options and thinking through the subtle dynamics of a situation.

The biggest mistake leaders make is setting their biases too early, deciding on the "likely suspect," and then putting all their resources into proving it. The one percent of leaders who are L.I.F.T. qualified don't do that. All scenarios, all suspects, all sides are equal—until they're not. It will soon become evident which one is the real suspect or the viable scenario.

Key # 4 Listening to the soft voices

I like to say, "Listen to the quiet ones." The soft and often ignored voices in an organization are often the ones with the most innovative ideas. When you are at the analysis stage, especially, look for those fresh faces, the new ideas. I often find those louder voices at the meetings are the ones without their own ideas. They might be good ideas, but they're probably not new ideas.

The marginalization of quiet people is sadly very common in corporate culture. We are taught to "stand out,"—but standing out doesn't mean we're creative. It just means we're loud.

Jack Welch, in his book "Winning," told the story of the quiet employee who admonished him during one of his factory tours: "For twenty-five years, you paid for my hands when you could have had my brain as well – for nothing." Precious information went to waste. Of course, Jack made that a turning point in his approach to people within his organization. It changed everything.

I have found that in my own leadership scenarios. You learn more "walking the line and talking to the soldiers" as Mehmed did—and as we should.

Leaders listen.

Key # 5 Four steps to decisions and mental processing

We covered the four aspects of transformative decision-making. It can be overwhelming. All of this analysis and collecting and sorting, and processing can lead to "analysis paralysis." To help with that, here's a handy exercise in the four steps of decision processing:

L.I.F.T. exercise: four steps to decisions

Step #1	Probe & Inquest Stage	Talk to every stakeholder and Find as many opinions on the matter
Step #2	Layered Analysis (Ask yourself 5 questions)	1 What information can be synthesized or falls into a similar pattern?
		2 What biases emerged from the parties in the probing stage, and why do they want to manipulate the end result?
		3 What concepts have I learned before that have a direct connection to this but in a slightly different context?
		4 What unique perspectives or innovative ideas did I learn in the past or from someone in the process?
		5 Is there a values implication or a higher purpose that should be considered?
Step #3	Facts and Evidence	What objective data do I have that needs to be considered?
Step #4	Options & Solutions	What are the three ways this could be solved?
		What are the pros and cons of each of the three options?

Reflections from the Conqueror

Even though Mehmed II was young—like Alexander the Great before him—he was famous for making hard, instant decisions in battle. Did he really rely on gut instinct in a battle situation, or, as is suggested in history, did he prepare and plan months ahead of those "instant" decisions?

Mehmed spent years learning the art of war, battlefield tactics, the technical details of weapons. He even studied how weather and terrain impacted all the other variants on the battlefield. Were their uniforms comfortable in the rain? Did their weaponry adapt well to defense as well as offense? Did the season impact the mental and emotional state of mind of his warriors?

He often quoted Alexander the Great's words, "Without knowledge, skill cannot be focused. Without skill, strength cannot be brought to bear and without strength, knowledge may not be applied."

Famous footballer Lionel Messi once said, "It took me 17 years to become an overnight success."

5

L.I.F.T. TRAJECTORY: DYNAMIC
FEEDBACK AND RECOGNITION

---

*In L.I.F.T., we call performance measures and enrichment L.I.F.T.
Trajectory – the process of immediate real-time feedback and 'course
correction' that facilitates corporate alignment and compensation—the
cycle of clarity and recognition.*

L.I.F.T. Facts

- It costs companies collectively up to $35 million a year (collectively) to undertake[27] formal annual reviews.

- Traditional annual reviews make performance worse one-third of the time.[28]

- In terms of feedback, the more frequent, the better, according to employees: in a Gallup poll, team-members said it was 5.2 times more likely they would receive meaningful feedback, and 3.2 times as likely they'd be more motivated.[29]

In this chapter

- **T**ransform performance with dynamic *L.I.F.T. Trajectory*—the process of frequent measures and enrichment, and "course corrections." Dynamic and active relationships with your team keep clarity and transparency, which are the foundations of trust and loyalty.

- How immediate real-time feedback and reporting transforms into business opportunities.

- Using frequent compensation and recognition loops—and making engagement a regular habit—minimizing frequency, depending on your business, at least every 90 days.

- Making recognition a mission—and making it happen in real-time, open, and from multiple sources.

- How to create clarity and accountability without pain or embarrassment.

Important Take-away

- ***"Transform your teams into eager climbers with feedback and recognition, and frequent course corrections to individual trajectories."***

Reflections from the Conqueror

- *Mehmed may have sent countless soldiers to their death, but they were always eager followers ready to charge. Why? Because he recognized the wins, promoting the winners, and connecting with all of his warriors. If you survived the battle, you would be recognized and well rewarded.*

Values of L.I.F.T.

Transformation through performance reward is the secret of L.I.F.T. Leadership—and what I like to call *L.I.F.T. Trajectory*.

Lead: Your team will follow if they know there is a substantial upside, reward—not just financial, but recognition or promotion.

Inspire: Nothing inspires individuals to be team-players more than recognition within the team.

Focus: Performance measures, reviews, rewards for accomplishment—this is the language of Focus.

Transform: Transformation is the goal of any review and reward. Nothing is more effective than incentives.

Usually, when I suggest Dynamic Trajectory—a concise formal review every 90-days—people assume I'm referring to new-hire or probationary reviews. I'm advocating a cycle of, no longer than 90-days, ongoing throughout the year for all team-members—with dynamic frequent, ongoing touchpoints. Ideally, your reviews and feedback loops with your direct-report team should be daily and weekly—I'm only referring here to the more formal *L.I.F.T. Trajectory: 90-Day Feedback and Recognition*. There's a reason we use language like "Trajectory" and "Dashboard." The key to maximizing opportunity, and minimizing lost opportunity, is near real-time control.

The term "feedback" originated in 1920 as an electronics term, connoting "sending out and returning" measurements. The term feedback is widely used in RF technologies. It was popularized in the context of trajectory by NASA, as Steve Roesler explains[30]:

"Feedback started as a term used to describe the signals sent from a rocket back to Earth in order to determine the accuracy of the rocket's course. By tracking speed and trajectory, ground crews could determine when and where to make corrections... At some point in time, the term

Feedback was incorporated into business language as a way to talk about performance. "

What's important about understanding the origination is the function. In NASA terms, you have to course correct in near real-time, instantly; otherwise, the deviation may be unrecoverable in the vastness of space. An off-course rocket could entirely miss an orbit trajectory—costing billions—or even lives in the case of manned space travel.

In business, we face the same issue. The longer we go before course correction, the more expensive the consequences. Feedback isn't just about knowledge, information, or planning—it's about the daily functioning of our business "mission." If your course correction is too delayed, it can cost millions of dollars, or lives, in the form of jobs.

The most common response to my call for frequent feedback is "Who has the time?" True, if you make the ninety-day reviews too formal and comprehensive—like the more common annual reviews—that would be unproductive.

Just as I advocate one-page plans and one-page *L.I.F.T. Dashboards* (see chapter 10), I likewise recommend frequent performance reviews as a *concise process*. Before you complain it's too much work or that your team will not respond—remember that not only is remediation tied to reviews (i.e., fixing ongoing problems before they gain momentum and spin out of control), but also incentives and reward. Your team will *look forward* to frequent reviews if they are tied to reward or recognition. They will also appreciate your "feedback" loop, allowing them to course-correct. It's a win-win for the team. Frequent course-corrections consume less of your time since you won't have to deal with "major" problems (trajectory changes), and your review process will be ultra-concise.

Don't make the mistake of thinking this is an "optional" chapter in the L.I.F.T. Leadership system. It's vitally important. Trajectory feedback loops and course corrections are vital to the dynamic, winning leader.

Real-life *L.I.F.T Trajectory* performance case study—Action tied to reviews is critical.

"Performance reviews and resets should take place every 90 days."

Performance Measures & Enrichment – corporate alignment

One of my early "lessons learned" was simply that review without action is meaningless. I already knew frequent reviews were critical when I hired a critically important executive along with a key technical executive from a competitor—a big win for us. (See poaching the "A-Team" in chapter 2). It was a great day when those two came through the front door, and we embarked on a game-changing turning-point in our company. The two came as a package, and they took comfort jumping over together.

I was more than delighted with our win, although I had some reservations about one of the executives. He liked to inspire laughs, always joking at others' expense—nothing wrong with being light-hearted—but there was a subtle tendency towards narcissism. This can be common with "A" types, but it often is a problem in a team environment.

In this case, as always, everyone starts with a fresh slate with me. My job as a leader is to define the rules, be clear about expectations, build a close relationship and be forthright about things I feel need improvement. Especially with new hires, particularly recruited "A-listers," that frequent feedback loop is vital. You don't want to waste your investment or shake up a productive team by letting issues gain momentum. A fresh slate, yes, but under a watchful eye.

With my daily and weekly feedback touchpoints, I started to see the trends almost right away. The technical executive I hired in the paired acquisition flourished in our environment, and he had a lot to offer. I saw he could be a person to reach extraordinary heights in his career. Unfortunately, the other executive almost immediately alienated himself from his peers, lashed out frequently at his team—often with "humor"—and deflected responsibility for his actions. Typical of someone who refused to take responsibility for his failures, there was plenty of blame to spread around. We tried the ongoing trajectory "course corrections," but as an "A-lister," there was resistance. My mistake, a lesson learned, was to overlook the opposition with a wait-and-see attitude. The stakes are high with "A" team recruits.

This is where my *L.I.F.T. Trajectory* 90-day Concise Feedback and Recognition resets are essential. In this case, I asked "open" questions, "what do you think you could have done better?" and "even if it's his fault, what could you as team-leader have done to minimize the issue?" Sometimes, you have to cut right to the issue, where someone refused to acknowledge their culpability. In this case, my "course corrections" included asking him to rebuild the bridges he'd burnt and to be humbler with his shortcomings. I asked him to listen more, to hear the underlying disagreements. I took the step to hire a coach and have him do a psychological performance evaluation. The next big warning sign came when the psychological results came in. The development plan was entirely rejected by that same executive with a dismissive "those things never know how to understand me," even though the list of concerns was long and detailed. The baby went out with the bathwater that day.

Sometimes, diplomacy, coaching, and best intentions aren't enough. In this case, our "A list" recruit did not listen. He was like the Teflon man. Nothing stuck.

The day came when my only option was to let him go—even though I had gone to such efforts to recruit him. It would mean a wasted investment in time and money. If I felt there was a way to bring him around to a more team-approach, I would have tried it since we'd invested a lot of time and money at this point. He wouldn't budge.

One thing I've learned is that the narcissist loves to hear themselves talk. They rely on their network of people to feed and create an aura of indispensability.

What I believe, though, is that no one person is indispensable. Only the team is imperative. The narcissist tendency to metaphorically "throw their people under the bus" is damaging to the team. A narcissist rarely, if ever, sees their failures or shortcomings.

Fortunately, when it came to this difficult decision, I had backup. Our frequent touchpoints and feedback loops were well-documented. By the time we arrived at the "no turning point" dismissal phase, I had conducted ten concise 90-day performance appraisals—with the goal of trajectory or course correction, not of dismissal. But, the thing about course corrections is they are well-documented. After final warnings and armed with ten written reviews, we took action to protect all the stakeholders: his team, my executive team, the company, and all our shareholders.

I did learn a hard lesson: I should never have let <u>ten</u> 90-day reviews go by without taking more decisive action earlier. Ten 90-day reviews are probably seven too many. Within three, the inevitable should be obvious. Especially for team-members in leadership roles, it can cost you multiple times their salary in collateral damage. The damage takes form in the direct loss of business, lack of performance in the team, the hasty departure of critical players, and the influence on others, and what I call the "aftermath." Other team members may emulate bad behavior or adopt a "who-cares" attitude because of the degrading atmosphere that the executive creates.

Hire slow and fire quickly is the old adage, and I cannot overstress that guidance when it comes to executives. As they say, the closer you are to the top, the closer you are to the door.

I'll use my NASA analogy of trajectory feedback. You are off course, but if you don't correct right away, you'll have to use a lot of fuel to plot your new trajectory into your target orbit. If you wait, you might not be able to course-correct. Your rocket might burn up in orbit. Or worse, it might crash and burn, taking others with it.

L.I.F.T.—Transforming Performance with Measures and Enrichment

"The powerful thing about recognition is that it reminds people of what matters most. This is a key part of engagement – to redirect employee effort and attention to the organization's top priorities. Regular recognition throughout the year is a reminder of what you need employees to keep doing."—Mary Ann Masarech [31]

Performance is an essential word in business but hard to define outside; hard-numbers and targets are easy to understand and track, but the team and personal performance aren't limited to decimal points, percentages, and dollars. You may not be able to tie every team member's goal to a budget, operational metrics, cost or finance, or some perceived measure of customer satisfaction through the number of re-orders, bookings, or satisfaction reviews. In many cases, performance is more about the intangibles and how your people capitalize on skills, abilities, and expertise in leadership or doing everyday tasks exceptionally well to achieve a superior result.

Another thing to bear in mind is "fit." I have seen scenarios where a top performer for another company, recruited to another team, could not replicate the performance. The dynamics of the team are often the reason. The person who can thrive in one environment may not do well in another.

There is, however, one secret to transforming performance with all team-members: incentives and enrichment tied to measures. In the same way, frequent reviews can help you spot course corrections; they can also identify opportunities for incentives and enrichment. Don't underestimate the power of "reputation enrichment." For most team members, with the notable exception of the rare narcissists, praise and the metaphorical pat on the back are often reward enough, especially if frequent. Waiting for an annual review tied to salary increases is too long if you want to see tangible gains and momentum.

Why? I'll draw on my reasonably extensive parenting experience with 11 children. Frequency of "course corrections" matters in parenting. It's critical to prevent the formation of bad habits and attitudes. Correcting is always more complex than good habituation. One thing you learn as a parent, though, is that out of sight is out of mind. Do you know what your kids are up to? These are clichés in parenting, but like most clichés, they contain gems of wisdom.

It's no different to valued team members. They are nearly as important to you as your family. If you genuinely care about people, then your team, whom you spend countless hours with, should be imperative, and their success and failure are in part orchestrated by you. The compassionate L.I.F.T. Leader treats the team as family. That means "course corrections" but also "reward." The little "ice-cream" enticement goes a long way towards correction without pain. It is not different in the workplace.

L.I.F.T. Entanglement and Reward: Training Team Engagement

Can you train "engagement?" In a leading study on team engagement[32], data indicated that recognizing small successes not only drove maximum satisfaction it created momentum for success. That is the definition of team engagement, according to the report: "...employee engagement is pragmatic: an engaged organization is one where employees reach maximum job satisfaction while at the same time make a significant contribution to the goals of their team and the organization as a whole."

I call this *L.I.F.T. Entanglement*. You can drive all aspects of Leadership, Inspiration, Focus, and Transformation with team entanglement. To maximize "employee satisfaction" and guide them towards "maximum contribution"—or engagement—you need to show that you value the team's contributors. It doesn't always have to be money. According to the cited research report[33], from the team-members point of view, the most important aspects of a manager are:

- Manager/Leader makes priorities clear for the team.

- Manager/Leader provides regular feedback.

- Manager/Leader facilitates training and resources.

In other words, it's all up to you, the leader, to create this leader/team entanglement—the environment where performance and "engagement" thrives.

Don't wait for the "report card."

Imagine not course-correcting your child until they bring you a disastrous report card from school at the end of the year—complete with ominous comments about social behavior in class and no homework assignments completed. The annual review is like the semester report card; it may already be too late.

The traditional annual performance appraisal system is an archaic business practice, much like stapling a business card to a Rolodex. If it weren't so dangerous to team performance, it would be quaint. In the vintage annual-review approach, since you didn't invest the time, you can't expect a high team engagement level. They are emulating you, and if your engagement factor with them is low, then don't expect anything more from them.

With frequent review and reward, team entanglement, you and the team invest in each other. You give them what they need: advice, feedback, help, positive and negative reinforcement as required. They will appreciate you because they see you care, you pat on the back, you reward them, you praise them, you buy them coffee (ice-cream) once in a while. You care. They care. It's a simple Entanglement formula. Review and reward, trains your team to be "engaged."

For the review process to be beneficial to our bottom-line business, you need to prioritize reviews, making them a dynamic process that allows course correction and fast recognition. Annually, you shouldn't spend more time on reviews and rewards. You'll simply be breaking the cycle down to frequent course corrections and reward sessions, many of them informal. Even the more formal *L.I.F.T. Trajectory* 90-Day process is still concise. If you want to grow fast as a company, everything you do should revolve around speed concepts, including reviews.

One reason managers despise reviews as much as employees are they are tedious, out-of-date, and time-consuming with sterile forms and rating methods. Make the process frequent, concise, and dynamic, two-way conversation—while incenting energetic performance at the same pace. It's human nature—we're inspired to perform for immediately tangible rewards, whether in sports, business, families, or school. Thinking about the trophy at the end of the year, or the annual pay raise, or the family holiday next year may seem long-term motivating, but the daily and weekly rewards are far more valuable to your business objectives. Waiting a year to find out you are on the wrong path is expensive. When the coach says, "great game, I'm taking you all out for a team dinner," it does more for the next few games than the hope of a distant winner's cup.

In case I haven't been clear, I'm advocating a different format—a feedback loop that is as close to dynamic and real-time as possible.

In addition to the daily/weekly feedback loops, I still believe in more formal but concise reviews and resets that should happen at least every 90 days.

How To L.I.F.T. Your Team: the Rule of Fives

Since I recommend and use concise, frequent 90-day *L.I.F.T. Trajectory* sessions—your near-real-time feedback loop—it is critical to emphasize working with both numerical and subjective goals. Not every goal translates into numbers, but you do have to make goals clear. In the previously cited report on team engagement—92 percent of top performers cite "clear work priorities" as the key[34]. Don't just tell them, "keep doing what you're doing." Help them find measurable ways to improve.

In these short transformative sessions (Transform, remember?), you want to cover all the key things that have been done (for reviewing performance), but also to set goals for the next 90 days (transforming future performance.) Ask, what will move the needle to accomplish a fundamental business goal?

L.I.F.T. and the Rule of Fives

Rules might be made to be broken, but as a rule-of-thumb, I advise you to stretch your conceptual thinking by focusing on *Five Objective Goals, Five Subjective Milestones*—and, optionally, *Five Stretch Objectives.* You don't have to do all the heavy mental lifting. I suggest you sit with your team members and encourage them to participate in their own goal setting. I often find they'll set more ambitious goals than you might otherwise have and can be more motivated to achieve goals they set for themselves.

In your L.I.F.T. Trajectory sessions, you will, of course, look back over the past 90 days. Then to manifest transformation, pivot, and look forward to the next 90 days. How did they do on their objectives? What wins pushed our business plan forward the most? What losses or setbacks impacted our plan? What do they promise to improve? What goals do they aspire to in the next 90 days?

Aim to set five key numerical numbers, the *Five Objective Goals*, something measurable as a goal—trust me, no matter what the team-members role, they can have some numerical measures. Sales, marketing, customer service, and engineering goals may seem more straightforward, but your leadership team, HR group, and administrative teams can also work to numeric goals.

Next, focus on Five Subjective Milestones for the next 90 days.

If you have no time for Stretch goals, so be it, but I suggest you try. Nothing flexes the mental muscles of you and your team members more than "stretch."

The interaction every 90 days is invaluable as you both get to reflect on the things you did, didn't do, or obstacles you faced. We agree if an item is dropped or changed to course correct towards completing our mission. We keep notes, debate things, outline any substandard behavior I see, and send the message about things I'd like to see improved that are not hitting the mark.

The Top Five Pain Points— Feedback Without Pain

Frequent feedback loops make everything less painful. At first glance, it seems like more work, but you'll find it amounts to less work. The clarity will drive enthusiasm and momentum. The frequency will eliminate the need for expensive "course corrections,"—which can be as costly as lost business or as significant as replacing a team-member who has gone too far off the path. Here are the top five pain points, regularly cited by HR Managers, stated from the point-of-view of the employee team-members:

Pain Point #1—I'm not valued

It's easy for team members to feel undervalued, especially if you're not recognizing them in small ways, in near real-time, and, at a minimum, every 90 days.

Pain Point #2—My ideas are not heard

Frequent feedback loops also feed the "agile" workplace. In today's business, a rigid, inflexible workplace results in declining returns on every HR return-on-investment. Not only that, feedback loops are just that—a loop. That means you'll have real-time feedback on your performance as a leader and be able to improve yourself. Finally, you'll create a dynamic, agile workplace that fosters creativity and ideas.

Pain Point #3—My workplace feels poisonous

Lack of morale and the "poisonous" workplace is a real phenomenon. You may not be able to remove stress from the workplace. It's the nature of any business to thrive in a stressful environment. But, you can remove much of the inter-team stress by being more dynamically watchful and interactive.

Pain Point #4—My team expects the impossible

Lack of recognition destroys the motivation to better the team. In turn, this feeds the momentum loop of failure. Failure leads to lowered expectations and results. To improve morale and exceed goals takes real-time leadership, not annual goal setting and merit reviews.

Pain Point #5—No one trains me

One of the most often cited complaints in HR is "lack of training." No matter how senior the hire, and regardless of their experience, each workplace requires training in how you want things done. Without training, it is unreasonable to demand performance.

L.I.F.T. Exercise —Three Times Five

In chapter 10, I demonstrate my one-page L.I.F.T. Dashboard. Each "component" of the business, including each team member, needs its own Dashboard. In preparation for that process, I find it helpful to work through this less-formal Three Times Five exercise. If this is for yourself, answer for yourself. If you are doing this with a team member, work on it together. Ultimately, you'll transfer this to your/their L.I.F.T. Dashboard, picking the top five priorities. But, it is helpful to brainstorm goals in this way:

What are your FIVE specific numeric goals for the next 90 days?

1.

2.

3.

4.

5.

What are your FIVE supporting and/or non-numeric goals for the next 90 days, as stated explicitly as possible:

1.

2.

3.

4.

5.

Without repeating anything from the previous lists, what are your FIVE stretch goals? These usually won't become part of your dashboard, other than as a footnote, but they help you think about longer-term achievements. These are goals that you would like to attain in the ultimate best-case scenario:

1.

2.

3.

4.

5.

What resources or help do I need to achieve my goals:

1.

2.

3.

4.

5.

Reflections from The Conqueror

Mehmed was determined to win at any cost, and he knew there would be setbacks and victories along the way. Constantinople represented the first battle in his journey. He had a grand vision of an Empire, where Constantinople was only the first significant milestone.

Mehmed understood performance reviews. His commanders in the field were his long-reaching arms. To track their performance once a year in a war would be unthinkable. He knew what each of them was doing every day. They would perform at risk of their lives. Yet, with each victory, his men would gain land and treasures—great performance rewards.

Mehmed, on the eve of the last great attack on Constantinople, spent the entire day walking through his camp and observed the preparations, reminded the people of the cause, and that this final push would result in treasures for all (who survived, but why dwell on the negative.) The troops were 52 days into a long battle, and spirits were low, energy sapped, and Mehmed needed to inspire his people and remind them that their last performance would lead to the tremendous financial gain he had promised.

Mehmed knew Alexander the Great's famous quote, "Toil and risk are the price of glory, but it is a lovely thing to live with courage and die, leaving an everlasting fame." More importantly, he understood human nature—the need for reward and feedback. Reward and fame are recognition. Treasures and plunders are rewards. Both come fast and furious on the battlefield, where the stakes are not only high but urgent.

Mehmed was willing to leave it all on the battlefield. His attitude "infected" the troops with the same outlook. He was a leader's leader. During campaigns, he was a constant presence.   To give your all, perform at the highest level, capture the prize—these are timeless concepts.

How to apply these lessons to 21st-century business

In business, modern, fast-paced leadership means your executive team and key people need real-time feedback and guidance to hit the mark. I believe in business plans, strategic plans, and tactical plans, but at the end of all the planning, your people need real-time guidance and advice. You cannot course correct a ship halfway through a journey and expect to reach your destination.

How I do it

I spend a lot of time working with everyone to plan and create their goals and objectives (See chapter 11 for more on this and the one-page L.I.F.T. Dashboard). In one of my roles I had direct reports in 5 different countries with vastly different time zones, but I scheduled weekly discussions, and then collectively, I pull in our global team every week for a worldwide huddle for 60 mins. The constant communication allows me and everyone on the team to understand where we are in the process. We attempt to streamline the discussion to what's working, what's not working, where I need assistance and forewarnings of dangers/opportunities that lie ahead. I can safely say that in those years, I was not seriously blindsided by anything not disclosed by my team nor hidden within the company.

You should consider this approach as well. As a leader, empower your teams with real-time guidance:

1. What's working?

2. What's not working?

3. Where do you need assistance?

4. What are the threats/dangers and opportunities ahead? (Think of this as a fundamental S.WO.T. analysis: Strengths, Weaknesses, Opportunities, Threats.)

Formally, every 90 days

I take that one step further to include a performance review every 90 days with all my direct reports. In my case, these last a minimum of 90 minutes because we ran a complex business with many moving parts.

How do I do this? We take their one-page strategic/tactical plan (see Chapter 11) and update it quarterly to include all the things they must accomplish that builds to their overall strategy and approved budget. We cover what they accomplished, what they learned, what they missed and the reasons, and what changed. Sometimes it's reasonable to change goals because things have changed. We cover this too.

We have excellent discussions, and it informs our thinking for the next quarter's objectives. We agree on their five key deliverables and put that on their one-page strategic plan.

Their frustrations—very important

I also make sure we cover their frustrations or feelings about the company. I make sure there is a very open dialogue about everything, giving them a platform for honest feedback.

Their rewards—very important

Accomplishments and performance must link to financial gain. We are all motivated to accomplish things in our business career, but that must be connected to tangible financial gain because it telegraphs your company's values and priorities. If the company is not willing to reward for it, how important can it be?

The amount is important in context, but it is not as crucial as simply the fact that bonuses were paid and that you were recognized for the things you did and the success you achieved. Variable compensation is critical to success.

Mini-Case: weekly huddles change a company trajectory

Over a decade ago, I took over leadership of a media company on a potentially deadly trajectory. To use my earlier analogy, this company had veered off its "reference trajectory" over a long period and was now so far off course they were in danger of running out of fuel.

The company was experiencing severe losses. The situation was untenable for the owners. The organization was not naïve to the realities of their trajectory—after all, they engaged me to work on the issues—but the company was on a collision course for insolvency.

I implemented a new performance management system, coupled with daily discussions, weekly huddles, and quarterly performance reviews. I did not have the luxury of moving to Europe at the time, and I could spend one to two weeks per month with them in the office, plus one week in Los Angeles or London negotiating content deals—while somehow keeping my family together at home. It was an enormously challenging time.

Managing a globally diverse business through your executive team requires a lot of depth to the relationships with your direct reports. It requires dynamic, real-time feedback loops. Our trajectory was dangerous.

With numerous, regular, almost daily "course corrections," we moved the company from losing seven figures per month to breakeven to profitability in 18 months. Our costs went down 63 percent.

It was a monumental shift in a record period with hundreds of moving parts managed by a team of five executives with a CEO on site less than 50 percent of the time. The active performance management, daily discussions, weekly huddles, and quarterly performance appraisals were the key to accomplishing so much in so little time.

Since then, this method became a backbone principle of my L.I.F.T. Leadership system. I have used this system for so many years, and I can say with 100 percent confidence that it makes all the difference on so many levels.

6

L.I.F.T. YOUR INSIGHT: FIVE ESSENTIAL METRICS

If you're relying on EBITDA as your primary metric, you may be charting the wrong trajectory. Metrics and True North Star: measuring success in a business comes down to five essential metrics: the "True North Star" of any company.

L.I.F.T. Facts

- There are five essential metrics—EBITDA is not one of them.

- "EBITDA is akin to a blender, into which go normal financial statements and out of which comes a number that always seems to make the subject company look better than it did when the numbers went into said blender." *Forbes.*

- EBITDA can make companies look healthier than they are. Where you are concerned with growing, competing, capturing new opportunities, and facing adverse downturns outside of your control, consider Free Cash Flow as a more transparent metric.

- Base your meaningful metrics on your business goals anchored to a specific timeline. If your goal involves the need for cash flow, many traditional metrics may fail to give you the needed insight.

In this chapter

- At face value: why EBITDA is NOT the metric that matters. In L.I.F.T. Leadership, five metrics are essential.

- Metrics only matter in context.

- Action requires foundation—use True North to reveal the path to success.

- Dealing with stakeholders—knowledge, and negotiation.

- Metrics can inform you—or send you in circles.

Important Take-away

- **"Rationalizing actions and plans with metrics is dangerous without knowing your True North Star."**

Reflections from the Conqueror

- *Mehmed's espionage network singularly focused on the conquest of Constantinople. Knowing the goal puts the metrics in context.*

L.I.F.T.

What do you know about your capacity, capabilities, product, service, and company?

Lead: In war, real context and knowledge help prevent loss of life. In business, it is no different.

Inspire: Your team can picture victory if you give them a reason to. Metrics can inspire the "troops."

Focus: Metrics are all about focus, but don't mistake facts for context.

Transform: With the right metrics, your own True North Star, transformation and success are inevitable.

Real Life L.I.F.T. Case:
Technology Forces a Pivot

In the early 2000s, I took over leadership of a break-even printing company struggling to find revenue. At the time, the entire printing industry underwent a massive seismic transformation to digitization, and countless printing companies simply collapsed. To survive the required conversion to digital technologies—a very cost-prohibitive investment in assets and training—demanded rapid deployment. We also faced shocking cultural change—the "press" industry measured in increments of decades rather than years. Vast "press experience" no longer carried weight in a sector that became digital almost overnight.

My company was over 120 years old. They had become very complacent about the realities of the market and their future. This was common in the industry, with many legacy owners thinking it was nothing but a passing trend.

The realities of extraordinary investments in new technology made metrics such as EBITDA, multiples, and other common valuations almost meaningless. EBITDA, especially with its blender-approach to metrics, puts too much emphasis on assets. My printing company certainly had expensive assets that were quickly becoming out of date. Unfortunately, what we needed were cash and cash flow.

Typical of legacy organizations, they didn't understand the fundamentals of modern valuation or finance. We needed to re-educate our finance team on the importance of cash flow.

In this case, especially in the face of massive, required infrastructure or asset investment, I had to train them to focus on the single most critical number—free cash flow. A company cannot exist for long without the underlying ability to generate cash through operations, less their cost of expenditures on assets. After paying the bills, the money left over had to be positive—even after capital expenditure investments. It's an invalid (or at best, misleading) metric to examine cash flow out of the context of capital investments and expenditures.

Where you are attempting to sell, expand or re-equip a company—or grow a business —you need to demonstrate one hard-core metric: an ability to produce sufficient cash.

Decisions made complicated by Union and history

Even without the seismic nature of the change to digitization, this company was not healthy in free cash flow. Planning a path to success became even more challenging in the face of the Union and a long history of "it's not done that way."

I pulled the executive team together. We had to face everything with grit and honesty. At the very first meeting, we worked around the clock on solutions. We focused on values, developed our goals, and mapped the ideal path forward. I challenged every notion held in the company, every convention, every metric. "Tradition" would not be a shield. We needed to break away from inhibiting traditions that had put the company in jeopardy.

The problem was "rose-colored glasses," as the saying goes. The past CEO had pumped up the teams, the Union, the managers, the investors with high-sounding goals and skewed analysis. What do I mean by skewed? By using the strength of expensive legacy assets, but ignoring low cash flow, everyone, and notably the Union, believed that there was no issue.

We were living through a seismic event, a virtual earthquake—but no one would acknowledge the walls were crumbling around them.

Why you should never say "Everything is great"

Ultimately, we developed a workable plan—and I was proud of my team. However, the more significant issue was buy-in from the union and salaried workers. For years, management told them: "everything is great." Suddenly, here's this new leader (me), no fancy suit, no fancy numbers, telling them the walls are shaking, and we need to start shoring up the foundations. Basically, after years of being told they were well-off, they found out they were almost broke. They faced an unaffordable technological shift at a time when everyone worked to the wrong metrics, based on their now-archaic 120-year history.

I knew this would be difficult. I decided to meet with every employee in the company, one-by-one, through a series of meetings where I only focused on a "reality check" session. The bottom line—I focused only on explaining the importance of bringing the business to positive free cash flow.

You'll hopefully remember my belief that performance should be tied to reward (from the last chapter.) It's no different when you are in the unenviable position of delivering terrible news. No one will carry in the face of "there's no hope and no reward."

One-by-one, I told each of my crew that there would be a reward for achieving the positive cash flow we so desperately needed—a reward that went beyond survival and good business. Yes, we had to upgrade to digital, a very costly process, but we also had to invest in the team.

I promised to invest ten percent of all <u>new</u> cash flow we generated in the next year in a new cafeteria with a popcorn machine, couches, cappuccino machine, and all the free kernels and coffee beans they could eat and drink. The other ninety percent would go to equipment upgrades, training, and other needed upgrades. I called it the 90-10 equation.

I even had our design group post renderings of the new cafeteria to help them visualize the 10-percent solution. We put up a graphic of a thermometer that rose week by week to demonstrate tangibly to everyone the Free Cash Flow (FCF) we generated—and how much of our goal went to the new cafeteria. Week-by-week they could see our progress. It re-affirmed the reward was actually within reach.

At the same time, I made profound changes in the workflow, job consolidation, yields, and numerous operational restructuring pieces necessary to generate the type of change required to make the company profitable and generating free cash flow.

Unbelievably, within 120 days—albeit 120 days of hard work—we reorganized our priorities. Within 180 days of those mandatory changes, we had generated enough positive cash flow to fund our needed changes—and to build the cafeteria of their dreams.

An essential element of performance rewards is to manifest them quickly. We built the cafeteria and even held a big party. We celebrated moving from negative six-figures of cashflow to positive seven-figures of cashflow per month—within an incredible six months! It was thanks to their hard work and discipline. It was undoubtedly worth a quarter-million-dollar cafeteria. The enhanced cash flow allowed us to pop buckets of kernels and brew gallons of cappuccino every month, and now having 100% of the free cash flow going towards our future.

Sold for nine figures

We sold the company a few years later for nine figures.

Transparency and reward are the keys to re-focusing a team to meaningful metrics.

Regardless of your industry and focus, L.I.F.T. Leaders always plan with true north metrics. Of those, free cash flow is one of the most important. It may seem rudimentary, but it is often overlooked—or in some cases, even deliberately "hidden." To the seller, it's like putting a fresh coat of paint on rotting walls. To the buyer, it looks good, but after you buy the house, you have to face expensive repairs. It's best to bring in a building inspector to dig deeper.

Be like the building inspector in the house sale—dig deep for the business's fundamental soundness. Avoid getting enamored by the paint choice on the shiny walls.

At Face Value: Why EBITDA is NOT the Metric That Matters

A "nickname" coined by one Union President early in my career was the "pivot CEO." I wear it like a little badge of honor because it reflects my philosophy. Whether you are "pivoting" a company due to competitive, technological or economic forces, you can be confident of one thing—your company will face an inevitable mandatory pivot. The need to pivot is an unavoidable force, like gravity. If you resist this natural force in business, be prepared to crash. This is why metrics and stress testing your company are critically important.

Let me punctuate my point: the metrics I believe all businesses should pay close attention to are those measures that "stress test" your company. Is your business "ready" to pivot? That pivot is going to happen. Even venerable companies with decades-long heritage will face a crisis—as I illustrate in this chapter's case study.

Will change be imposed on you, or by you, is the question. If it is imposed on you—and you haven't previously stress-tested your company—this can become a matter of survival. These market forces are gravitational: your market shrinks through no fault of your own, or the economy collapses, or technology drives intractable forces that changed your entire industry. More pro-active leaders use the pivot to develop new opportunities. In either case, without Free Cash Flow, you will not be able to weather these "pivots." Free Cash Flow is the first of the "five essential metrics" in L.I.F.T. Leadership. Just as we had "Five Pain Points."

The Five Essential Metrics

Every business has its own set of essential metrics. L.I.F.T. Metrics is all about customizing Metrics and Key Performance Indicators (KPIs) to your business goals. If your goal is gross sales above all else, you'll have different goals to a company focused on reputation—and you'll focus on a different set of metrics.

Business Leaders, certainly L.I.F.T. Leaders, will keep four categories of metrics in front of them at all times—and one "wild card" metric, I call the *L.I.F.T. Stress Test*.

Usually, these four categories are indicated by 13 performance indicators. (More on this later.) We've added a dynamic real-time metric to the four main categories, we call the *L.I.F.T. Stress Test*, arguably the most important of all.

We'll discuss your particular customized metrics in the section True North metrics. Regardless of the various metrics, you land on as critical to your business, you will have at least these five essential metrics. If you group the 13 performance indicators, you'll end up with four categories of metrics:

- Liquidity

- Profitability

- Leverage

- Efficiency

- To which, we add the *L.I.F.T. Stress Test*. If you only measure one thing, this is the one to spend your time on—in real-time, since crisis and stress are fluid and dynamic.

No Manipulated Metrics

In any company, industry, or market, there is no universal metric or ratio that perfectly sums up the financial health of your enterprise.

There are, however, some metrics that can be manipulated, intentionally or unintentionally. I've mentioned one, EBITDA, which might be useful for its blender-approach (as an "overview"), but which should never be relied on for any critical decisions or enterprise valuations. Metrics are best analyzed in context, which by definition means that one number is rarely sufficient for any decision.

The L.I.F.T. Leader is vigilant against any manipulated metrics. It's not uncommon for team-members—especially in sales metrics—to unconsciously manipulate analysis to make their team or project "look good." It's human nature. Everything should be auditable and arms-length verifiable if you are making important decisions.

Fit the Metric to the Goal

We often fixate on specific metrics. My best advice is to fit the metrics to the goal. This is why the "blender" approach, EBITDA, tends to be misleading, even though it is the central default metric many investors or analysts use to evaluate performance. The simple fact is that EBITDA doesn't tell you the one thing most businesses need to focus on: can we handle inevitable downturns and crises? It also doesn't give context. When you start to ask "what if..." questions, common in management planning, there are no answers in EBITDA. A company rich in assets can fail in the face of a significant market change. I demonstrated how that almost happened to my printing company.

Lean culture and True North Metrics

True North Metrics implies you have a destination and goals. A "purpose-driven" company. If you don't, start there. One of the upsides of my diverse career as a "Pivot CEO" is versatility. I've led companies in technology, communications, printing, automotive, broadcast media, and some even more niched categories. Although all of these companies are guided by those five key metrics, they also have their own important set of "True North Metrics."

These "True North Metrics" reflect company valuations: automotive businesses are valued far differently from software companies, which is entirely different from media content companies. For example, you may think running a charity might have simplified metrics. You'd be wrong. Different priorities, certainly, but Charities still need cash flow and liquidity like any other organization.

True North metrics isn't my concept, but I subscribe to it entirely, without reservation. In the bibliography, I'll refer you to books on the topic. Some of your metrics may differ from mine. Why? Because you customize True North Metrics to your own "purpose-driven culture"—and your purpose will not be the same as mine.

Your True North Metrics or, to use another vernacular, Key Performance Indicators (KPIs), may not be the same as mine. If you lead a quality assurance department, your measures will be very different. Some highly vertical KPIs might include:

- Acquisition and client growth

- Intellectual property capture

- Subscribers

- Active users

- Various productivity metrics

- Percentage of donations that reaches recipients.

I encourage you to build your own critical, customized True North KPIs and metrics. But—with any business, always start with the basics: the five key metrics. Why? Because they measure your financial capacity, your ability to withstand the stresses of market dynamics, competition, regulation, and the ups-and-downs of the economy.

Always Assume You're in Danger—
Build Your Spy Network

Face facts—as a business leader, you must always be ready for war. Even if you are on "cold war" footing in business, you are still under some sort of threat: regulatory, competitive, economic, market forces, natural disasters, politics, investor withdrawal. A stress-free "peace" environment is not feasible in a competitive scenario in any industry. The best you'll manage will be the occasional "peace treaty." If you are not war-capable, you should give up the notion of being a business leader. As a war-leader, this does not mean you lack compassion or empathy. Only that you realize you must manage the threats to "protect" your people, your stakeholders.

For this reason, I always coach L.I.F.T. Leaders to "always assume you are in danger."

What is the one thing a war-time (or cold-war-time) leader needs to plan to launch great campaigns? Spies. Espionage. The base of your intelligence-gathering effort is business metrics. Later, in chapters 8 and 9, I will show you how to expand your "spy network" to gather insights into competitors and target audiences.

Entanglement: Rationalization Metrics

In a company, there is the additional danger of limited vision: focusing on one metric, the wrong metric, or worse, a "spun" metric. I call these "Rationalization Metrics." Entangle your critical planning to rationalized metrics at your peril.

EBITDA is unreliable for planning strategy because it is vulnerable to "spin"—it can be presented as fact when it is more a "perspective." To finish off my analogy, in war, reliance on war propaganda instead of your espionage network will only help you plot a course to defeat.

First rule, then, of espionage—never rely on one source. Believing that a single metric contains the essential picture of your financial health is misguided at best; depending on any single metric for a critical decision is just foolish. Don't entangle yourself in "rationalization metrics," or the art of only presenting specific metrics that support your cause or mission, while hiding or discrediting those measures that oppose your position.

In other words, you're not a salesperson; you're a leader. Decide based on the relevant facts. You don't need "all" the facts, but you definitely must know what is relevant.

Later, you may have to pitch your plan to your employees, team, board members, investors, shareholders—but it should be fact-based tactical planning, supported by more than one metric. In the absence of definitive, relevant metrics, you should assume the worst.

As in war, always have a contingency plan.

EBITDA Should be Abolished from Leader Insights

To make the EBITDA's blender-approach worse, some financial "gurus" layered in another aspect to EBITDA, making it even more open to manipulation. Described as *Adjusted EBITDA*, it enables "spin analysis." With Adjusted EBITDA, you can strip out what you believe are one-time adjustments—things you "rationalize" as single occurrence events or transactions—that you assert won't repeat.

How valuable is a metric where you can adjust it at will? How different is "adjustment" to "manipulation"? Yes, they are different since the presumption is that adjustment is factual, but you are still, in this case, manipulating your appraisal based on selected facts. Even if these adjustments are legitimate, which they most often are, it still serpentines reasoning. A measure is only of value if it's consistently applied and formulaically repeatable. I'd go further and state, *Adjusted EBITDA* simply magnifies a problem. EBITDA in any form is a weak metric for crucial decision making and should be banished for three reasons:

1. EBITDA does NOT give you insight into cash flow.

Even novice business leaders understand that cash is the lifeblood of a company. What if you are posting positive EBITDA—but burning cash. Your skewed analysis, like war-time propaganda, gives you an unclear picture. The accurate picture may not emerge until it's too late.

The underlying engine of a company is its ability to generate cash. Don't fall into the trap of pretending everything's okay because EBITDA is positive. Even if you work with EBITDA, it should be one of "confirming" your insight. Start with and rely upon the more important measures.

2. EBITDA does NOT consider working capital

EBITDA does NOT take into consideration the working capital and capital expenditures in a business. Here's a straight-up fact all L.I.F.T. Leaders understand: if you are not investing in your company, then you have no future.

For this reason, if you ignore the cost of that needed investment, you are rationalizing and spinning. We don't put lipstick on a pig!

EBITDA ignores depreciation and amortization, essential indicators of the level of investment in a company. If the company isn't investing in the future—if your leadership is limited to the present moment—then your underlying trajectory is dangerous as a company—and earnings are inflated.

Working capital is also an essential factor that EBITDA doesn't contemplate. The ability to fund and harness that growth is your working capital. Suppose you are underfunded, or you're burning cash, and you hit a sales or performance lull in your inevitable cycle. In that case, you then have to fund dips with financing, or worse, use your suppliers' balance sheet—delaying your Accounts Payable to finance your operations. Either option—and there are a few others—only masks the problem and becomes an on-going shell game to hide your mistakes. Once you start that shell-game, you can't easily come "clean."

The major shell game players can further mask the game by taking out loans against receivables, bringing cash forward in the flow, but at a very high-interest rate. The more significant risk is overextending, for example, when a receivable is not collectible. It's like going to a cheque cashing company before payday, and after you spent the money, you find out your company went bankrupt, and now you can't pay that loan. Promised money only becomes money when it is collected.

3. EBITDA does NOT give you insight into debt servicing.

Can you service your debt? Will your line of credit max out? Can you pay your suppliers? You may never know if you rely solely on EBITDA.

There's a big difference in financial planning depending on your debt structure. If your debt is a mezzanine-type facility—where you have to pay a high-interest rate with no principal payments—your cash flow and capacity are significantly limited compared to a company using a traditional senior debt facility low-interest rate and a principal payment schedule. Here are some examples:

- If you have a company with $500M in revenue and $40M in Adjusted EBITDA, with a traditional senior loan and lines of credit that equate to $120M in credit, the bank would be satisfied because the debt covenant ratio is $120M/$40M or 3.0 times—a fair amount of leverage in a public company but low leverage for a private equity group.

- However, in the case of adjusted EBITDA of $40M, less CAPEX of $17M, less $12M of adjustments (these cost you money—and will likely continue to cost you), less working capital and inventory changes of $8M; as a result, you have less than $3M of free cash flow. If you are paying a blended

6.5% interest on the $120M in debt, you need $7.8M to service the debt, and you only have $3M to pay for it.

If a person looks at the $40M of adjusted EBITDA, it's easy to think they have lots of money. Still, it means nothing as you are degrading your balance sheet every single month with ultimately negative cashflow.

Valuations and EBITDA

To make matters worse, Investment Bankers often use Adjusted EBITDA to establish the valuation of a company for sale. The business could easily be burning cash, but never-the-less show positive EBITDA in the millions. When these millions are used as a valuation multiple, it significantly inflates the value.

As an investor or buyer, you'll quickly experience "buyer's remorse" shortly after you acquire that over-valued business—a company burning cash (your cash). If you bought the business based on an EBITDA multiple—and you didn't properly capitalize the business on day one with appropriate working capital or took on too much debt to complete the transaction—then you will not have enough staying power to fund the cash burn and restructuring costs. Yes, you can value future "synergies" in a company purchase, but you may run out of cash before you realize those "synergies."

Many deals fail after two years because they overpaid on an EBITDA multiple, underfunded the real underlying cash burn, over-levered with debt, and didn't have sufficient capitalization to transform the company.

Metrics from the Point-of-View of Acquisitions

Acquisitions can be accretive and bolster a company's position in its market or adjacent markets, but you have to prepare your balance sheet to do this well.

Going into an acquisition, here's what you should consider before proceeding:

- You determine you have properly capitalized the acquired business,

- The target is net free cash flow positive or your post-close capitalization structure makes it positive,

- Debt levels for the deal are reasonable to low, and

- You did NOT rely on synergies as "funding" or the sole justification.

In this case—and especially if you have stress-tested the business (see *L.I.F.T. Stress Test* below)—then you've prepared yourself to weather the storm and get the acquired business integrated and producing cash to drive future value to your original business.

Determine if a company is managing costs

Profits do not equal cash, and in business, you need both—profits and cash. The best way to evaluate whether an acquisition target company is managing its costs correctly—is genuinely planning for a promising future:

Take EBITDA for the past three years—together with ending cash at the end of each year—and if they are converting 80 percent of EBITDA into Free Cash Flow, then the company is being managed well.

This is a basic determination. It ignores a number of things, but at the end of the day, cash is the lifeblood of a company, and if you're generating 80 percent of your EBITDA into cash, and this has gone on for three years historically, then you are properly managing your business well.

I encourage all leaders to stress test their company or their acquisition targets. The quick form, the L.I.F.T. Stress Test (see below), can help you determine if you can weather financial storms—or afford to tap into opportunities. Stress Test your existing companies—and any you plan to acquire.

L.I.F.T. Stress Test: Are You Ready for Financial Storms?

To determine if you are ready for an acquisition, or prepared to weather a financial storm of any sort, or, even if you can afford to exploit business opportunities, it is important to stress test the company.

The *L.I.F.T. Stress Test* is deliberately simple, but it considers essential aspects in a concise tool. By now, you'll know that I always recommend concise formats for everything from business plans to employee reviews—one-page dashboards for everything. It's no different here. Clear information need not be complicated.

Always stress test your company. Do it often. Your L.I.F.T. Stress Test will tell you if you're ready to exploit opportunities. Refresh whenever you are considering a costly tactic since it will give you a better picture of your current state and cost structure. As the name implies, the L.I.F.T. stress test measures your capability and fortitude to nimbly manage ups and downs—especially through lean times or setbacks or broader economic turbulence.

How to stress test

Start by asking the head of your finance department for seven numbers:

1) What are the average sales per month for the company in the past 12 months?

2) What are our average Gross Profit margins in the past three months?

3) What are the current monthly operating expenses: OPEX including sales, marketing, general, administration, R&D—but excluding depreciation and amortization?

4) What are the average monthly interest expenses from all our debts, lines of credit, and others?

5) What are our average monthly Capital Expenses: spending on property, plant, and equipment (CAPEX)?

6) What is the closing cash balance from our most recent month's balance sheet?

7) What is the available credit and unused room in all our facilities at the end of last month?

Lift Method Stress Test

		Monthly Figures		Margin
Revenue		1	9.0	
	75% factor		6.8	
	x18 mths		121.5	
Gross Profit			2.6	2 39.0%
Total Opex (excluding Depreciation and Amortization)		3	4.3	47.8%
EBIT			-1.7	-18.5%
Interest Expense		4	0.1	
capex		5	0.3	
Plus Available Total Cash		6	13.7	
Plus Available Credit		7	5.1	
Burn Rate				
	x18 mths		-32.7	
Cash/Credit availability at month 18			-13.9	
Months of Cash before liquidity crisis			10.3	
If fail above (line 26)			FAIL	
TOTAL COST monthly reduction required			-1.8	

The formula and model are available on our website at www.
randydewey.com, but you can do the math manually by taking the numbers and using these three steps:

Step One

((Average Revenue x Gross Profit Margin x 0.75) – OPEX) = A **New EBIT level**

Step Two

Interest Expense + CAPEX expense = B **Financing and investment costs**

Step Three

Cash on Balance Sheet + Available Credit = C **Overall availability**

Step Four

$((A - B - C) \times 18) = D$ (*A,B,C, from steps 1-3 above*) **Burn Rate**

Evaluation of result

If Positive

If the final result (D, or Burn Rate) is **positive,** you are structured to weather challenges that may lie ahead

If Negative

If the final result (D or Burn Rate) is **negative,** then further calculate your "months to the wall"—that is, how many months until your cash drain burns the business out or you hit the wall.

Step Five

$((C / (A - B)) = E$

Evaluation of E

If the result in E is less than 18—then you have too much cost in your business to endure difficult times—you have less than 18 months before you hit the proverbial wall. Less than 18 months is not long enough to sustain most businesses for the long-term, provide the needed time to restructure all the costs out of the business, and/or it's also not long enough to integrate a newly acquired company. Additionally, credit markets can dry up during difficult economies, and it typically takes 12-18 months to free up credit. Either way, your balance sheet is not prepared for this type of turbulence and it puts the future at risk.

What to do if you fail the stress test?

If you are evaluating a potential acquisition, weigh a failure in this test seriously. If, on the other hand, you already operate the tested company—and you failed the **L.I.F.T. Stress Test**—then you should consider taking some of the following seven steps:

1. Share the bad news

Share the bad news with your immediate leadership team, and ultimately all key stakeholders. You have the insights, but you need to let your troops know in order to manage the necessary change. It is important to conscript your people into the mission. Don't sugar-coat the problems—chances are, that's how you landed in this difficult place. Your leadership team and stakeholders will realize the need and realities.

Need is an excellent motivator for your team. As for other stakeholders; banks, board members, investors, shareholders or others, it is good to keep them in your corner. How much time do you gain by hiding an unfortunate truth? In difficult times, face the problem.

Turn your stakeholders into major allies by showing them what you're going to do about it. Show them you are going to act now and take steps. In ten company turnarounds, I've never seen a scenario where hiding an uncomfortable truth helps. It almost always makes matters worse.

You may think *if I share the problem, won't my competitors exploit our weakness?* This is always a risk; however, you should know that they'll eventually discover this independently. Inevitably, your suppliers will leak your situation. The offset to this issue is working with allies, being honest, asking for support. As long as you have a plan of action, you'll find more supporters than detractors.

2. Reduce costs immediately

You need to review all your costs and take steps to reduce them (S, G &A, OPEX, and COGS)—as aggressively as you can until you get the burn rate to *at least* neutral—ideally a lot better.

3. Preemptively diversify

Preemptively and gradually pull down all your available credit and diversify banks and institutions. Don't rush or jump on this; your current banks that hold your debt, lines of credit, or revolvers will be very concerned about this type of quick preemptive action. However, if you have time and can deliberately, methodically, and gradually make this change, it can bolster your reserves. The cost of interest on regular credit is less than the cost of emergency capital in the middle of a crisis, so pre-emptive financial reorganization is best. Evaluate the options in light of your stress test above. One subjective analysis will be your relationship with your current financial institutions. You don't want to trigger a review. Your bank is well versed in scenarios and knows when to trigger reviews, so try not to be abrupt on this step—unless you face an urgent situation requiring maximum flexibility. The bank is your most important financial partner, and forthrightness and directness are critical to gaining support. Never undermine or take advantage of this relationship.

4. Freeze, freeze, freeze

Freeze all discretionary hiring, wage increases, tradeshow, and marketing expenses. Sometimes you're hampered by agreements or plans with commitments and penalties, or you need sales or marketing to close new business—but the key is to freeze anything discretionary that doesn't immediately help solve your problem. Cut or eliminate CAPEX and limit travel and expenses to necessities only. Put in a high-level approval and a temporary policy to curtail the behavior. An email asking people to "synch the belt" never works. You need concrete change.

5. Inventory all sources of cash

Inventory everything that is convertible to cash, for example, unneeded inventory or assets that you can sell. This is your quickest source of cash. Develop an aggressive plan to free up cash from aged inventory.

6. Evaluate accruals and allocations

Review in detail all your accruals and allocated costs. Here, you'll find many costs that are not regularly reviewed and are often hidden in your statements. Scrutinize these costs closely to make sure they are required.

7. Delay payables and pressure receivables

Delay Account Payables where possible—but be forthright and honest with suppliers, as you're technically asking them to finance your business for future gain. Find ways to push for faster cash flow from your customers. They may be old "tricks," but in all likelihood, you'll need to do both. There are some helpful ways to speed up cash flow, such as "point of revenue recognition." Evaluate your agreements for this language. If the "revenue recognition" and ownership transfers at your dock or your distribution centers dock, then air freighting, or emergency Less-than-load (LTL) may be a cost-effective way to speed up cash receipts. You may pay more to ship, but you can convert to revenue and cash faster. The more you can trim your cash conversion cycle and build your cash and flexibility, the better off you are in a crisis.

The Short and Long Trajectories

We've covered the concise indicator, *your L.I.F.T. Stress Test*, but never lose sight of the metrics needed to chart the overall trajectory, both long and short. Yes, we have to plan for contingencies, urgent situations, and stress—after all, the nature of business is competitive. L.I.F.T. Leaders also plan for the long trajectory, planning for future endgames. Handling crisis is one thing. Charting a course to industry leadership—or your long-term specific goals—is arguably even more critical. Yes, in war and crisis, we have to step up and become the war-leaders, but most of the time, *L.I.F.T. Leaders* focus on visionary aspirational goals. Building long-term share-holder value. To achieve this, we need our "True North Star" objective metrics to accurately chart and check our trajectory.

Stress Test is all about testing your readiness for a crisis. Repeat the test frequently, especially during times of fast burn or rapid change (In fact, repeatedly performing it monthly as the previous month closes and tracking the trend is equally as insightful.)

The various trajectory metrics are grouped into the four remaining critical metrics, loosely grouped as "Short Term Trajectory Metrics" and "Long Term Trajectory Metrics.

Short Trajectory Metrics include:

- Liquidity

- Profitability

Long Trajectory Metrics include:

- Leverage

- Efficiency

Are you an Income Statement or a Balance Sheet Leader?

A L.I.F.T. Leader embraces both the Income Statement and the Balance Sheet, but it's a sad truth in business that the "view out the windshield"—the Income Sheet—tends to be more heavily emphasized by short-sighted business leaders. The average large-cap CEO, according to Equilar, in 2017 was 5.0 years. The reality is these CEOs tend to be Income Statement leaders because they never make it long-term, and it shifts their perspective and creates a view that often ignores the Balance Sheet.

If the Income Statement is your "windshield view"—your short trajectory report—then your Balance Sheet is your compass or GPS, or your long trajectory.

Many executives tend to want to run the company exclusively from the Income Statement—as it measures the immediate performance. You can get by for a while if you're a good driver, the roads are dry, and it's not rush-hour. But when the bad weather comes, or the crazy drivers are on the road, you might find it dangerously limiting. You'll find yourself fumbling with your GPS—perhaps too late. You'll recognize this type of leadership in companies with compensation measures built around the income statement.

On the other hand, investors, bankers, and acquisitions managers grab the Balance Sheet first. They look at all the metrics but focus first on the extended trajectory metrics.

Both are important.

The Short Trajectory Metrics: Liquidity and Profitability

As a foundation, always start with your company's financial capacity or strength—determined by the underlying cash-generating ability of your company. Liquidity and cash connect to everything in the company and ties back to most lines on your income statement, balance sheet, and cash flow statement.

What do we mean by liquidity? It is the company's fundamental ability to meet its obligations both now and, in the future, or in accounting terms: do your current assets have the undiscounted ability or quickness to convert to cash to meet all your current liabilities.

Liquidity Ratios

- **Current Ratio (current assets/current liabilities).** Can you pay your short-term obligations? This metric indicates whether you could pay all your obligations over the next year with your current assets. A current ratio below one indicates the company does NOT have enough liquid assets to cover short-term liabilities.

- **Quick Ratio (cash + marketable securities + accounts receivable/current liabilities).** Even if an asset is deemed short-term in the Current Ratio, it doesn't mean you could convert them to cash quickly—at least not without a discount or penalty. The quick ratio more accurately shows your ability to liquefy assets versus your current liabilities that probably require real cash to service or lay off. It is a more conservative view of liquidity, but it's the best test of your financial flexibility.

Profit Metrics—Are you a Commodity?

The second short-term looking metric shows your company's ability to command pricing in the market, and financial strength is the gross profit margins. If you have margins consistently under 30 percent, then, by conventional analysis, you are selling a commodity with little protection. Low-margin products can typically be replicated by a competitor or a new market entrant.

On the other hand, if you are over 50 percent in gross margin, this indicates you have something very unique or special. If you command a high gross margin, it signifies replaceability is difficult. This can be a "home run" if your revenue is recurring versus the "one-and-done" product or service.

These indicators help in many ways. For potential acquisitions, it tells you if the product or service is worth buying. For valuation, it typically adds to the equation. For your line of products, if you have high margins but aren't exploiting it in sales or marketing, now's the time to start. If you have a real winner, where you can't fully exploit the market, or you can even look at exclusive licensing opportunities. Profit metrics are significant in all areas of business planning. Are you considering taking on debt? A lender is more likely to loan to a high-margin product or service with predictable cash flow.

Profitability Ratios

- **Free Cash Flow Margin (Cash flows from operating activities / net revenue)** This measurement gauges a company's ability to convert sales into cash. Pro-active L.I.F.T. Leaders will work with the entire statement of cash flows—but this quick Free Cash Flow Margin indicator is a valuable snapshot. As long as it is over 50 percent, it indicates you are generating meaningful cash. L.I.F.T. Leaders must know their Free Cash Flow. It helps them decide on—to exploit—future investments or opportunities that can enhance shareholder value or erode it. A solid ability to generate Free Cash Flow shows that a company can navigate difficulties well or harness opportunities quickly without leveraging or taking on significant risk.

- **Net Profit Margin (net income/rev)** This is the simplest profit ratio and a quick indicator of your ability to command a premium or not. If you have a high gross or net profit margin compared to your competitors, you are likely providing more value. This may be perceived or real—for instance, a strong brand name adds to perceived value—but the market believes you have a stronger solution, and they are willing to pay for it. For investors, Diluted Earnings per Share (EPS) is a good indicator of how the company manages their profits and the direction they are going. If the company buys back stock with excess cash or grows quickly even with dilutive equity offerings, you can easily discern that in the Earnings per Share.

- **Return on Assets - ROA (net income/average total assets).** ROA is a good indicator of management's ability to leverage their assets into business activities. If a company has significant capital needs, and you're concerned about how the world is judging your ability to manage these investments, then ROA is the metric to watch. If you are looking for future capital and want to demonstrate your ability to manage your assets, then ROA is the best unfettered measure of your capability.

- **EBIT Margin (EBIT/revenue).** Operating margin is EBIT divided by Revenue, and it measures how much profit a company generates from a dollar of sales once it has paid for all variable operating costs.

- **Return on Equity - ROE (net income/shareholders' equity).** ROE takes net income and divides it by shareholder's equity, bringing forward the actual return to shareholders. Company executives, even if they are the founders, must always consider the shareholders even if they are the only one—because when you go to sell the company, the ROE is an important metric. ROE shows shareholders how much the company is making for every dollar invested. Are you using your resources wisely? ROE can be a little murky, especially vis a vis debt leverage or stock buybacks, but on the whole, it is a measure of value.

The Longer Trajectories— Leverage and Efficiency

Pro-active leaders pay close attention to the leverage and efficiency indicators, the longer trajectory metrics.

An investor or financial partner will always grab the balance sheet before the income statement because they need the big picture/long view.

This is why L.I.F.T. Leaders never focus on one tool for metrics. In L.I.F.T. Leadership, you embrace both the long and the short trajectory metrics. The long-term metrics important to leadership are the leverage ratios and the efficiency ratios.

Leverage Ratios

- **Fixed Assets (total fixed assets – accumulated depreciation) / Tangible Net Worth.** This ratio shows how the shareholder's capital has been invested in fixed assets and what that investment has generated.

- **Debt/Net Worth (total debt/net worth).** This is the amount of debt relative to the amount of equity from shareholders. If the debt ratio is over 3.0 times net income, or relative to its asset base, the company is very vulnerable. In this situation, they will want to convert as much of their EBITDA into Free Cash Flow as they can to avoid potential disaster.

Efficiency Ratios

The next long-term ratio indicators on a company's balance sheet are the efficiency ratios. This is a view of how a company can use its assets to make money. How much do you have to spend to make a dollar? Bottom line—if you need more than 50 cents to make a dollar, you're not managing well.

- **Asset Turnover (sales/av. total assets).** Measures the value of a company's revenue in relation to the value of its assets.

- **Inventory Turnover (cogs/av. inventory).** Measures the number of times inventory is turned over during the year.

- **Days' Sales Turnover ((sales/receivables)/365)** Measures the average number of days a company takes to turn its inventory into sales.

- **Return on Invested Capital (ROIC)** An assessment of the company's ability to allocate capital to sensible investments that drive returns. It is management's responsibility to create value over time and care for the shareholders' capital entrusted to them.

Four main metrics and 13 indicators

L.I.F.T. Leaders must keep all four categories of metrics—liquidity, profitability, leverage, and efficiency—and the related 13 performance indicators in front of them at all times. Add a live dashboard of these metrics to your computer screensaver. Or keep your excel sheets open all day. Whatever form you "dashboard" your metrics to, keep it handy and up-to-date. Better yet, commit them to live-memory. If you don't know what's going on in the company, who does?

These metrics and the LIFT stress test will help you understand where your business needs work and ways to help you.

To review, in addition to our L.I.F.T Stress Test, have ready access to these metrics at all times:

Liquidity Ratios

- Current Ratios

- Quick Ratios

Profitability Ratios

- Free Cash Flow Margin

- Net Profit Margin

- Return on Assets

- Operating Profit Margin

- Return on Equity

Leverage Ratios

- Fixed assets to net worth

- Debt to Equity

Efficiency Ratios

- Asset Turnover

- Inventory Turnover

- Days Sales Turnover

- Return on Invested Capital

Reflections from The Conqueror

Mehmed was clear about his goal, take Constantinople or die trying. To say the stakes were high would be a gross understatement.

Although he was driven by the desire to build an Ottoman Empire, the first step was to extinguish the remnants of Rome's last great stronghold outside Italy.

While court advisors, and many military generals, wanted to compromise and negotiate with the Byzantines, King Mehmed was relentless in his goals. To him, there could be no compromise.

From a "True North" point-of-view, he had his unique positional goals established. However, imagine the logistics of fighting a war, one empire against the other. Thousands of men, food, accommodations, health care, weapons, money, and countless other logistics. The metrics Mehmed used to manage this vast war engine were precise. He deployed spies, collected information, commissioned a technology for new cannons, knew the placement of all enemy troops, managed his troops' resources, and politically planted his Step-Mother in Hungary to keep an external threat at bay. Collating all this data without modern-day computers, cameras, and radar to help him meant he was a military genius. He engineered innovative ways to collect, understand and act on his war-time metrics.

Alexander the Great said, "In the end, when it's over, all that matters is what you've done." Mehmed was obsessed with getting it done and building his vision.

7

L.I.F.T. NETWORK: AND AGILE TEAMS

One thing every L.I.F.T. Leader values above all else is what I call the L.I.F.T. Network—communications, huddles and relentless messaging. To facilitate this, I recommend developing L.I.F.T. Agile Teams. Break it down, and you'll see productivity increase.

"For 20 years you paid for my hands, but all those years you had my mind for free and you never used it."—an employee, to Jack Welch in his book Winning.[35]

LIFT FACTS

- Unproductive meetings waste more than $37 billion per year in the U.S.[36]

- There are 25 million meetings per day in the U.S.

- Middle managers spend 35 percent of their time in meetings.

- 67 percent of meetings do not meet their stated objectives.

In this chapter

- L.I.F.T. Network: Your internal L.I.F.T. Communication Network is the most critical infrastructure in your company—every communication channel should be open.

- L.I.F.T. Agile Teams: The key to action and productivity is agility. In meetings, this means, brevity and frequency. To make that a reality, break your departments and bigger teams into agile teams.

- Embrace the whistleblower. Anonymity brings out insights you really need.

- The divided team is set to fail.

- Town halls, team huddles and one-on-ones: use what works.

- Most limitations to success are misunderstandings. Clarify, communicate, command.

Important Take-away

- Alexander the Great famously said, "With the right attitude, self-imposed limitations vanish."

Reflections from the Conqueror

- *Mehmed understood there could be only one commander. He was famous for "consulting the troops"—but when the orders came down, they marched. In war, the biggest army doesn't win—the best-informed troops usually prevail.*

L.I.F.T.

It's fine to know everything—but does everyone else know what you know? And, do you really know everything? You'll only find out if you huddle.

Lead: Your team will follow your lead if they understand what's at stake. Inform them.

Inspire: Your team is waiting to be inspired.

Focus: To communicate with a "team mind" requires a mission that all team-members embrace enthusiastically.

Transform: When the team is of one mind, what isn't possible?

Why do we call our business corporations "companies"? I'm sure you know the answer, but in case you didn't, its etymology is the French word compagnie, meaning "body of soldiers." We name our companies after armed forces companies for a reason. It's not just because of organizational structure—squads, teams, platoons—and chain-of-command; it has a lot to do with mission, agility and action. We speak the same language. "Intelligence-gathering," and "risk assessment" and "chain-of-command."

The reason I focus on Mehmed the Conqueror as a metaphor for business management is that he avoided the mistakes made by other military commanders—failure to communicate. You could easily reverse this.

History is replete with battles lost due to blunders in communication:

- 1788: Austria lost the battle of Karansebes against the Ottoman Turkish Empire because they split their superior army of 100,000 into two—based clumsy on communications and poor intelligence. This mistake led to a tragedy-of-errors, resulting in the deaths of 10,000.

- The most famous example of blunders in communication is the "Charge of the Light Brigade", immortalized in the poem of the same name by Lord Alfred Tennyson. Information, corrupted by a long chain of command through four separate commanders, was so vague that by the time it reached General George Bingham, that the calvary commander ended up charging the wrong battery. As a result, scores of British perished. Today, the Charge is used in military school to illustrate the consequence of "poor intelligence and command structure."

- In 1815, at the Battle of New Orleans, British troops lost because one team failed in basic logistics. The team's sole job was to set up "forward redoubt" with ladders. Because they didn't complete their task—for want of a few ladders—the British were beaten back with huge losses.

You get the idea. The stakes are no less in business. Causalities might be measured in revenue loss or job loss, but both can be devastating. There are three lessons, business leaders can learn from these famous military blunders:

1. Armies move better as "agile" fireteams, inside nimble squads, in-turn part of the force of a dynamic platoon, who in-turn stay connected to the entire chain-of-command. (Why this metaphor? The U.S. Army knows a few things about the benefits of agility, real-time communication, and good intelligence.)

2. Leaders communicate better without layers (See Charge of the Light Brigade) above.

3. Timely information is critical. No battle can be won with old information.

This is why Mehmed remains my ideal model for the "agile" and "networked" leader. He suffered none of the issues experienced by Austria or the British in my three examples.

Real-life L.I.F.T. Case: Agile Teams and Real-Time Networking Transforms a Global Company

I took over a company that was spread across the globe, in multiple countries employing thousands of people, distributed across three different lines of business. On a small scale, the logistics of a global company, regardless of size, is not dissimilar to the issues faced by the army. In this company, one business unit in Asia had significant, and unique complexities in technology and product development. The need for frequent communication and weekly huddles in this company was an urgent priority.

We gave the general managers in all countries reasonable autonomy, but soon realized that to reinforce unity and action, the messaging required relentless repetition. The leadership team went through the values exercise and reset the expectations; we all agreed, and everyone was committed to the new mission and methods. However, here's reality of larger organizations—or even disorganized mid-sized teams: you cannot change business operations or values in one day, one week, or even a month—not even in a year—if you don't break the cycle of habit that automatically forms within any organization. Team consensus only goes as far as inspiration; implementation requires repetition, frequency, feedback, more repetition, more feedback—until the new "better" habits form. In one sense, habit and repetition is a key to productivity. It can equally be the biggest barrier to productivity, if those habits and repetitive patterns are off-mission.

This is challenging in a company, such as this, spread over nine countries, separated by time zones, language and cultural differences. Even in a smaller single-office company it would be unreasonable to expect everyone to change after one consensus meeting. To move forward as a global unit and coordinate, without reverting to old habits would require weekly and daily "huddles."

Our main operation in Asia, was widely differentiated from our head-office mission and standards. The leadership was not used to doing business with our renewed commitment to values; for instance, it was common and an acceptable practice in this country to incent suppliers or clients. As a brand with a mission and position, it was critical we all operate with the same values and ethics.

We needed to drive this "new way" of doing things—in all parts of the globe—on a weekly basis. This didn't have to be in-person, and could be facilitated with video calls, telephone, online conferences, and even live chat. The key was regularity and interactivity.

It did become evident in the first 90 days that we needed to send an executive champion on-site to assist with the daily efforts to change our business. Old habits and a "culture of hidden deals"—is not easy to break. The possibility of losing a client over these new deals only encouraged a new layer of "concealing things." We acted quickly. I rolled out a whistleblower policy and an "anonymous reporting" online portal to help ensure any hidden issues were revealed quickly. Being able to report concerns anonymously ensured people would come forward with questionable practices.

After these changes, it became apparent that the local workforce embraced our new values. After due diligence, we released the general manager and left our temporary executive there in the transition period, as we looked for a replacement. The next 30 days was eye-opening. When we audited the GM's expenses, we found many shocking claims including $1000 exotic cats, Chauffeur parking tickets, three-times-a week massage parlour "treatments"—and even a live-in "house guest" who turned out to be an HR contractor he engaged to monitor our plant workers.

The damage was done, but after we removed the issue from our workplace, and revealed the excesses and abuses of the executive, there was a palpable momentum in our facility. I'd have to call it a serious rebound, and it paved the way for needed positive change. We carefully recruited a replacement GM—someone not previously indoctrinated in the previous bad habits—and this individual was able to ride the very positive wave of change and championed a recovery that was unprecedented for this factory.

Over the next few years, we engineered our changes with frequent "huddles" and relentless reaffirmation of our values—and how to lead the way to exciting change.

L.I.F.T. A-Teams—Agile Squads and Why You Need Them

The fastest growing companies—by any metrics—are almost always agile companies. Large cumbersome Fortune 500 companies may be stable, and growing predictably, but that doesn't mean they're growing "fast." If you desire to fast growth, give strong consideration to my approach—L.I.F.T. Network and the L.I.F.T. Agile Team.

Basically, in L.I.F.T. Leadership the entire company is organized around agility. Agility means putting aside quaint notions like the "all-hands-on-deck" meetings and quarterly town halls—other than as a formal touchpoint. To make action happen—you need agility.

L.I.F.T. Leaders are Agile.

I'm going to pre-empt what I know will be your immediate gut response to my premise of frequent, short meetings. We all know that "meetings interrupt" productivity. Even though I advocate for frequent meetings, I also know it can be an interruption—if handled incorrectly. Instead of interrupting the flow of work, I argue it facilitates momentum—if you handle it right.

I'm going to stay with my "army" metaphor here. Who knows more about organizing for precision and agility more than the U.S. Army? I'm not talking about chain-of-command and discipline—those can be important.

Critically, I'm also not talking about introducing layers-upon-layers of management. That just becomes cumbersome, the opposite of nimbleness. In fact, as I discuss in another chapter, L.I.F.T. Leaders flatten hierarchies and management levels. But, I am talking about groups and teams who depend on each other to facilitate action and dexterity.

I'm speaking solely of responsiveness. I think armed forces generals of today learned lessons from the "Charge of the Light Brigade," Alexander the Great, and Mehmed the Conqueror. They know that speed means lives saved. They know all about flat chain-of-command and communication. One wrong word in a communique can cost lives.

So, how does the massive infrastructure of the vast U.S. Army operate with agility? They break it down. Communications is all-day-long, not once-a-month. Troops are broken down into team-sizes that can be effective and agile at the same time:

- A fireteam is four or less soldiers, a very intimate group who depend on each other to survive.

- Two fireteams typically make up a squad of soldiers—and you can bet the effective squad know each other, like family. Usually, a squad is led by a sergeant.

- Three of four squads make up a platoon of 20-50 soldiers, usually in the charge of a lieutenant.

- Two or more platoons make up a *company*—interesting word, isn't it?

The L.I.F.T. Network: Town halls, Team Huddles and One-on-Ones: Use What Works

Here's the bottom line in business: network or die. This applies equally to working with your teams. L.I.F.T. Network is just a word, but it describes your lines of communication as a vast omni-directional network. One mistake business leaders make is thinking "top down" or one-dimensionally. Communications and networking moves in all directions, is interactive and active. It's not just about frequent huddles, but it certainly starts there. Why?

Communications in a company defines a company. A L.I.F.T. Leader engineers a company ready to seize opportunities. You cannot seize what you do not perceive. You cannot create opportunity without dialogue. Leadership might include "chain of command" but it's not defined by it. Leadership is more readily associated with communication and networking.

Today, thanks to technology, we have no excuses for avoiding the daily or weekly huddle in action teams. If your teams are in different countries, embrace the online conference. Pick up the phone. Live chat. For bigger teams, try a virtual town-hall format. Whatever works. There's no need to book a flight and hotels just for your regular huddle.

It's about what I call the L.I.F.T. Network. I describe it this way because you obviously cannot meet personally with thousands of team-members in multiple countries every day. You can facilitate real-time feedback loops, networked communication, and urgency by de-structuring your meeting format. Use what works.

Daily to Direct Reports

Make it your mission to have a daily touchpoint with all your direct reports. Encourage and insist your direct-reports have daily touchpoints with their direct-reports. And so on. Daily networking. Weekly, try to "huddle" with the wider team. Again, be creative. If your meeting is facilitated by online conferencing, that's still a huddle.

If it's only 15 minutes or less—count that as a triumph. If each "huddle" discusses and resolves five key points and puts forward five mini-goals for the next huddle—that's momentum. If you decide on a daily touch point instead of weekly—for example, in your small action squads—you can cover the same content in 5 minute "huddles" each day—and actually double productivity (see examples below.) Why? Because there's no need for recaps and reviews.

As an exercise "log it" over the next 10 weeks. Break teams into smaller action groups and try weekly and daily formats. Track how many actionable goals you discuss and act upon. (See the exercise in this chapter.)

Why is frequency important? Here's a few reasons (there are many more):

- In a daily meeting, you only need to focus on the action points for the day, perhaps one or two. No need for review or debate. All about action.

- In a weekly meeting, you only need to focus on the action points for the week. That might amount to seven to twelve action points. Some small amount of review and recap may be required, but minimal.

- In a weekly meeting you'll have to try to cover 30 to 40 action points, once a month. Some opportunities will have already been missed. You'll have to spend more time on review and history than on the actual action points. In this scenario, information is now dated, and requires updating. Many of the action points are dated and no longer require action—or worse, the opportunity is now gone!

In the typical monthly 120-minute meeting, you'll likely spend:

- 10 minutes bringing the team up to speed with minutes of the last meeting and backgrounds

- An average of 5 minutes per action point (takes into account some topics are long-topics and others are quick review topics).

- 15 minutes: setting goals for next month and action recaps.

On the other hand, the weekly meeting, 30 minutes in length, can easily get by on 5 minutes for both "review" and "goal setting" because the action-points are "in play" and the last meeting was only days ago. For daily meetings, you can skip the recaps, jumping right to: "How are we doing with…"—it's much more fluid and top-of-mind and make sure you respect the end time and call the meeting to a close when the allotted time has arrived.

Examples of L.I.F.T. Network Momentum

In other words, a two-hour meeting, once a month, not only covers stale and redundant material, it also cannot accommodate as much action/discussion. Real-life scenarios:

- **One 120-minute meeting once a month**: 120 minutes spent in total time of which 95 minutes is spent on action/points and decisions, at an average of five minutes each: 19 action topics can be covered (several of which will be historical, non-active by the time of this meeting.) These meetings become post-mortems instead of action meetings.

- **Four 30-minute meetings per month** (one per week): 30 minutes—five minutes on recaps and goal setting, and an average of five minutes per topic: five topics per week. This translates into 20 topics per month covered, but these are covered while still in motion (active).

- **20 five-minute meetings per month** (one per day, five days per week)—no formal recaps, recap and cover goals as you go along on each topic. Since the topics are "alive", just spend two minutes on each topic: two topics per meeting. This translates into forty topics per month, no extra time spent, and the action-points are in motion. Simply ask, "what has changed since yesterday" and "what do we have to do to complete this action-point."

L.I.F.T. Cadences for Meetings by Scenario

Not every team or scenario is the same, and it varies by industry and service—although if in doubt, plan on a cadence of short weekly meetings for any department or group.

More formally, in every company you'll have a mix of what I call L.I.F.T. Cadences—a music metaphor this time (taking a break from the military!)—and if you break them down, they can be associated by the activeness of its assigned team. I start with the most frequent cadence—your A-Teams (Agile Teams, remember?)—ending with the least nimble cadence:

1. **L.I.F.T. Daily Huddle Cadence**: Agile Teams need the short daily huddle. [This is the "Fireteam" in my military metaphor.] These are action teams, built in fairly intimate groups of three or four. They typically meet five minutes each morning over coffee or tea, to hit the top-level action topics.

2. **L.I.F.T. Informal Cadence**: usually informal one-on-ones for special projects, alliances and other tighter groups. This could be daily (on urgent projects), weekly (more likely, biweekly or monthly.

3. **L.I.F.T. Weekly Project or Production Cadence**: Projects and Production units are almost always at least weekly in an action-oriented company, but could also be daily, biweekly or monthly. [These are your "squads" in my military metaphor.]

4. **L.I.F.T. Bi-Weekly Departmental Cadence**: Almost always bi-weekly in an action-oriented company, typically monthly in cumbersome corporations not focused on fast growth. [These are your "platoons" in the military metaphor.]

5. **L.I.F.T. Weekly Leadership and Steering Teams Cadence:** Usually weekly, daily in times of crisis or for special project implementation. [These are your commanders and generals.]

6. L.I.F.T. Bi-Weekly Account Management Cadence: Ideally bi-weekly, or monthly in larger corporations, quarterly in some enterprises.

7. L.I.F.T. Monthly Town Halls (All-Hands): Even in nimble L.I.F.T. organizations, I advocate regular townhalls—monthly or quarterly—although this can just be as simple as a five minute up-date video with an invitation to feedback by email.

8. Committees: widely vary, depending on how action-oriented they are, from weekly to monthly to quarterly.

9. Boards—Usually quarterly and annually, but sometimes monthly.

If you can think of others, they likely fall into an area combining two of the above. I break them down this way simply because it helps guide the frequency. Obviously, boards and committees don't meet daily. Customer Relations tends to be historical review and goal setting. The real action is in what I call "L.I.F.T. A-Teams: Agile Teams."

Even the largest of teams require frequent huddles

The key to corporate success is communications, clarity and inspiration. All of these require the frequent "huddle." Daily, biweekly, weekly—whatever you define as frequent in the context of that action group (see the nine cadences above).

Basically, the rule of thumb is: action-oriented teams meet more often. If you're not an active team—isn't that a problem?

It's About Action!

Don't make the mistake of assuming the daily or weekly meeting is an unproductive waste of time. It's only a waste of time if you make it so.

Huddles, as in sports huddles, are all about action. Quick and concise. You are about to engage in a major game-play—huddle quickly and make sure all the players are together on the play. The huddle is about action, not bureaucracy. Sometimes, it's also about fresh top of mind. Or "rah-rah-rah" inspiration.

What does the war-leader need—that the corporate leader also needs? Action. Quick, insightful, action. A large, unmotivated army is much less effective on the field than an energized, focused, and skilled troop of elites. L.I.F.T. is about being the elite war-leader.

Why is the smaller army, potentially effective against the larger force? Through communications, movement, strategy, coordinated action.

And it starts with frequent huddles.

L.I.F.T. Out—Get Out in the Tent!

Mehmed didn't isolate himself in a palace. He was out with his troops, living in a tent, dusty and dirty with the troops. His authority was unquestioned, but so was the loyalty of his troops. They knew him. They understood him. They knew his thoughts—because he told them. He huddled with his war-leaders. Those war-leaders huddled with his squadron-leaders. They huddled with their troops. Every day. He lived in tents alongside his army. Metaphorically, so should you.

In business, the war never ends. Sorry to tell you that, but if you believe the battle for customers and business is ever over, you will lose the next engagement. Even cumbersome Fortune 500s can't rely on the concrete bunker of their reputation. Concrete cracks. Bombs can pierce bunkers. Assume you live in a tent, not a bunker.

In other words, there is never a time when the need for the urgent, frequent huddle is ended.

The secret of the frequent huddle is a simple one—but potentially a game-changer in business. Embrace brevity. No one complains about a daily or weekly huddle if it's short, to the point and useful.

L.I.F.T. Top Tips to Great Huddles

Here are some quick ways to ensure productive, frequent, useful, actionable "team huddles."

1. Lead from the top down.

However, you structure your teams, you will ultimately end up breaking down your teams into more and more actionable groups. To encourage frequent, action huddles, lead from the top down. As leader, make sure you meet with your leadership team as often as you would like to see them meet with their teams.

2. Break it down into A-Teams.

Agile Teams, remember? Forget the big Departmental meeting. It's a relic. If you have them, make them touchpoints for all the Agile Teams to report in. Agile Teams meet more often and work on the mandate of action-points. A-Teams also tend to be more "intimate" and get to know each other, learning to work well together.

3. Frequency to duration ratio.

To get buy-in from the teams on "increased frequency of meetings" convince them with "no extra time in meetings." Reduce the length of meetings. Five 5-minute daily meetings are actually less time committed than one 30-minute weekly session. Four 30-minute sessions are less than one 2.5-hour mammoth session.

4. "Resistance is futile."

It's inevitable that any change in meeting frequency will be met with resistance—even if you assure them, they can join by online conference. Be understanding, say, "I understand your concern, but let's do it my way and see..." But, regardless of push back on the idea of, never give in. You are the leader.

5. Avoid problem solving.

Meetings are not where you solve problems, unless they are specifically brain-storming sessions or project meetings. Meetings are about identifying the problem, the resources to handle the problem, the obstacles and challenges. Assign the resource, set a goal, and move on to the next item.

6. Recognize habits with kind firmness.

Be patient with changes to routine. It may take up to 90 days or longer for the new routine to "sink in." Persist, patiently and kindly, but without flexibility.

7. Tie incentives to the meetings

No, I don't mean incent them for attending. But, make recognition and reward part of your meetings so team members have some good news to look forward to. "Congrats to Team-A, on closing the $6 million-dollar contract." Praise in public meetings is already reward.

8. Make it fun

I know, it's easy to say. How you do it, depends on the team-groups and what they respond to. But, just keep it top-of-mind that most people dread meetings, either because they think it's a "waste of time" or a forum for criticism. Don't fulfill either of these expectations. Cut the meeting the moment it's no longer productive. Move it along. Praise the team. Bring in doughnuts. The point is making it fun.

9. Try a stand-up meeting?

This tip is only for the daily five-minute 'check-ins' for the A-Team folks. Obviously, you don't force people with arthritis to stand in a meeting, but the concept is to illustrate the idea that the daily meeting is just a stop-in and go—a check-in. In this format, try a standing format around a whiteboard. Psychologically, it really motivates a short, productive session.

Embrace the whistle-blower

I know, whistleblowers are pariahs. That's the common thinking, right? If you think that way, you're on the wrong side of a potential whistleblower's wrath. L.I.F.T. Leaders embrace the anonymous whistleblower.

And, that, fellow L.I.F.T. Leaders, is the secret—anonymous. Ideally, use an arms-length, outside "whistleblower" reporting agency. Your team should never feel they will be punished for being honest. One way to ensure that, is to keep their identity a secret.

Yes, it's true, you invite criticisms of your own leadership. So be it. Honest insight is valuable, even if you don't agree with it.

Another Lesson From the Army—Never Down Braid Your Subordinates

Criticism and honest feedback are vital at all levels of your organization. This is why we embrace the whistleblower. But—there's a time and place. The time is not the weekly or daily meeting. It is most definitely not in front of your subordinates' team-mates. It only takes one break of public trust to destroy your hard-built relationship with your subordinates.

In my chapter case study, I mentioned how we discovered the abuse of the General Manager through a Whistleblower. Enough said?

L.I.F.T Exercise: 1 to 5 to 30

Bear with me. Try out this exercise—or ask your team leaders to try it out.

List all your goals for the next 30 days as specifically as possible:

1.

2.

3.

4.

5.

6.

7.

8.

9.

10.

11.

12.

13.

14.

15.

16.

17.

18.

19.

20.

Now, put aside the 30-day list. List instead all your priorities for the next 7 days:

1.

2.

3.

4.

5.

Now, if you put those aside and just listed what you needed to do tomorrow, how would the list change?

1.

2.

That's probably it, right? Two, three at a stretch.

Which plan would you rather write? A plan for the 20 thirty-day goals, or a plan for the 5 seven-day goals? Would you rather write a one-paragraph plan for tomorrow, or a PowerPoint for next week's meeting?

I'm not suggesting you limit yourself to short-term thinking. My point is to show you how your thinking and language changes when you list your immediate goals versus your longer-term goals.

Now, write an agenda for your one-day goals, as if you're having a meeting in the morning—just a five-minute stand-up meeting:

1.

2.

Now, write the agenda for the weekly meeting (sit-down, of course.)

1.

2.

3.

4.

5.

I won't ask you to write your agenda for the 30-day meeting, because by now you probably realize how generic and time-consuming it will become. You'll probably notice from this exercise, that short-term, specific goals tend to be driven action.

L.I.F.T. How-To: Monthly Townhalls.

Repetition is the mother of learning. Implementing change is a slow process, especially in a mature team undergoing a transition.

If you've embraced the A-Team, the Action Team, and concept of shorter action-oriented meetings, you will soon find that clarity and consistency are critical. You can save time in meetings, and in productivity time-flows, by being clear and consistent—and by formalizing a short "all-hands" town hall session on a regular basis.

For example, you shouldn't need to spend time on things like values and corporate vision, at regular weekly meetings. Instead, surround the teams with those reinforcing messages—on the walls, in emails, vision boards, mission statements, and lunchroom message board.

This way, you can make the weekly or daily huddle all about project work and key milestones. Save the bigger values messages, progress reports and motivational touchpoints for a monthly, or quarterly, town-hall format. Today, it can be a virtual townhall, a live streamed conference, or even in the form of a short-pre-recorded video to the team. Again, make it short, meaningful and information packed.

Think of your town halls as your cultural events, your "all hands" we're-in-this-together, rah-rah-rah sessions. There are several ways to instill enthusiasm for the townhall.

Think of the Town Hall as a very important stage for the CEO and C-suite to communicate to the broader internal stakeholder audience. This can be especially beneficial in companies with multiple offices in various locations, and especially for international companies.   I t ' s about sharing with all stakeholders—the employees on a manufacturing floor, or a supervisor in an isolated department, or a procurement buyer placing orders—of the sales team in a remote city. They can often be left in the dark on the broader company initiatives and efforts. It serves the same purpose it does in politics—reaching all the constituents—but without the politics. We pitch our stated values, our goals, our mission, our plans, and ask for feedback from people we otherwise won't have an opportunity to meet with directly due to the logistics of scale and geography. Let all the teams see your face, hear your thoughts, and be inspired by your plans.

As the CEO/C-suite/VP or Director you cannot assume that the "chain of command" filtered the full picture down to the entire team. Remember, the "Charge of the Light Brigade" and how General George

Bingham charged the wrong hill due to misinformation passed through four commanders. One of those commanders got it wrong, and it ended up being the "other hill."

A Town Hall, like your website, like the mission posted on the lunch-room wall—all of these make sure everyone knows who we are, what we stand for, and where we are going.

So, here's the simple format for a 10-minute town hall for each month or so. Remember some ground rules: be honest and direct, since speculation and rumours are worse than any bad news ever can be; invite anonymous feedback and also open questions; and explain "we're all in this together."

If you decide to go live online, modify this, and allow for some inter-activity for an online conference. For this simple format, I'm structuring a pre-recorded video format Town Hall with an invitation to ask questions:

1. Introduce the theme and your main topics, and make sure you mention the content is for internal team-members only.

2. Answer any questions from the last pre-recorded townhall. Don't miss this step, or your team will feel like you're not listening.

3. Share news, especially any "good news" such as new large con-tracts, or the opening of a new factory, or a new initiative.

4. If there are any "bad news" bits, share them honestly. Hiding bad news benefits no one. Instead, explain the "action steps" you plan to take to overcome the obstacle or issue.

5. Covering goals, milestones and mission that affect the entire team—especially over the next month—assuming you're adopt-ing a monthly format.

6. Invite people to submit questions that you'll answer at the next townhall.

7. Explain your whistleblower policy and how to anonymously report.

8. Thank everyone until the next time.

We need to provide an opportunity for everyone to understand the direction, and what is important to us and where we are going. Go transparent—since ambiguity and haziness will lead to speculation and criticism. The dialogue should be two-way. Make sure in each town hall you answer questions. In a live online townhall, that might be an actual incoming live question. In pre-recorded format, make sure you answer questions from the previous townhall on the next one.

A good well-rounded approach to internal corporate communications can provide a platform for harmony with the value and vision of a company.

Reflections from the Conqueror

Mehmed II was known to talk openly to his troops, gathering his advisors, secretly meeting his enemies' leaders, using spies tactically, and befriending a possible ally. He had many "frenemies"—people he was "friendly with" and used, but who were really his enemies. He never tired of speaking with his troops, his commanders, even captured enemies. He felt every conversation could produce a nugget of information or give him insight into the efforts of his enemy.

Mehmed II was a master communicator.

Alexander the Great famously said, "With the right attitude, self-imposed limitations vanish," and Mehmed II had the right attitude, precise focus on the prize, and managed a vast flow of information. Like any great commander he knew how to filter the bad from the good, the useless from the hidden nugget of critical information. Above all, Mehmed kept his mind open and his relationships wide—to make sure he always had enough information to make the tough decisions that would win the battle.

8

L.I.F.T. TARGETS—EVERYBODY NEEDS AN ENEMY

The "Art of War" is written into the DNA of every top business Leader. Challenge is Inspiration. Nothing brings your plan into Focus faster than an enemy—the larger and nastier the better. Learning to deal with "enemies" will lead to your Transformative moments.

L.I.F.T. Facts

"85 *percent of employees have to deal with conflict to some degree… however, conflict can also lead to positive emotions, when it's managed correctly. Over three quarters (76 percent) of employees have identified a good end result from conflict."—CPP Global Human Capital Report.*

Conflict is inescapable in business. You either embrace the conflict as an engine for Inspiration, Focus and Transformation, or you are crushed by the stress and uncertainty. A "healthy" respect for conflict helps the great leader thrive. L.I.F.T. Leaders see conflict, enemies, and rising competitive threats as engines for invention.

Embrace your enemies as opportunities. They are the driving force of your leadership strategies. Capitalism is adversarial. Invest energy and inspiration when "times are tough." Try to think—you are fortunate to lead in desperate times.

In this chapter

L.I.F.T. and the "enemy":

- Your enemy—your opposite number, whether competitor—gives you the momentum to succeed, the drive to win.

- Know your enemy—to know is to win. No battle is won without reconnaissance.

- Service is enhanced by the business battlefield: the need to succeed and win drives the best in customer service, the best in recruitment, the highest level of leadership excellence.

Important Take-away

- **"Keep your enemies closer."**

Reflections from the Conqueror

- *Mehmed, as the master tactician, was extraordinary at tapping opportunities. He "competed" with the Emperor of Rome by offering the people of Constantinople a "better deal": keep their homes and possessions instead of being destroyed.*

Values of L.I.F.T.

Lean thinking is the driving force of L.I.F.T.

Lead: The greatest business leaders and war leaders in history excelled when they were honed on the battlefield.

Inspire: Competition inspires the best in performance. If you don't have the threat of an enemy ready to inspire the troops—find one.

Focus: Now you have the enemy, the target, focus on the solution. Competition refines all processes into their highest form.

Transform: The need to survive is the most transformative of forces.

Harvard Professor Porter's "five forces" are as valid today as they were thirty years ago. The dynamic nature of competitive forces keeps leaders and companies and brands at their best. If not, for the pressures of markets, would there be printing presses, vaccines, light bulbs, personal computers and smart phones? We need enemies for focus. We need competitors to pressure us to grow, anticipate and thrive.

Professor Michael Porter's famous five forces are widely embraced, although I restate them here as threats in more 21st century context, those "threats" being:

- Supplier threat—your suppliers can drive up your prices.

- Buyer threats—buyers drive prices down and demand constant innovation.

- Competitive threats – the other guy can drop prices and drive the products towards a commodity, eroding ultimate value.

- Technology threats—demand for better technology to solve problems.

- New enemy threats—new enemies and threats arise constantly.

HR Enemies

These threats can also be put in the context of HR. We compete for team-members. I mentioned how I poach other companies for top team members in chapter two. HR is also subject to supply and demand, competition, and even technology. HR is also subject to friend and enemy scenarios. In your career as a leader, you will be forced to let team-members "go." All leaders do this, but they often forget a basic lesson—the former employees remain part of your network. Former employees don't just "go away." They end up working at your competitors, show up at industry tradeshows or the lobby of a customer. They appear in your wider social circle. They are still in the "trade." Never assume a separation means you'll never cross paths again.

In fact, I suggest that all of your "foes" be treated with respect. Keep in mind the ancient proverb, variously attributed to Sun Tzu or Niccolo Machiavelli (and sometimes Al Pacino in the Godfather movie.)

"Keep your friends close, keep your enemies closer."

In other words, as a L.I.F.T. Leader, it can be more important to watch your enemies, than your own team and friends. Whether you are planning for HR (recruitment or union negotiations) or for marketing, you are always in competition for resources. As Sun Tzu wrote in the Art of War:

"Know your enemy."

Real-life L.I.F.T Inspiration Case Study—"Keep your enemies closer."

A most difficult union negotiation becomes an opportunity to grow.

A number of years ago I worked with a company that had a tremendous amount of turnover. There was a virtual revolving door in the HR department. The dynamic was unusual, since our company was located in a small town. Working in a small town never lets you forget that former employees remain part of your circle of influence. I've always believed that all people I meet and engage with are valuable and important to some degree.

I kept that in mind when I unintendedly ran across the former HR Manager of our company at a social occasion. Even though I knew he had hastily departed from my company—and that my company had a very negative view of his departure—I was eager to spend time with him. Whenever someone is rushed out the door, they usually have valuable information and perspective. At this time, I was dealing with a union issue in my company.

So, I spent time getting to know him on this occasion, and I found him very generous with his time. He shared his perspective on the union and the people involved. We chatted that day—and remained in contact.

I didn't think much more of it at the time, but, as with all of my relationships, I felt good about having made a new associate. I could hardly have anticipated how important that would be, until six months later.

At that time, our company headed into a very difficult contract negotiation. The company's situation required us to request deep concessions from the union. At the time the company was losing $27M per year—one of the main reasons I was brought into the company. Legacy language, constrictive work rules and inefficient costs associated with the union contract represented our biggest expenses. Our employee expenses were the highest in the industry—and it threatened to "bury" the company, possibly leading to liquidation.

I was given the mandate by the shareholders to do whatever it took to save the company—or push it from Chapter 11 into Chapter 7. The Management Team and I spent an enormous amount of time developing an agenda, outlining all the language required in the new contract. The stakes were high.

We spent four months creating a comprehensive "survival" document to present to the Union, explaining every problem, variant and nuance, all the scenarios proving how these issues made us unprofitable and threatened our existence. The stakes were high, and this would set a precedent in the industry. For the union to agree to even some of our demands would be beyond difficult for them. We understood that. At the same time, we had no alternative. Concessions were absolutely essential and not optional in any way.

The first day of the negotiations I sat across from the National Representative of the Union, who came in for the opener of the contract negotiations—because they knew this contract would set precedence in the industry.

A leader listens. It's a defining characteristic of the L.I.F.T. leader. So, I listened. He delivered a passionate opener, and it was clear why he was the National Representative. "The union wants every company to succeed," he said, grandly. He explained how they were not interested in taking any steps backwards financially—but they had to deliver a long and secure contract for the betterment of all the members of the union.

After an hour-long opener the stage was mine. The fact our company was in Chapter 11 bankruptcy proceedings was well known. I walked through the financial position of the company, and how risky the future was at this time. In the opening slides I attempted to explain the uncertainty of our survival the need for us to work together during these negotiations because it played an integral part the shareholders decision for the future. My team handed out nicely prepared three-ring binders that contained over 400 pages of data and proposals. We showed how we could restructure the entire collective agreement to not take a dollar from the members, and to create flexibility for management to maximize worker efficiency. We showed how we could deliver eight hours of work for eight hours of pay, and how we had the ability to meet our customer's needs and requirements. It was a fulsome proposal that addressed the monetary interests of the union members and the essential needs of management to improve the cost structure of the business. Members would not lose any money but achieving an increased level of productivity would be their role in our survival.

I'm used to dramatic presentation, and I'd say I was eloquent in my opener. I enthusiastically demonstrated how everyone would be kept intact and whole, could be given reasonable rest times, and create a culture of productivity and success.

The fact is, in these types of negotiations, I expected hostility—and the members in the room met this expectation. Their faces were non-receptive to say the least. I think I made a compelling case for a reasonable agreement, and win-win negotiations.

From their dramatic response, I assume they didn't see it that way. The National Representative stood up, whispered a few words to his team, and the entire union team walked over to the garbage bin next to the conference room door and threw out all our nice binders and hundreds of pages of work into that bin which filled it to the rim. Just so much garbage.

The National Representative was the last to exit the room and, as he was leaving, he said, a little over-dramatically, "it will be a cold day in hell." The stalemate began.

The next several weeks were obviously difficult. Our employees "worked to rule" in a concerted effort to slow operations, production and sales. We were at a stand-still, with no likely end in sight. Cold day in hell, indeed.

A surprise call—

One late evening, at our headquarters, my cell phone rang, and a familiar, cheerful voice said, "Hi Randy, how are you?"

Yes, it was our cheerful previous HR Manager, the one I had met socially six months previously. He had heard about the situation and wanted to offer some advice.

I was all ears—which is a good thing in any leadership position. Over the next few days, this former HR Manager walked me through some backdoor channels. Thanks to his insights, contacts, and knowledge, over the next three months I managed to bring the Union back to the table.

I won't bore you with details—the point of my story being how important it is to remain networked with everyone, including past employees—but ultimately, we were able to make enough changes to the agreement to get it ratified with 98% approval by the members.

Bottom line—we were able to offer a slight economic increase to the employee's compensation, but our cost per hour dropped by 62 percent, and our throughput increased a whopping 212 percent. We were able to move from -$27M in EBITDA to +$35M in EBITDA over the next 24 months.

This company, which was insolvent in Chapter 11, sold for several hundred million dollars within a four-year period of time.

And the lesson to be learned: all relationships matter. Never burn any bridges, to use the cliché. In this case, our unlikely hero was a former employee who gave me the information needed to break the impasse. A hundred-year-old company had almost vanished some 15 years ago—but thanks to some information, a little networking, and months of negotiating, I am happy to report it is alive and thriving today.

Your enemy gives you wings

There are two main analogies used in business schools—warfare, and sports. Both are valid, because they deal with issues familiar in business. In war, we have the opposite side. In sports, we have the other teams. In business, we have competitors. It is this "enemy" who gives you the inspiration not only to succeed, but to innovate. Or, as I described in my case study, to break the unmovable impasse.

In keeping with the "warfare" analogy, the first thing to learn is a lesson expressed by Bill Gates: "Sometimes the lambs have to lie down with the wolves." He was speaking of the cooperation between Microsoft and Apple at the time. Of course, many ventures find they have to cooperate with their competitors. In warfare, this might be expressed in unlikely alliances against a greater enemy.

This is what I meant by "Keep your enemies closer" in paraphrasing Sun Tzu and the Art of War. Remember, even within a single company, you can have rivalries between departments—metaphorical "enemies"—but you must work together in order to achieve.

Why do I make such a big point of this? Because, "enemies give you wings." Don't fear the enemy. Embrace the opportunity and energy of competition. It can be used to inspire your 'troops' to innovate solutions. It's not just about new ideas or innovation, but also speed and urgency.

Adaptability and change. All of these things are handily pushed along with a little nudge from your enemies.

Here's the longer list of what you stand to gain from constructive conflict in your company or in your market:

- A heightened sense of urgency.

- Higher team productivity.

- Employee retention—volatility can inspire loyalty when handled the right way.

- Innovating and new ideas.

- Enhanced problem-solving—from competitive scenarios.

- Enhanced communications—when you are in a "war-footing" you tend to communicate more frequently.

- Speed to market—because the stakes are high.

- Higher level of client/customer satisfaction—because everyone tries harder in the face of competition.

- A more motivated workforce.

- A positive brand reputation derived from the "try harder" attitude.

There are downsides, of course. For some people the stress of conflict can be de-motivating and actually hurt productivity or creativity. But, for the savvy L.I.F.T. Leader who embraces the conflict, it can give your team wings.

When conflict is demotivating

L.I.F.T. Leaders know how to use conflict to motivate and empower. Conflict can be our worst enemy if handled incorrectly. Usually, the *worst* ways to handle conflict are:

- **Compromising**—Too much give and take weakens the momentum. When competitors attack with lower prices or better products, the solution is not to compromise your own situation. The key is to use the situation to inspire better products and solutions.

- **Dominating**—Trying to dominate the market with supplier leverage and other methods usually backfires. Don't concentrate on your own needs, domination, but on solving the needs of others, your customers. Knee-jerk reactions rarely lead to creative solutions to conflicts.

- **Avoiding**—Avoiding is not the secret to success in any part of business. It's just failure. We cannot afford to put our head in the sand, take the conflicts and face them head-on with a calm demeanor that is orientated towards solving the issue.

- **Giving-in**—What's the point of having an opportunity to innovate if all you're going to do is give-in: for example, price-matching. It's a loser's game. I refuse to play "race to the bottom" in any business, it's a lose-lose proposition.

The secret—know your enemy

There is only one big secret, and you saw it in action in my case study. My friend, the past HR Manager shared information on my "enemy" that I was able to use. In warfare, this would be analogous to "espionage." (By the way, we're not advocating illegal corporate espionage. Just the ordinary sources of information that are ethically obtained, but often overlooked).

Regardless of who your enemy is, knowing them is the secret to overcoming them. This is why the wisdom of the great war-sage Sun Tzu is embraced by business and sales professionals alike.

The problem is, by the time you research your competitors—with the goal of "getting in their head" you're probably already out-of-date. Do you want to discover what they'll do next? It isn't easy, but chances are many of Google's tools can help. You can run deep analytics on competitor websites. You can check out your competitors online Google Ads keyword campaign and results. You can discern strategies of public companies from their public reports. You can recruit their team-members. You can try to "think" like your competitors, by brainstorming what you would do in their place, with their market position and resources. The tradeshows are notorious highways of gossip and speculations that are often very close to the truth.

Of course, one of the most important sources of insight will be your shared suppliers. Chances are, if you are in the same industry, you share suppliers.

The point is, this is "war" and you have to think like a general, without breaking any laws and living your company's values in every sense of the word. Reputation as a fierce competitor is not necessarily synonymous with being an unprincipled competitor. It is winning while taking the high road that makes for the sweetest victory.

Sage advice from Sun Tzu

This timeless advice is from the 5th Century writings, *The Art of War*:

"He will win who knows when to fight and when not to fight."

In other words, hold on to your resources until you know you can win. There's no point in wasting money on a campaign when your competitors are out-spending you two-to-one. You either wait for the right timing, or you have to spend intelligently to win. Big competitors with endless money and resources for marketing can overshadow you, but their apathy can be their nemesis and a smart, well-timed, economical and brilliant marketing effort can seize the day.

"All warfare is based on deception."

I know this sounds awkward in the context of business. But the fact is, you should never reveal your plans and secrets. But, the more profound truth in this saying, from the point-of-view of business, is that you must have a "unique idea"—so unique and powerful no one could anticipate it. The unique idea is gold in business and in marketing. And, as this chapter I hope made clear, your team should be motivated to creativity and innovation by the challenge of your competitor. To best them, means to be better. Everyone loves the David and Goliath story, where the underdog wins against the odds.

"In the midst of chaos, there is opportunity"

So now you know where "Transform" comes from. Transforming the opportunity is ancient advice, predating L.I.F.T. Sun Tzu taught that to change the course of a battle, one should be ready for the worst case. The company who has a contingency plan for a particular disaster can win the battle. For example, in economic downturns there are opportunities in certain niches. During the Covid-19 disaster, many companies rose to the challenge—for example, quickly changing production lines to produce face-masks. Companies with contingency plans covering various crisis situations are well-positioned to seize the opportunity and "win the war." Remember, change is inevitable in business—so plan for as many change scenarios as possible and have a readiness plan to seize the moment.

"Know yourself, know the enemy"

The fuller quote is: "It is said that if you know your enemies and know yourself, you will not be imperiled in a hundred battles; if you do not know your enemies but do know yourself, you will win one and lose one; if you do not know your enemies nor yourself, you will be imperiled in every single battle."

Facts are better than educated guesses. Educated guesses are better than intuition. It should be your mission to continually collect information on your competitors (or your opposite numbers—in my earlier case study, the Union.)

Enhanced service—everyone's secret weapon

If you're stuck for ideas, there's one area you can always tap into in almost any industry. The company with the best customer service is almost always going to win in business wars. It may sound trite, but it's absolutely a fact, that—all other factors being equal—the company with the best customer service will be the number one player.

L.I.F.T. exercise—What do you know?

Rate all from 1-10, where 10 is the highest, and 1 the lowest.

1. Our industry has many competitors (choose 1 for many competitors, 10 for none): _____

List all your competitors in order

_____

_____

_____

_____

_____

2. Our knowledge of our direct competitor (10 is high): _____

What are your main insights? _____

_____

3. Our knowledge of our secondary competitor (10 is high): _____

What are your main insights? _____

_____

4. Our knowledge of our main target audience (10 is high): _____

What are your main insights? _____
_____

5. Our knowledge of our secondary audience (10 is high)

What are your main insights? _____
_____

6. Our knowledge of the management team members for our direct main competitor (10 is high) _____

List : _____
_____

7. Our knowledge of the management team members for our second main competitor (10 is high) _____

List : _____
_____

8. We have a pipeline of services or products unique in our industry soon to launch (10 is high)

List : _____
_____

9. We know exactly what pipeline of services or products our competitors have ready to launch (10 is high)

List: _____
_____

9. We know exactly what pipeline of services or products our competitors have ready to launch (10 is high)

List: _____
_____

You get where we're going with this. As you start to list what you know, you'll soon see the information you're missing. If you score under 75 on this, you have a lot of work to do—but don't give up hope, since, you have every incentive to work harder, to innovate more, and to beat your competitors. It is worth the investment to hire a research firm, coupled with your market facing team members and dive deep into reconnaissance work. In the end, you will know more about your competitors, their approach, their strengths and weaknesses, and the potential angles you can develop that will separate you from the pack. We don't run our business in isolation, serving our customers, with racehorse blinders on, ignoring the field. We must never lose sight of the customers we serve and why they choose us, but bolstering your competitive moat, and creating impenetrable walls is good business.

Reflections from the Conqueror

When two armies engage in long warfare, the battle is often won or lost based on the focus. Mehmed II was very focused on reversing the humiliation of history. As the aggressor, the motivation was strong. Was it strong enough to endure a long battle?

Mehmed was also able to keep the excitement of his troops high with superior lines of information.

There were many scenarios in the battle for Constantinople where "know your enemy" came into play as a decisive, or strategy-changing scenario. One weakness in Constantinople's defence was the defender's war-leader Giovanni Giustiniani. (*See the full story of Mehmed in Appendix for more on this story.*)

In short, the Italian mercenary had a pirate-like ambiance and a fierce resolve to protect the city—but it was inspired by greed, rather than loyalty or love. He was offered the island of Lemnos in the Mediterranean Sea as payment to protect and defend Constantinople.

When Mehmed II learned that Giustiniani was motivated by payment, and not the love of the country or Empire, he sought a private meeting. In the history records it stood that he was tempted to switch sides in exchange for a vast fortune. A pivotal moment for a "mercenary."

Since Giustiniani was a proud man, he declined, concerned about reputation and legacy. He chose the more noble goal of protecting the

Roman Empire. The knowledge of this meeting and the mystery of what was said spread concern amongst the Romans, seeds of doubt were planted that maybe their leader was not committed to their cause. Did Mehmed promise to Giustiniani mean something to him? Is there a potential coup underway or has Giustiniani become a traitor or given a higher price? A paid mercenary at the helm with no loyalty to the flag creates questions of faithfulness.

Additionally, the valiant attempt by Mehmed II to sway Giustiniani did leave an impression on him. He realized the young King's tenacious spirit and resolve left little hope for early surrender or withdrawal. Mehmed II may not have convinced his adversary to join his side, both parties learned about the other—and the psychological war continued. Mehmed had succeeded in seeding doubt within the Military Leader and doubt within the people under that leader, important in any war.

9

L.I.F.T. MARKETING: FIRST "HAND" OF THE LEADER

In Mehmed's medieval era the term "Hand of the King" is one that is indispensable to the empire's leader. In L.I.F.T. there must always be two "hands" of the leader: Marketing and Sales. You need the "Tag-Team" of Sales and Marketing. It takes two hands to clap. In this chapter, we focus on the first hand, Marketing.

L.I.F.T. Facts

- The top brands—just by name alone—are worth Billions in 2020: Amazon $220B, Google $160B, Apple $140B, Microsoft $117B, ICBC $80B, Facebook $79B, Walmart $77B. L.I.F.T. Leaders value their brand equity above all else.[37] Most of the top brands have single one-line slogans or loglines, expressing their unique position.

- Global B2C ecommerce "is expected to reach $4.5 trillion by 2020." Consumer confidence is higher in companies with a credible ecommerce footprint.[38]

- 70% of marketers focus heavily on "content marketing"—ensuring content on their websites is rich and fact-based.[39]

- Ignore social media at your peril: social media users are expected to reach 3.43 billion by 2023. [40]

In this chapter

- One hand clapping? Sales without marketing, or marketing without sales, is like one hand clapping—no one can hear you. Why the L.I.F.T. Leader needs both hands.

- L.I.F.T Loglines: the one-line solution: brilliance is a matter of focus—if you can't say it in ten words or less, don't bother—the core story.

- L.I.F.T. Separators: don't ask in what ways you compare to your competitors—leaders "separate" and differentiate, they don't emulate.

- L.I.F.T.: The effectiveness of "education-based marketing."

- L.I.F.T. Influencers: Influence the Influencers. Using your unique voice and "logline", reach out to the influencers in your industry—through social media, the trade, mainstream media, and content online.

Important Take-away

- A marketplace always has room for a company that serves it well, creates value and answers the need and pre-empts the needs it has. But—there is only room for one leader. To be that leader, we need to find a way to serve that separates us from our competent competitors.

Reflections from The Conqueror

- "You shall, I question not, find a way to the top if you diligently seek for it; for nature hath placed nothing so high that is out of the reach of industry and valor."—*Alexander the Great*

The Marketing of L.I.F.T.

Marketing is at the core of L.I.F.T.

Lead: Leaders think in "loglines"—or well-defined niches that can be described in one sentence. The smaller the better. The Leader asks, "What can I own?" The follower asks, "what can I do well?" Ownership cuts out competition, simplifies your message, and helps you build a unique team-culture.

Inspire: Think Hollywood! Yes, movies. Producers have perfected the art of the one-line pitch—known as a "logline"—and so should you. The clarity of the pitch will inspire not only your customers, but all of your stakeholders: investors, internal teams, suppliers and influencers.

Focus: Defining your central theme—your owned «logline—and building all of your strategies around your unique position will bring clarity of your value to all audiences.

Transform: To transform a company requires confidence in where you fit in the market, and the humble pride or confidence your company telegraphs to all stakeholders begins a transformation that is enduring.

Real-life L.I.F.T Values Case Study

You could argue it's not so hard in many technology-driven industries to find your niche, however in a market with countless competitors you are often vying not only for top-of-mind and market share, but also for innovation leadership—what I call the patent race.

One of the many technology companies I had the privilege to lead had a serious patent track record, and a massive portfolio, yet still found it had to fight for market share a very fast-changing industry. This company faced a transformation challenge: being good alone was no longer good enough. History, track record and patents only take a company so far.

When I took over leadership, I knew we needed a "brand"—not just a name. I understood that we needed to be remembered as a leader, not just recalled as a "oh, they're good too" company.

This company was typical of a company with "one hand clapping"—a strong sales force and a wide network, but no brand or marketing presence. That was about to change. We had invested substantially in the development of the company, and now was the time to invest further—to manifest that "second hand"—marketing—so that we could be heard around the world.

Going from Easy-Cheesy to "Tech leadership"

The company's brand, at the time of I took over, sported a generic clip-art logo from the 70's. This is fairly typical for a sales-driven company, where the sale-team governs. Fair enough, since an aggressive sales team had helped them grow into a global force. Going forward, it would not be enough, not in the face of rapidly changing technology and intense competitors with deep pockets.

The most innovative aspect of the brand, at the time, was the historical name, based on decades of equity.

But—not to sound harsh—we had a great brand name, but an "easy cheesy" clip art logo. And no central focusing theme or "logline" as I call it.

There really was no point in hiring a designer to create just an "award-winning" logo—not yet. Our scope was the wider strategic brand. We needed everything to speak together—two hands clapping. We needed a position to own in the marketplace before we designed a logo to fit. We needed the entire brand—as expressed in every part of the company— from sales to engineering to distribution to communications—to speak in one unified, differentiated voice. And, that voice had to have the authority of a leader.

A Niche in a Crowded Competitive Field

It is always a challenge to carve out a niche you can "own" in a crowded field. The bigger problem was our technology, patents, engineering capability and history separated us from 95%+ of the competitive field but we didn't distinguish ourselves in the marketing aspect in the same manner as we did in the marketplace. We needed a helicopter to rise above the noisy competitive landscape full of amateurs.

Believe me, it's not easy to distill such a big proposition to one statement. What I learned, though, is to tough it out until you discover your differentiator. For us, through a grueling process of elimination and discovery, we drilled down until we found that we actually did have a unique and exceptional position. Every company has one, it takes determination and resilience with your team to figure it out.

It doesn't matter if at the end you think it's splitting hairs. Your differentiator, what makes you stand out is key to leverage.

Don't underestimate the importance of distilling your differences down to one elevator pitch line—what I call a logline. It doesn't have to be a million-dollar slogan, but it does have to strongly separate you from your competitors, not only for your client audiences, but for your internal teams and stakeholders.

Pitch vs slogan?

The best loglines are pitches that can be delivered in a one sentence burst: on the telephone, in a board room, on a website, tv commercial, tweet—the "elevator pitch." Whether you are pitching a movie (loglines) or a venture capitalist in an elevator (elevator pitch) it comes down to one sentence or less. That's all the time you have to "pitch" it. (In the case of tweets, you have 160 characters!)

I want to say it was "easy" to take a company down to one pitch line. Clearly, it's not. The end result certainly appears simple. The key purpose of your logline was to nail that articulated differentiation to make sure all audiences are unified in direction.

In our case, once we had our vision and mission, things started to click into place. We needed a snappy new logo. Brilliant. Now that we knew what we were all about, we could tell our story much more simply—great new website. Our vision, and our move to concise clarity and flat management structure.

The key, though, is that none of it is guess work or trial-and-error. Once you have the vision, the rest of the mission and venture falls into place.

Two-hands clapping

Here's where it becomes more difficult, especially in mature companies with two separate silos for marketing and sales. There's a reason many companies flatten the VP position to Sales and Marketing. The key though, is balance. If you recruit a sales top gun to that position, you may find sales priorities overwhelm marketing—and vice versa.

For many decades, sales led our company. But, to grow beyond the wide network, and the sales channels, we needed to bring in that second hand—so people could hear us.

This company is not a consumer products company. Our audiences are necessarily narrow—a few hundred very large companies.

Credibility versus Comradery

It's a bit cliche to say this, but sales are often about the relationships. Marketing initiatives are also about relationships, but often with a focus on creating new relationships. That requires credibility. The website must reflect the audiences. The logo must be the right persona for our position. In our case, since we sell to large companies, and our transactions are large, credibility is arguably the most important aspect in the relationship.

In the past, marketing budgets focused heavily on tradeshows, hospitality suites, wining and dining clients—comradery. Yet, when you go big, when you focus globally, credibility becomes equally important. Like I said, two hands clapping.

I knew what mattered the most was first impressions: logo, slogan, website, a re-branded tradeshow booth design, rigid corporate standards for everything from approved type to whitespace on a page to colours.

Distillation—the critical skill of L.I.F.T. Leaders

In almost every chapter in this book you've heard about distillation:

- Chapter 2—90-Day one-page distilled L.I.F.T. Personal Dashboard plans.

- Chapter 3—"What can you do without?" exercise (lean-management distillation).

- Chapter 4—Five keys to Great Decisions (distillation for decision-making).

- Chapter 5—The Rule of Fives (distilling to the essence in feedback loops.)

- Chapter 6—Stress test your company—a one-page distilled metric.

- Chapter 7—Agile Teams (distilled teams.)

- Chapter 8—What's the one thing you know about your enemy?

- Chapter 10—Why sales have to distill their core one-line pitch.

- To come, in chapter 11—The L.I.F.T. Dashboard, one-page strategic plan.

In other words, L.I.F.T. Leaders know how to distill to the essence. It's an acquired, learned skill, not an innate talent.

Distillation is the key not only the sales and marketing success, but also to Business Leadership success. Here's the bottom line, I often reinforce with my teams:

"If you can't tell me in one sentence, you're not trying hard enough."
I'll demonstrate this "logline" principle with examples.

L.I.F.T. Loglines—Distillation of Position

I like the term "loglines" borrowed from the movie industry. In that vertical, the logline is critical. Whether you're a script writer pitching an idea for a movie, or an executive producer pitching investors or distributors for that same movie, or a marketer trying to create a trailer and advertising for the movie when it's ready to release—all of them, without exception, rely on the logline.

In business (outside of Hollywood) it's no different, except we tend to borrow the term "elevator pitch" from venture capitalists. Tomato, tom-ah-toe. The point is, you need to pitch in in ten to twenty seconds. Later, it will prove invaluable in sales calls. (Chapter 10.)

The logline is, in one line, how we're different. To keep it concise, if there are predefined paradigms or icons, you can just compare to that icon with a "difference." Literally, you are not invited to pitch or sell or market a movie or television show without a logline.

Here are some famous movie loglines, that sold massive franchises[41]:

The Shawshank Redemption

Two imprisoned men bond over a number of years, finding solace and eventual redemption through acts of common decency.

The Matrix

A computer hacker learns from mysterious rebels about the true nature of his reality and his role in the war against its controllers.

Godfather

The aging patriarch of an organized crime dynasty transfers control of his clandestine empire to his reluctant son.

How do you know if a logline is good? Simple. After the fact—after a movie's gone big—you can read a logline to someone, without telling them the name of the movie, and ask them to identify it? If they can, wow, great logline.

Just for fun, can you name these movies from their loglines (these are real ones, used by the script writer to successfully pitch the movie):

- The lives of two mob hit men, a boxer, a gangster's wife, and a pair of bandits intertwine in four tales of violence and redemption.

- A science-fiction fantasy about a naive but ambitious farm boy from a backwater desert who discovers powers he never knew he had when he teams up with a feisty princess, a mercenary space pilot and an old wizard warrior to lead a ragtag rebellion against the sinister forces of the evil Galactic Empire. (Okay, this is long, but it's one sentence!)

- Lion cub and future king Simba searches for his identity.

- A wheelchair bound photographer spies on his neighbours from his apartment window and becomes convinced one of them has committed murder.

If you're an avid movie fan, you guessed, in order: *Pulp Fiction, Star Wars, The Lion King,* and *Rear Window.* You might have missed one or the other because it's not your "genre" but you probably knew most of them.

It's no different in sales or marketing of anything else. If your "logline" is the right "genre"—i.e. the audience has an interest—you'll get the sale or at least top of mind as a choice.

I use loglines in "everything." I'm being literal here. If I'm getting ready for a board meeting, I have my introductory logline, so they know what's coming. If I'm pitching a business plan, that plan has a logline. My sales team have their own loglines for their particular customers.

I demonstrated our logline in the above company case study, and how that's different from a slogan. I'll discuss the "slogan" or "tagline in a moment, but first, let's explore the "what if" question.

The "What if" Question

The "What if" question "counterfactual" thinking, but we all do it. In Hollywood, novels, and our own personal reflections. We all ask that question "What if I didn't go to that customer's office that day?", "What if my Mother wouldn't have told me to apologize?", or "What if our engineers didn't finish that project on time?" In this chapter's context, the question is asked when searching for the marketing or sales position; later, it becomes the logline once it's refined and developed.

The "What if" question is another form of distillation. How can you use it? Here are some top-level simple ways:

- Sales meeting: "**What if** we offered longer terms to our customers?"

- Marketing meeting: "**What if** we target engineers instead of designers?"

- Business planning meeting "**What if** we consolidate the customer relations division to another location?"

I like to "what if" everything I can. But, more importantly, the "what if" is a challenge. You think of scenarios. Once you land on a scenario—in sales, marketing, business planning or anything else—you ask the "what if." If it's promising, you test. If it tests well, you distill it down to a logline and build a plan around that.

L.I.F.T. Leaders become the masters of distillation and the "what if."

How to: L.I.F.T. Loglines in One Sentence

Writing a L.I.F.T. logline is a big proposition—even though the end result is only one sentence. You have to do this for your business, proposition, product, service. The four things a Logline must contain:

1. Tell them who you are.

2. What you do.

3. What's unique about your proposition.

4. Write it to grab their attention.

Easy right? The truth is, your business (or campaign, or product) L.I.F.T. Logline may be the most difficult challenge you meet as a leader, department head, pitch person or salesperson.

Classic One-Liners

Here's a classic example, from Mastercard:

"There are some things money can't buy"

This line is memorable. Okay, here are some other top-notch Loglines in business:

- "Gawker—Daily Manhattan media news and gossip; reporting live from the center of the universe."

- " Merchant Machine helps small businesses quickly and easily save money on their credit card processing costs by comparing the leading options in the market."

- "Cigarette Pollution Solutions makes energy from cigarette butts."[42]

Notice how each of these states "who" in their line, what's unique, and "grabs attention." It's all about trying to make it part of your loglines (implied or stated.) In the case of Gawker, above, for example, it's implied.

How do Slogans and Loglines Differ?

As I mentioned, your L.I.F.T. Logline is the equivalent of an elevator pitch or a logline. Slogans and taglines have different missions, no less important. They serve the same purpose as name and logo. In fact, in L.I.F.T. we say it is the third point of the brand triangle:

- Name: is "what we remember" when identifying a brand.

- Logo: is "how we remember it."

- Slogan or tagline is "what we associate with that brand when we remember it."

There's a reason you don't have to search hard in your memory for great slogans in the corporate world. They become part of modern culture. The most famous slogans of all time are:

- Just Do It.

- Think different.

- Where's the beef.

- Open happiness.

- Because you're worth it.

- Melts in your mouth, not in your hands.

- A diamond is forever.

- The breakfast of champions.

I didn't have to tell you the company names, did I? Their cultural and recall power is so vast you probably knew which brand they were associated with. In case you've been living as a hermit in a cave, the above slogans (in order) were for: Nike, Apple, Wendy's, Coca-Cola, L'Oreal, M&Ms, DeBeers, Wheaties cereal.

Make sure you tick off all the boxes for a great slogan/tagline:

1. Must be short: ideally two to four words, no more than eight

2. Contains the "gist" of differentiation.

3. Is impactful.

4. It conveys an "emotion" about the brand.

If you look at the top slogans (historical list above) the emotion is always there as well. "A diamond is forever" from DeBeers is obvious.

"Open happiness" from Coke is clear. "Because you're worth it" carries strong emotional context, with the "you" in the slogan.

In other words, Slogans are not exactly the same as L.I.F.T. Loglines. Loglines or elevator pitches need to be more complete—stating the corporate name and precise differentiator. With a slogan you do not repeat the name, because it invariably appears with name and logo. With L.I.F.T. Logline, the name must be there.

Slogan vs Tagline?

Marketing experts tend to differentiate between slogans and taglines, but they are two parts of a whole. Usually, in an ad, on a website, in videos and other content you'll see both. A tagline, typically, is a punch "finisher"—a short sound bite for recall. However, some companies, such as Nike, for all intents-and-purposes combine both into "Just do it."

If you want the technical difference, Slogans are meant to contain more of the L.I.F.T. Logline—at least enough to differentiate, but not so much it's hard to remember. Taglines, on the other hand, tend to be all about impact and recall.

A few classic **slogans**:

- California Milk Processor Board: "Got Milk? "

- BMW: "Designed for Driving Pleasure."

- Bounty: "The quicker picker upper."

- U.S. Marines (yes, they have a slogan!): "The Few. The Proud. The Marines."

- Dunkin' Donuts: "America runs on Dunkin'"

You get the idea. It's nuanced.

Why is "America runs on Dunkin'" a slogan while McDonald's "I'm lovin' it" a tagline? The Dunkin' donuts short punchline states their name and their difference. The tagline from McDonald's doesn't attempt that.

Basically, taglines are designed for narrower campaigns and might be tied to shorter timelines. Taglines are more campaign specific than slogans—which, like logos, tend to endure.

In other words, for L.I.F.T. Leadership purposes, it's sufficient to just think in terms of Distilled slogan and L.I.F.T. Loglines.

Although this chapter could have rolled into rules for this and rules for that, and how-to market online, and the importance of social media, and a dozen other topics, the L.I.F.T. Leader knows, first-and-foremost, that concise distillation is the secret in leadership.

Now Prove it: Rule of Fives

You remember the *L.I.F.T. Rule of Fives*—not just one, we have many of them. We try to coach you to think in short lists, as part of distilling the message. Five is a good number. For example, if you're trying to prove something to a prospect on the phone as a salesperson, the shorter you make your "proof" the better. In advertising, you have even less time and space. Marketing is expensive, and attention spans are short. Today, tiny elevator side-bar ads replace the full-page ads of twenty-years ago. Concise is in.

So, here's a mini exercise in distillation for you:

List your top five "provable points" for your product or service. In other words what five points do you bring up when you "sell your product or service":

1.

2.

3.

4.

5.

Great, that was easy, right? Now, here's the hard part. **Prove them.** Take the same five points and give us the proof. Score ten for each if you can prove it in five words or less but deduct two points for each word over five words.

Does that seem arbitrary? It's not. I've found, for the same reason that elevator pitches work, concise proof is required. People don't have time to listen to long explanations. So, now list your "five proofs (use the same numbers as above for easy reference):

1.

2.

3.

4.

5.

Score: (50 is perfect, anything below 40 is weak, below 30 is hopeless.):

_____

L.I.F.T. Exercise: Let's do Loglines

You guessed it, time to buckle up and distill your own Logline for your business or business unit/product. You can start with the above "five" truth lists and expand on it if you like. As you'll see in step 2, you'll start eliminating them quickly.

Name of brand:

Current Logline or slogans (if any):

List every feature and benefit for your product/service or company. Try to list 20.

1.

2.

3.

4.

5.

6.

7.

8.

9.

10.

11.

12.

13.

14.

15.

16.

17.

18.

19.

20.

Now, go back through your list and draw a line through all of the ones you've listed above that are matched by a competitor. *Note: This negating process doesn't mean this feature has no value; only, that it has no value for your logline.*

Chances are you're left with less than three:

1.

2.

3.

Those above three items are the base from which you'll build a logline. Were you left with nothing at all? In that case, either think again—chances are you missed a feature/benefit—or think about "spinning the feature."

How to spin

I know, spinning's a bad word. In the era of "fake news" and so on, we don't want to invent anything. Spinning is about using a core truth and emphasizing a differentiating point—at least that's what it should be. If there's no fact, there's nothing to spin (unless you're engaging in Fake Facts, which I vehemently discourage you from considering.)

If your list above was empty, go back to your list of twenty, that you drew lines through, and see if you can combine two of them to create a uniqueness.

_____ plus _____ is unique

_____ plus _____ is unique

_____ plus _____ is unique

It is crucial that you distill down to a unique element of what you do, and that takes thoughtfulness and time to refine the list to the one or two things that make you stand out from the rest. Keep refining the list until you've got your keywords. You know where you're going. You've distilled.

Now, take all those uniquely blended keywords and turn it into one-high impact sensible sentence:

_____

_____

Realistically, you'll probably spend days on this part. Language and impact are not an equation. It's more an art. Chances are good, though, that your company has people who are great wordsmiths. Or, you have a marketing department or an agency to work with. The key thing is to give them the right keywords to start with.

Congratulations, you're on the way to a strong L.I.F.T. Logline that will help you compete and beat your competition.

L.I.F.T Out

Here's a hard truth for L.I.F.T. Leaders of growing enterprises. It is less expensive—generally—to earn sales than to acquire them. What do I mean? If you are in the fortunate position to have the cash needed to acquire a company, with the goal of strengthening your top line, consider first investing in sales and marketing in your current portfolio. I don't advise enterprise leaders to solve their problems with acquisition. If your goal is to fill in capabilities, bring in complimentary teams, or vertical niches that you don't currently own which are complimentary to your own—then go for it. But, for a given investment dollar, you will earn almost double the return by investing in selling and marketing your existing portfolio, before you bravely move into acquisition.

Five Marketing Rules

Tired of my five rules for this and that? That's too bad. I'm giving you five more cardinal rules, this time related to Marketing.

1. Central Mission

Regardless of your niches and verticals, remember there is momentum in the central mission. This has less to do with outward-facing positions—which we discussed above—than it has to do with vision. If you have a central mission, you will know what other niches you need to build-out. If you randomly build out, your scattered approach will lead your mission—a sure path to ultimate oblivion.

Even companies like Nestlé—who make and sell everything from ice cream to dog food, very broad portfolios—have central, driving mission. They may have a hundred verticals, but they are anchored in "leader in food and beverage." They have plays in health sciences, coffee (Nespresso), pet care (Purina), cereal (General Mills)—but they don't stray from "food and beverage." This is from their global website: " Good food, good life – that is what we stand for."

2. Real Research and Real Market Data

Especially in marketing and sales, where each move is costly, every-thing should be developed and planned on a solid base of reliable research and market data. Ignore your own history at your peril, but at the same time recognize markets change, economies collapse or expand, competi-tors change, and you can't control every outcome. But—you can anticipate scenarios based on real data, not just as a mitigation factor, but to make sure your marketing and sales investments are in the right areas.

3. Marketing and Sales: 90 percent Education Rule

Unless you're marketing a whimsical unrealistic proposition—if you've reached this chapter in L.I.F.T. that's dubious—you should base most of your marketing and sales on "education." Firstly, educate your own teams, immersing them in the research, data and competitive scenario. Then, educate the prospective clients. Customers prefer to buy from people who know what they're doing. For this reason, don't engage in exaggeration, fake facts or hyperbole. If you educate honestly and fairly, you will earn your share of the market. Part of education is risk assessments, both your own, and the other stakeholders. No solution is one hundred percent. But show them how you mitigate most of the risks—by acknowledging first that you know the risks.

At the same time, do you really know, with certainty, that all of your teams, in all of your offices, in all of your companies, are on the same page? Educating the internal teams comes first. We talked about how to do this in earlier chapters.

4. Your Brand is Your Flag

Once you've established the brand always be sure your teams—sales, marketing and you—treat the brand as "too important or valuable to be interfered with." In other words, sacrosanct. Brand is like the flag of a nation. Protect it with everything you have. Brand is an equity position. The outward facing "trinity" of brand is: name, logo, slogan/tagline which are the "flags" standing in for your unique position in the market, your L.I.F.T. Logline. You don't have unlimited budgets, so you reinforce and protect the equity in your brand with everything you have. This is why we trademark and copyright.

This means you must make sure everything in your company is regulated. All companies should have a brand standard. At all the companies I lead, we have consistent typefaces and colours. As long as everything is clear, the brand is "flag"—to be protected as you would the Nation's flag. Even the CEO of the company should not be permitted to "play" with the brand.

For these reasons, it's a good idea to assign a "brand sheriff."

Especially important, in our real-time communications age, is social media, live-streamed events and other dynamic media. Brand is no less important on Twitter than it is in your trade show booth. Brand is brand. No exceptions.

5. Incent your "Hunters

Not to sound too primitive, but I firmly believe that marketing and sales, both, should be made up of hunters, not farmers. We talked about A-Teams in chapter two. This is another way of putting it. Supporting teams, such as customer service and technical support teams may be more about cultivation and farming—but in sales and marketing we're on the hunt. You'll want to recruit hunters. Your agencies and partners should be aggressive and hunt oriented.

When you deal with A-Teams and hunters, you'll need strong incentives. A-Team hunters like rewards and recognition both. They're motivated also by challenge and the win.

To use a sports-oriented analogy, your business is not little league—where it's about learning, growing, and having fun. This is big-business sports: competitive, aggressive, dangerous, thrilling, and all about the win, not the challenge. In little league there's plenty of motivation to try hard and do your best. That's just not good enough for the A-Team hunter-killer sales/marketing group.

Bottom line—aggressively reward and incent your sales and marketing group. If they do well, you do well.

10

L.I.F.T. SALES: THE SECOND "HAND" OF THE LEADER

Sales is the co-equal of Marketing, the L.I.F.T. Leaders second hand. Just as you need A-Team members in other areas, in sales look for a special sort of A-Team: Apex Predator Sales Teams

L.I.F.T. Facts

- According to analysis of one million "sales calls" only 20 percent of a team generate 60 percent of the sales.[43]

- 46 percent of salespeople never wanted to be in sales.[44] If you have any of these on your team, please go back to chapter two—you need A-Teams!

- What do buyers want from sales professionals? 69 percent want a rep who "listens."[45] Stop talking!

- The cross-industry sales conversion rate is 2.46 percent.[46] Are you over 5 percent? You're a L.I.F.T. winner. Remember to "incent your hunters" (Chapter 9.)

- 92 percent of sales pros remove prospects from their list after the 4th call. Research indicates most prospects say yes only after four nos.

In this chapter

- Why you need Apex Predators on your sales team; say no to farmers.

- L.I.F.T Distillation—How distillation is equally important in selling.

- L.I.F.T. Sales Rule of Fives—is sales a numbers game? Yes, but not in the way you think.

- L.I.F.T.: Selling remains a strategic process. Apex Sales reps are both strategic and tactical.

- L.I.F.T. Predator Rule of Five—What it takes to be a hunter-killer in sales.

Important Take-away

- Knowing the numbers means you won't take it personally when you are told "no." Not everyone is in buying cycle. But Apex hunters always find the ones who are ready to buy.

The Sales and Marketing of L.I.F.T.

Sales is the co-equal partner of marketing.

Lead: L.I.F.T. Sales Leaders are hunter predators, not farmers or trappers. Like the Apex hunters in nature, they average a high kill rate through the combined skills of perception, intelligence and opportunistic patience.

Inspire: Inspire your sales team with strategic vision as well as tactics. Tactical sales leaders tend to demotivate teams with quarterly goals, resulting in a useless flurry of activity in the last month of the quarter. Be the inspiring strategic visionary.

Focus: Focus your teams on priorities—key among them is timeliness. Sales is often about timing—being there when the buying cycle finally arrives—and likewise responding to leads within minutes, not hours. Predators, above all focus. They never let their prey out of their sight.

Transform: Transform teams with the Sales Rule of Five and the Predator Rule of Five.

Apex Predators—A-List Sales are Hunters, Not Farmers

What makes an apex hunter in nature successful? It's not speed, muscle, teeth or claws. It's eyes, nose, ears. I hope you're not too squeamish; my L.I.F.T. metaphor for sales is the predator. I mentioned the metaphor "hunters, not farmers" in the context of your leadership team in chapter two. This principal applies equally to sales teams.

For sales teams, especially their leaders, you need Apex-level hunters on your team. They have the highest "kill rates." In the next section, *L.I.F.T. Sales Rule of Fives*, I mention the famous three percent statistic—that at any given time, three percent of your prospects are ready to buy (on average.) If you are competing with numerous companies for that three percent, you definitely need Apex predator sales representatives who have at least 25 percent "kill" rates.

What makes the Apex predator's "kill" rate so high? It's not because they're always running and roaring and clawing and biting. They're waiting in stillness—until they're sure they can strike and succeed. Have you ever noticed the haunting eyes of a lion or tiger—or even your house cat?

Cats eyes, whether lions, tigers, or house cats, glitter with unblinking intensity—focused with precision on their prey. Not a muscle moves—until the moment is right. Then, there is a flurry of claws and teeth, but only then.

Take these Apex examples in nature (if you're squeamish, jump to the "*L.I.F.T. Sales Rule of Five*")[47]:

1. African wild dogs—85 percent successful kills

2. Black-footed cat—60 percent successful kills

3. Cheetah—58 percent successful kills.

4. Leopard—38 percent successful kills.

5. House cat —32 percent successful kills (Didn't expect that, did you? That's right, the world's fifth most effective Apex predator is your house cat!)

Don't mistake my metaphor for an invitation to brutality or carnage. We'll cover five rules in sales based on how we're using the word "predator." (See the L.I.F.T. Predator Rule of Five, below.) But remember, we're describing the "noble and honourable hunter."

Predatory instincts are not an invitation for bad ethics or conduct. Apex hunters kill to survive, and they serve a purpose in nature. Equally, your Apex sales representatives' noble purpose is to serve your company.

L.I.F.T. Sales Rule of Five—and Sales is a Numbers Game?

You've heard various sales gurus tell you sales is a numbers game. Others say, "Numbers don't matter, quality matters."

Here's the bottom line: "sales is a qualified numbers game." Numbers will always be important simply because at any given time less than three percent of your audience is in the buying cycle—on average since buying cycles vary widely by industry. In other words, you need numbers, yes, but quality is important. Or, put another way, you need a good quantity of quality leads. How do you calculate your quality/quantity base? Using the Sales Rule of Five.

Knowing the numbers means you won't take it personally when you are told "no." Not everyone is in a buying cycle. Bear in mind, buying cycles vary not only by product/service category, but also by client psychographic. Early adopters are shorter buying cycles. Consumable commodities have short buying cycles.

You'll have many "nos" on your way to a resounding and rewarding "yes." How can you not? In your audience, according to national statistics, an average of three percent are ready to buy at a given time.[48] (Again, remember this is a national average, so it varies by category.) Interestingly, those numbers are similar (separate research) for ecommerce visitors landing on your site. The actual numbers are:

- 2.46% to 3.26% is the national sales conversion rate (Statista).

- 2.86% is the national ecommerce conversion from visitor's rate.[49]

A separate study indicated that "92% of sales pros give up after the 4th call, but 80% of prospects say no four times before they say yes."

Why they say no more than yes is obvious if you look at that three percent statistic. It's nothing personal. They are saying "no" because they're not in the buying cycle right now. Be respectful, polite, log it, and make sure you call them the fifth time. Or sixth. Make sure it isn't your competitor who happens to call when they enter the three-percent zone.

For all of these reasons, the L.I.F.T. Sales Rule of Five is simply "make the fifth call."

Remember, too, the two-hands clapping: sales and marketing together. Marketing exposures—your social campaigns, web content, advertising, tradeshows—are also part of the L.I.F.T. Sales Rule of Five. If you increase your exposures, you are more likely to find the three percent who are ready to buy.

This all sounds very tactical, but it also works towards your overall strategy. If you are the market leader, you are going to be in touch with qualified prospects regularly.

You can rely on this number: five. Putting it in the context of method:

"It takes a minimum of five sales exposures to a message to trigger a needs-based response."

For example, my car dealership, where I've bought my cars for years, still contact me at least five times a year. That's not so often as to be annoying, and just often enough to be there when I'm ready to trade in my vehicle. No hard sell. They check in with me. They give me a little news—after all, the market leaders are also the market educators. They let me know the annual "last year's model" sale is on. Otherwise, I don't feel they pressure me unduly. Who do I call when I'm ready? Of course, I call them.

This is where A-Team sales teams excel. I've never seen a top sales professional remove a valid prospect from a list. Yes, they removed unqualified contacts, but never a valid buyer prospect. Numbers are important, but it's still a process of quality numbers. Don't just add prospects to your list in hopes of hitting a qualified buyer.

[To see the *L.I.F.T. Tips for the Apex Sales Rep*, see the last section of this chapter.]

This is not an invitation to lazy selling and B-Team practices such as: "Spamming by phone, email, mail, any media users in hopes of reaching the magic five."

Selling Remains a Strategic Process

One thing that distinguishes a strategic Apex Sales Representative from a Tactical B-Sales Representative is timing. Apex Sales Representatives keep in touch—just staying in touch, being helpful, sending educational information, no pressure—all through the year. Tactical B-Sales Representatives pump up the calling in the last month of every quarter, when their sales manager is putting on the pressure to meet the quarterly targets.

In a Gong data[50] science project, 15 months of data was analyzing and found that most salespeople make more calls in the third month of a quarter than in the first two months put together. In the L.I.F.T. Leadership System we'd call this poor leadership rather than poor sales representation. It starts with the expectations, incentives and conduct of the team leader.

If this is your team, pouring on the high-pressure calls in the last month of a quarter, you're to blame. Now's the time to restructure your team with *L.I.F.T. Apex Hunter Strategic* concepts.

Selling remains a strategic process, even if you know it's a numbers game. Strategic sellers know this better than the B-Team—the tactical sellers. Opportunistic B-Team tactical sellers are easy to recognize they play the game taught by sales gurus at workshops around the country. You know the gambit:

"It's Susan at ABC Corporation. How are you today, Tony?"—making a point of saying the name—relying on the politeness of strangers to answer.

"That's great," you say, even if they said, "Terrible!" Relentless, you carry on: "I know how valuable your time is. Is now a good time to talk about X?"

"No!"

"Oh, how about I call you back. Is Wednesday at 2pm good, or is Thursday at 1pm better..."

You know, a script: if prospect says A, answer with two choices C or D. That sort of nonsense. Tactical. Rubbish.

Or, worse, real amateur hour: you launch into a memorized spiel/pitch only to discover two minutes later they hung up. They probably hung up in the first fifteen seconds, but you were too busy making a speech to listen, so you'll never know.

If either of these is your style, you'll need to quadruple your lead numbers just to scrape by. Of course, the script above is the worst possible example of a cold call. Unless you're brand new to the business, you may not need the cold call. Even if you are calling cold, there are strategies for pre-warming them. Why go in with a hammer and chisel to break up the "ice" when you can use 30 seconds in the microwave instead?

So, what is the answer? Strategic selling. Tactics have their place, in service of strategy. Strategic selling doesn't work to a script. Never. Ever. Unless you're spamming through a call centre, you should never need a script for a quality product or service. If you are spamming your prospects this way, you're probably reading the wrong book.

The first thing you'll want to do is "distill your message" to the essence, just as we did in marketing in chapter 9—only this time, tweak your core messages to your specific target audiences. The key is to deliver a message in one sentence that delivers the core, unique message and grabs their attention.

Distillation in Sales: it's Power

Slogans and L.I.F.T. Loglines are ultimately about distillation—and they're essential for your sales teams. Hopefully, sales and marketing and leadership worked together on the distilled Loglines and slogans—two hands clapping.

The ultimate demonstration of the distilled logline pitch in sales is often honed on the dreaded "cold call." This is arguably the hardest thing a person can do in business.

When you call cold to a prospect, even the best salespeople feel uncertainty, perhaps even fear or anxiety. I have demonstrated countless times to salespeople how the fear "goes away" when you have a one-sentence logline the uncertainty is removed. If that cold prospect finds something of interest in your one-line pitch, they'll listen. If not, they'll say "not interested" or worse.

What do I mean? Statistics indicate you have less than 5 seconds to grab them. So, you need impact at the front end. We're all trained to "hang up" on telemarketers. Don't be one. When I say, "cold call" I don't mean random calls to a random wide list in hopes of a "hit." Cold calls, if you do them—some business models have no other options—should be as targeted as any other part of your sales and marketing.

Assuming you have a good list of "qualified" prospects, how do you know if your logline is effective. Time how long before they "hang up" on you. That tells you all you need to know.

Distillation is also dynamic. In a sales call, you should "listen" more than you talk. In the survey I cited, the top 20 percent of sales reps talked on 48 percent of the call versus listening for 54 percent of the call. The bottom reps were the opposite—talking 72 percent of the time, only listening 28 percent. This was measured by AI on one million sales calls.[51] My own experience over many years tells me it's right on the money. Listen at least as much as you talk.

Dictating the agenda

Distillation is also about "dictating the agenda." Whether for marketing or sales—and remember, they are equal partners—you need to "dictate the agenda." By that, I mean, you have to try to control the agenda. In a sales call this means, you bring up pricing, or typical obstacles on your own terms. For example, in a survey of one million recorded sales calls, the top representative brought up pricing—rather than the prospect—and it was normally three-quarters of the way into the call.[52] Why? Because you know pricing is the last thing you discuss. Often, for a client, though, it's the first thing they think of. What does this indicate? That top sales reps can control the agenda in a call or a meeting.

It's no different in a board meeting, a conference call, or any meeting of any team working to an agenda—you, the leader, control the agenda if you want to succeed. Once you lose that control, the results can spin off in any direction.

One hand clapping? Why marketing and sales Loglines should be the same.

Sales and marketing are momentum forces in your company. Give them concise messaging, mission, slogans, Loglines, logo and so on to work with—so that they always have a consistent core message. Nothing is more confusing to a potential customer than one message from marketing, and a different message from their contact in sales. Sales and Marketing are your two hands—the hands that reach out to your customers, clients and accounts. They are co-equal, regardless of your sector or niche, and they must be on the same page.

Do you remember we spoke about top guns and A-Teams in Chapter two? Hopefully you've done that, and filled both sales and marketing with A-players—but not, as we discussed in that chapter—prima donnas and narcissists.

If you suddenly find yourself as mediator between sales and marketing, you know you have a problem. Neither should be dominant. Neither should control the other. Often, they are one department in a company—and for good reason. But assuming there are still marketing and sales pillars within that department, foster the partner relationship. Think marriage here, not just good buddies. Marriage is hard work, right? You commit to a lifetime together. You work through all the problems together. "Friends" is a less satisfying metaphor because it's not about "in good times and bad times" in the way marriage is supposed to be.

Brand Loyalty Versus Closing the Sale

We all know brand loyalty and awareness and "closing the sale" are not mutually exclusive, but you wouldn't guess that from the goals and manoeuvres of the classical Tactical sales reps. I'm not saying Tactical Sales Representatives are B-Level and Strategic Sales Reps are A-Level. They're actually both B-Level. What does it take to be an A-Level Sales Representative or—in your case Sales Team Leader? Both.

Plenty of sales representatives make a "good living" as B-Level sellers. The key is, you, as leader, should never be satisfied with a team at that level. That doesn't mean replace them—it means train them, work together with them, using all the same leadership methods we've discussed throughout this book.

What do we mean by "Tactical" and "Strategic" Sales Professionals? This is my one-liner description:

- Tactical Professionals look for opportunities to close the deal, then attempt a close.

- Strategic Professionals educate prospects and build brand loyalty, hoping they will engage and self-close—when they are ready.

Typically, in short buying cycles, such as consumable commodities, sale representatives lean towards tactical—always hunting for a close, because they know they are competing, and the prospect is in the buying cycle. In longer buying cycles (typically, harder assets, houses, cars, commercial products, equipment, anything with long leases) selling tends to be more strategic and brand oriented.

I'd argue that you need to have a tactical and strategic representative in both scenarios.

Short buying cycles may mean they are always ready to buy, but brand loyalty and education may be the only edge you have in hyper-competitive markets like consumables. (Classical examples: Nestle, Kraft, Avery labels, etc.) On the other hand, the long buying cycle has plenty of time to research their solution, the price point is higher, and if you miss the opportunity you have to wait months or years for another; this means being purely strategic is a bad play. If you don't act tactical and close you won't have the deal, no matter how loyal they are to your brand.

Bottom line, both scenarios require both approaches: Strategic Educational and Tactical Close.

L.I.F.T. Predator Rule of Five

Especially today, when "fake merchants" are common on online selling sites, consumers and BTB prospects tend to be suspicious by default. Have you ever walked into a furniture store, only to be circled by salespeople-like hungry sharks? Do you run from the store? If a sales representative for any product or service looks too hungry, the fish will hide. The zebras aren't necessarily afraid of the leopard if he recently fed.

It may sound ruthless to call this rule the *L.I.F.T. Predator Rule of Five*, in sales, as I explained in chapter two, A-List team members—not just in sales—are usually hunters rather than farmers. There are times, as I explained previously, when farming is appropriate, but most companies benefit from a strong predator sales team.

Let me be clear though—predators may be ruthless, but the successful ones don't look that way. The fox may sit for hours, watching the rabbit, before the right moment comes to pounce—then, there is no hesitation. The shark may circle, but its intention is cloaked in silence. The lion may not be a threat when he has recently fed (my metaphor for the long-sales cycle salesperson.) Another metaphor that works in this context is fishing— using a lure to catch your "prey."

The hunting methods we're talking about aren't brute force. They are the clever, primal Apex predator—top of the food chain because they're smart.

In this set of "five rules" we're focused on the combination of predatory instincts under the camouflage of credible friendliness. Can't you be genuinely friendly? Of course. You can even play golf and exchange seasonal gifts. But—when it's time to close, predators are ready for the pounce.

Here are the guidelines (call them your metaphorical weapons) for almost any market you sell to—from consumer products to business to consumables to services—and, of course, there are five of them:

1. Positive brand image offsets most price differences.

This is about being the Apex predator. Top of the food chain. In marketing terms, that means positive brand image. Without it you have to "hunt" with clumsy weapons such as "discounts." Don't assume your ten percent discount will overcome the positive reputation of a competitor. Be diligent in building your own reputation. That means a number of things: handle every complaint from customers, respond to all communication requests, even on social media, pro-actively prevent or mitigate damage to your brand.

2. Educate prospects

In Chet Holmes' great book, The Ultimate Sales Machine—which I highly recommend—he gives the example of two furniture stores, competing in the same town, who opened on the same day. "If you go in to look at couches in store 1, the salesperson tries to sell you a couch. Tactical. Over a four-year period this store grows at about 10 percent per year, mostly driven by increasing costs of furniture... In store 2, of course, they try to sell you a couch, but management constantly trains the salespeople to sell the store. "First time in our store? Well let me tell you about it." And while the salespeople are on their way to couches, they pitch the heck out of that store."[53] He goes on to point out store 2 opened up six more locations in the next four years due to their success.

3. "Cult of the Expert."

Cults, sounds creepy doesn't it? What I mean here is just teach the prospect how to buy. Isn't this the same as Educating? It deserves its own discussion. Here, I'm referring to the "cult of the expert." This doesn't mean you should belittle your prospect, showing them how much more you know than them. What it does mean is you listen twice as much as you speak. You ask questions. You invite their questions. You answer their questions. If you do not know the answer, you don't make it up—you find out. Because, you guessed it, you are an expert.

If you're not an expert in your product or service, get out now. You as leader should be an expert. The people you recruit should be experts. Not in selling—although that is highly desirable—but in whatever you are selling. Prospects buy from experts who know more than they do.

You know the type of person I mean. Your favourite car dealer, who you return to for each car. The salesperson at your local technology store who knows everything about everything technology—they're walking Wikipedias—who you go back to just whenever you have a burning question. They always have time to chat. They'll always answer your questions, even when you're not in a buying cycle.

Remember, the Sales Rule of Fives, earlier in this chapter. Only three percent (on average) are ready to buy at any given time. If your prospect is one of the 97 percent, take the time to impress them with your expertise. Later, when they are ready to buy, they will remember.

What is a White-paper, but an opportunity to educate—with the goal of capturing a lead, and keeping in touch until they are ready to buy? What is an informative blog—but an opportunity to inform? Why do you bother writing a newsletter? The companies, and sales teams, willing to invest in educating the prospect will close the majority of the three percent of buyers ready to buy in any given cycle.

4. Camouflage and Stillness

One of the finer skills of Apex hunters is their use of either camouflage or stillness. Orchid mantis's look like orchid flowers—until you get too close. As an example of stillness—the spider and her web. Or seagulls, who "trample on the ground" to mimic the sound of rain to lure worms to the surface. Or, weirdest lure of all, the anglerfish, who mutated to generate light-emitting bacteria that draws in curious prey to its gaping mouth.

No, I'm certainly not recommending you cheat, or that you make your brand invisible. This is about making the "salesperson" role invisible by emphasizing another role of the salesperson: educator, or problem-solver, or expert, or resource.

Now you think I've lost it. The Pivot CEO who advocates ethics is suggesting we cheat. Hide. Disguise.

Let me be clear. I'm not advocating any form of dishonesty in sales. Period.

On the other hand, does a hunter tell his prey "Hey, hunter over here, watch out!" Since terms like "sales representative" have negative initial first impressions—and since first impressions can make or break a pitch—why advertise you're a hunter?

In other words, a B-Type sales representative calls up a prospect and says, "Hi Susan, I'm with ABC Corporation, and I'd love a chance to sell you some Gadgets." The B-type "tactical hunter" approach is "I'd like to offer you a one-time only discount." That's a clumsy hunter at best.

Chet Homes, in bestselling book *The Ultimate Sales Machine*, demonstrated how he handled this issue with one of his clients:

"...To meet this challenge, I changed the titles of the salespeople to sound less salesy—for example, "director of corporate communications." This enabled a salesperson to call a prospect and say something like: "Hi. I'm Jennifer Smith, the director of corporate communications here at *XYZ Magazine*. As part of our ongoing effort to continually serve the market, we like to learn more about other companies in our market..."[54]

Chet was not advocating dishonesty. He was re-focusing sales on their function as experts, representatives, informers, and communicators.

5. Confidence of the Predator

The confidence of an Apex Predator does not arise from being "faster" or "better." Predators, contrary to what you might think, aren't always faster than their prey. They are certainly quick when they "strike," but most of their prey, in the wild, are faster than they are at sustained runs. Lions are faster than most of their prey, at 80 km/h, but only for very short bursts. Their typical prey, zebras, run 64 km/h, but can sustain it.

The confidence of the lion lies in its sharp perceptions and its intellect. Apex hunters calculate probabilities. They attack the slowest and weakest. They plan an interception trajectory. They wait for the moment when their short burst of speed will be enough.

They watch. They listen. They use all their senses. Only when they're 90 percent certain of success do they strike. The shark may circle for hours before it hits. So should you. Watch, listen, and wait for the right timing. Then, strike with confidence.

Before I lose you with all my gruesome metaphors, the key thing to remember is that hunters strike when they're sure of the kill. If your audience is in the 97 percent phase—not ready to buy—you watch, make friends, convey expertise, warmly invite them to return to your "lair" at a later time when they are ready. You don't haphazardly strike at anyone who comes within reach. Hunters are precise, careful and intelligent.

L.I.F.T. Tips for the Leader of Apex Sales Reps

The *L.I.F.T. Tips for the Apex Sales Rep* is updated regularly, based on statistics. Check the website for more up to date data. Just as the Apex Predator studies its prey for long periods before deciding to "leap", Apex A-Team Sales members also study the sales and marketing data. (Visit the

RandyDewey.com website for latest statistics.) These L.I.F.T. Apex Sales Tips are based on 2020 data[55]:

1. Being a Helper: Earning Trust is the Primary Mission

Only three percent of buyers (cross-industry average) trust their sales representatives, even the ones they've worked with for years.

The only professions with lower trust rates are politicians and lobbyists. On the other hand, the trust rates for a doctor is 49 percent, firefighters 48 percent, teachers 38 percent, nurses 36 percent, accountants 19 percent.

What do teachers, firefighters and nurses have that we don't? Trust. Why? Because we know they're job is to help us. Even accountants help us. What do sales professionals do? Take our money, right?

The first, critical tip for all salespeople is to turn yourself into a "helper." No, not like a politician, who only during election years volunteers at the food bank. Apex Salespeople are out in the community—volunteering at the school, at the church, at the food bank, or just helping their past customers move. Being a genuine helper anytime, all the time—and not just at the end of the quarter when you need the deals to close.

Mostly, in the context of the typical Apex Sales Rep, this means education:

- White papers

- Newsletters

- Blog

- Social Media

- Interviews with community networks or trade journals

- Community service

- Anything that is "no strings attached" helpful education relative to you and your product/service.

2. Don't stall on pricing.

Many sales gurus for years have coached sales representatives to hit all the value propositions, and to de-emphasize price. Or, to pre-emptively hit all the value points before the pricing. This is fairly dated advice.

According to broad-ranging data, 58 percent of prospects—who qualify as buyers—want the price up front, in the initial call. Many don't want to wait for elaborate quoting and pitches.

If they ask, that's a bonus—Apex Sale Reps know this is a hot "buying signal." Stop hiding—now, is the time to leap.

Clearly, this statistic tells us that price matters. Unless you sell a pure commodity, value is clearly made up of a number of factors, including brand-quality, service, support, delivery time and other factors. Yes, you should cover all this, but don't stall on pricing. Confidently say your prices and this telegraphs the message that there is more to the story and you can back your prices with value they may not realize. Never be apologetic about price. Remember a dodgy answer or delaying them will only frustrate your customer, which will create more skepticism and by the time you say the price you've lost what little trust you had with them.

Strategic sales representatives will have been in touch with their prospect for weeks, months or years, patiently educating. By the time of the "quote" price, delivery and support might be all that's left to discuss. Don't frustrate the prospect.

Other information prospects want in the first sales call (in person or phone) are:

- How the product works (or a demo) 54 percent

- How it solves my company's problem 47 percent

- Examples of other organizations who have used the product successfully 44 percent

- Timeline for purchase 24 percent.

3. Hunt when it's not busy

Since we know that the majority of sales representatives will be making calls in the last month of the quarter [Gong Data]—make sure you're not among them.

Sell equally in all three months of the quarter. You'll have less competition for attention.

Although this data refers to "calls" it applies equally to however you contact your prospects, including, of course, your educational efforts.

4. Persistently Persuade—Don't Push

No one likes the pushy sales representative. On the other hand, in a Hubspot survey[56] of buyers, the majority of buyers would prefer to be in touch with the representative at the "consideration stage." Only 20 percent want to "talk" during the "decision stage." 19 percent would like to connect with salespeople at the "awareness stage."

In other words, last minute pressure—for example the last month in the quarter—isn't going to cut it.

We're back to "educating the client." In the same survey[57], the preferred method of obtaining information on a product or service was:

- Fact sheets, product information on web, pdf or print 57 percent at the "learn more" stage and 51 percent at the "buy" stage

- Ratings or reviews from customers 52 percent at the "learn more" stage and 48 percent at the "buy" stage

- Peer referrals 42 percent at the "learn more" stage and 41 percent at the "buy" stage

- Case studies of customers 42 percent at the "learn more" stage and 36 percent at the "buy" stage

- Demonstrations (virtual or in-person, as applies) 38 percent at the "learn more" stage and 36 percent at the "buy" stage

- Brand and best practices 35 percent at the "learn more" stage and 32 percent at the "buy" stage.

5. Be an information hoarder

Considering the importance of how buyers want information—see data in 4 above—it's critical for Apex Sales Teams and leaders to be information hoarders.

Collect case studies, testimonials, referral letters, articles mentioning your product, reviews, competitor reviews, assessment and diagnostic data, service and quality data—you name it. You are the expert, and your prospect expects you to have all this information at your virtual fingertips.

6. Don't wait to follow up—you have minutes!

Minutes not hours. Hours not days. Days not weeks. Following up on a lead—especially an online lead—is the most important role you, as Apex Team Leader or Apex Sale Rep can play.

In a survey of 2,200 American companies published in the *Harvard Business Review*, they reported that sales professionals were ***seven times more likely to have meaningful conversations with decision-makers within an hour of the lead***—more even, than those who waited 60 minutes[58].

It gets worse—especially if you wait 24 hours, as many companies do. In the same report, the company that gets back to the lead in one hour is 60 times more likely to close the lead than the company that waited 24 hours.

In other words:
Responding to the lead within five minutes—solid opportunity
Responding in one hour: 1/7th the opportunity
Responding in 24 hours: 1/60th the opportunity.

This is bad news for most companies—although it could be good for you, if you are one of the L.I.F.T. Leadership companies that makes minutes the rule. In a separate study of 433 companies ***only 7 percent of companies responded in the first five minutes.***[59]

This is where the "marriage" of sales and marketing is critical. If your company is spending a small fortune on marketing, the leads are coming in, but you follow up within hours—rather than minutes—you've squandered the seven-time factor. Within 24 hours, the 60-time factor. By the time you get back to them, they've contacted someone else.

Worse, if your sales team is "too busy" to handle the live chat or the online leads—and you outsource all of this to a call centre for screening—you'll likely lose the lead. You'll lose the investment you made in earning that lead.

Especially for a lead—regardless of source—you have minutes, not hours. You, as leader of an Apex Team need to ensure it happens.

7. Use videos for sales

If your sales lead and marketing initiatives include online, video is likely a major component. If it's not, work with your marketing team to build video content. Google indexes and emphasizes video content.

Especially today, the need for product videos, or features/benefits videos, or educational and support videos is high. Here's some data:

Seven in 10 business-to-business buyers prefer to watch a video prior to buying. This is according to "Think with Google."

YouTube data: 895,000 hours of B2B videos were watched.

Half of buyers watch at least 30 minutes of related videos prior to buying in B2B. Another 20 percent watch more than an hour of videos.

---

8. Ask the right number of questions

Asking questions and listening for opportunities is critically important selling. Strategic sellers ask questions and solve problems. But—there's a fine line between being "helpful" and being "annoying."

According to a Gong study of 519,000 "discovery" sales calls[60]:

"Asking 15-18 questions in a discovery calls was only slightly more effective than asking 7-10 questions."

11-14 was optimal.

The same study indicated that the role of the "discovery" call or visit should focus on discovery of 3-4 problems you can solve for them: 81 percent for three problems uncovered, versus 85 percent for four problems. This is based on analysis of 519,000 calls and seems about right.

The process of selling is largely about uncovering the genuine problems to be solved—everything can be stated as a problem—and offering precise, properly timed and executed solutions.

Your questions should be short, but data from the same report indicates the answers should be long. In other words—structure your questions so that your buyer will have to invest a lot of time answering. While they are answering, never interrupt.

Buyers are educated—you beware.

The old cliche was "buyer beware." In L.I.F.T. we spin this around:

"Buyers are educated—you beware."

There are basically five types of selling, which I've touched on in this chapter. They go by various names—and Apex reps will use more than one. In L.I.F.T. we call them:

1. **Educational Selling**: Your mission is to be informative, the educator, the leading expert.

2. **Pain-Point Selling**: You ask questions, discover problem, solve them.

3. **Trusted Advisor Selling**: You, the Apex Rep, focus on being the trusted, valued partner, visible in the community, in touch with meaningful information, helpful long before the sales cycle.

4. **Lure Selling**: This includes the Apex hunter who use various lures. It could be pricing, offers, but it equally can be an offer of information, seminars, values-adds, and service support.

5. **Lead-Jump Selling**: Where the marketing and sales teams are in full synch, leads are coming in through marketing—today, often online—and sales jump on the leads within minutes, not hours, not days.

Regardless of the source of the lead, or your approach to selling, never forget that buyers today are already well-educated. With online resources, they've done their research, watched the competitor videos, studied the specs—likely without your help. Ideally, as an Apex Rep you have pro-actively been the source of much information.

We say "you beware" because data in the last three years has indicated:

- Buyers are experts at blocking cold and interruptive techniques—which is why "Educational Selling" works so well.

- Buyers have higher expectations today versus five years ago. They are in total control through access to data and information online. The best weapon we have against this shift of dependence is pro-active education-based marketing and selling.

- Buyers likely have most of the information (from online or elsewhere) on your products and services as well as your competitors—long before they engage with a salesperson.

This informs our approach in L.I.F.T. Leadership. It is this data and trend that makes the Apex hunter the right approach in selling. The source of the information should be you and your company. The leads should be jumped on within minutes—like a pouncing cheetah.

L.I.F.T. Exercise—Strategic Vs. Tactical

Try this exercise as the leader of a sales team, answering for the team. Or, if you are an aspiring Apex Rep, try this exercise for yourself. List at least 10 strategic objectives of the sales team. Don't confuse these with tactical objectives and metrics. Strategic, for example, by topic (make them more specific) are: brand loyalty, establishing the sales team as experts, long term relationships, increasing customer satisfaction.

Strategic Objectives

1.

2.

3.

4.

5.

6.

7.

8.

9.

10.

Tactical Objectives each quarter (sales volume goals, conversion goals and so on.)

1.

2.

3.

4.

5.

Ignoring the tactical objectives, focusing only on strategic, develop a method to help you achieve the strategic goals. For example, an educational blog or newsletter for your market.

1.

2.

3.

4.

5.

6.

7.

8.

9.

10.

11

L.I.F.T. STRATEGY: ONE DASHBOARD TO RULE THEM ALL

Don't be a tactical genius, but a strategic fool. A dualistic single dashboard—combining top strategic goals and vision with tactical action—helps distill the essence of strategy to actionable tactics that can drive momentum.

L.I.F.T. Facts

Here are some alarming leadership facts:

- Only two percent of leaders are confident they will achieve 80-100 percent of their goals.[61]

- 50 percent of leaders rate implementation as equal in importance to strategy.[62]

- 67 percent of well-formulated strategies failed due to poor execution.[63]

- 85 percent of leadership spend less than one hour a month discussing strategy.[64]

In this chapter

- Why a tactical genius is not necessarily a strategic genius— why you need to be both.

- L.I.F.T. is all about distillation: break the multi-page business or operations plan habit: one-page rule.

- The Three D's of L.I.F.T. Strategic Tactical Planning: Defining, Development, Determination.

- Why dashboards can serve both strategic and tactical goals— and how to create your one-page dashboard.

- Why strategy is visionary, and tactical is activity-oriented, and remembering activities serve the vision.

Important Take-away

- If you can't explain your goals and plans in one-page you're not at your best as a leader. Exemplary Leaders know how to work with the "essence." Top Leaders know how to pitch in one or two sentences. Why use four pages when one will do? Why use one page, when a paragraph will do? In business, momentum is everything.

Reflections from the Conqueror

- The name Erich Ludendorff is a military commander famous for in World War I for being a "tactical genius but a strategic fool." His tactics on combat extended the brutal war which wreaked chaos on Germany. He was recognized as a military genius with exceptional tactical prowess. Of course, as history demonstrated, his brilliant tactics led to ruin and defeat, in the first world war, but also planted the seeds that led to the rise of Hitler and a far more catastrophic defeat and mass loss of life. His example led to the saying, "Don't be a tactical genius but a strategic fool." [65]

The Concise L.I.F.T.

Brevity, distillation, essence define the L.I.F.T. leader.

Lead: Lead with "show" rather than "tell." An image, chart, graph or PowerPoint slide is worth a thousand words—to paraphrase the cliché proverb.

Inspire: A concise narrative and images—charts, graphs, data—will inspire your teams, shareholders, stakeholders. A lengthy plan will put them to sleep.

Focus: If a picture is worth one-thousand words, a L.I.F.T. one-page business dashboard plan is worth a thousand-page business plan. (Metaphorically speaking, since I trust your business plans are nowhere near one-thousand pages!)

Transform: Transformation is about activity: action and reaction. To manifest both, embrace brevity.

Most of our business terminology, such as "strategy" and "tactics" derive from military labels—a key reason you see Mehmed, Alexander the Great and Sun Tzu so prominently mentioned in this book. One thing "war" cases teach us, as businesspeople, is that strategy and tactics are mutually interdependent. You cannot win a war with one alone. Germany lost World War I, and one of the reasons (among many) was the disconnect between strategy and tactics. The German Chief of Staff, Eric Lundendorff, prolonged World War I with his revolutionary tactics—brilliant tactics still deployed in the field to this day—but without service to a strategy, it was inevitable the war would be lost. Lundendorff is sometimes cited as the example for the advice

"Don't be a tactical genius, but a strategic fool."[66]

In my career, I have been brought into many companies full of tactical genius—inevitably resulting in great products or services, strong customer service, access to financing—but hampered by a lack of strategic vision. Tactics without vision, as with Lunderdorff in World War I, almost always leads to a major crisis.

I'll illustrate this with a case study of a company facing bankruptcy, despite fantastic products, high revenue and four international factories—and how the one-page dashboard was one of the tools I used to instill the strategic vision—combined with great tactics—into a one-page action-dashboard. The dashboard was only a tool, in service of strategy and tactics—but it is an important one, in service of vital activities.

Real-life L.I.F.T. Strategy case study— facing bankruptcy: 90 days or bust

I took over leadership of a company with operations across Canada, USA, and the UK—and 3,500 employees resulting in a half-billion in revenue—facing a rapidly shrinking market. Our team-size, and international scale meant we could not exactly "turn on a dime," although it was clear that urgent changes were needed. We produced designer materials for the home décor market—and the style and trend fell out of favour on both the residential side and the commercial sides of this market.

The company faced incredible financial challenges, with negative $15M in EBITDA and a market growth rate of -10% over the prior year— and realistic projections was that the trend would continue.

With the company facing Chapter 11, our licenses with Disney, Warner Bros, Marvel and others were at risk. This financial reality, inherited when I took over, would certainly lead to turmoil with our channels: Walmart, Home Depot and the rest of the big box stores we supplied.

Since the market pressures were consumer-driven, the inescapable cost impact would have to come from operations and logistics. At the same time, new product innovation and product offerings were key to diversification, but with long product-development cycles, we needed time to stabilize the company—just to survive long enough to exploit our strengths in those areas.

In emergency-mode, we raced to develop a comprehensive—yet concise—business operations restructuring plan that would buy us the time we needed. After extensive analysis of all options, it became clear we could not hit the "breakeven" plateau simply by trimming up the existing facilities and making them operationally better. There was no way to avoid it: plant closures and massive operational consolidations remained the sole option. The massive undertaking required very precise planning—but at the same time we needed rapid action, and a blueprint that everyone could follow. We needed clarity and momentum!

The Game Plan

We distilled our plans into a single double-sided page plan with all the most important action points, which I referred to as "The Game Plan". You can't expect an emergency deployment team to work to a fifty-page restructuring plan, it's not realistic or helpful.

I came in like a Football coach, with a one-page play sketched out. A football coach spends hours, even days, preparing for a game: understanding the opponent, watching videos of old games, charting their strengths and weaknesses—and importantly, mapping that against your own player's vulnerabilities and capabilities—then, the coach develops a plan. Great players are important, you rely on their skills, but a team can't win without a great coach. Here's something else a great football coach can do. He can explain the needed tactical plays to his team concisely, clearly, perfectly, and with inspirational vigor. The plays might be a single sheet of paper— or a whiteboard when explaining it to the team—that allows the coach in a game to have one central reference—to manage that moment in time. The coach knows where the team needs to be, how they need to play, how they need to respond—and so his team.

In this case, we had our Game Plan and it required four factories to be consolidated into one, located in the least expensive area, with the most factory floor available. From the point of view of our stakeholders, including customers, it would be a win; for some team-members it would mean life-changing decisions.

This time it even more personal

This time it became more personal for me, because one of the factories I was forced to close was in my hometown. My office, along with my family, would have to move to the new factory town location. My family issues, of course, was the least among complications and sacrifices made by the entire team—but we all knew it had to be completed.

The bigger pressure, for everyone, was the timeline. We had 90 days to complete the mission. Strategic planning and tactical execution would have to be exactly on the mark, without a single slip-up or mistake. There was no time for mitigation and further problem-solving. That one-page action plan, developed after we exhaustively went through every contingency, opportunity and issue, would have to be immutable to the end if we were to accomplish the nearly impossible in 90 days.

We simply didn't have time to work from a more complicated, longer, wordier plan document. We just needed to all work to the one "Game Plan".

The most difficult 90 days in my career

You can imagine the raw emotion and angst our team went through over the next 90 days. Consolidating from four production factories to one, reorganizing the entire team—it is no small feat on a timeline that tight. Everyone had the Game Plan in hand, and we spoke every day without fail. Let's face it, this is ambitious. Everything had to be accomplished—logistics, flights, layoffs, closures, equipment moves, start-up and training, testing—all within the most difficult 90-days in my career.

The fate of the company literally relied on this one-page plan succeeding, so there was no question of contingencies or changes of direction. Drive to the end, course correct quickly with new information, be clear and concise, communicate with openness, rally the troops in the darkest moments, and don't lose sight of the prize.

Did we make it? We did, 90 sleepless nights later. We completed the mission. It may shock you to learn that we executed the Game Plan perfectly—and the unity of our team was incredible. Many of us moved cities, uprooted our lives. Others moved on to new careers. Everyone knew what was needed. Like top players in the last quarter of a game, we all rallied against all odds, and we won. We did it by staying a team. We had our plays. We had our setbacks and adversities. The team did anything they had to, to win.

Change is hard, but during a crisis there can be an advantage in the momentum of speed. No one has too much time to stress-out or worry. There's also a feeling of immense satisfaction at the end. Imagine the exuberance of a football team, the underdogs, when they win against all odds, taking the trophy.

What I've learned, a key lesson learned out of those 90 days, is there's never a reason to have an operational plan longer than a page or two. Think Game Plan. We call it the L.I.F.T. Dashboard—but it's the same idea. We not only track results as we go, we can see at a glance where we're going. You don't want your team hunting through 50 pages of text when they should be in full action mode. Action means Game Plan.

"Many Strategies Fail Because They're Not Actually Strategies."

"One major reason for the lack of action is that "new strategies" are often not strategies at all," writes Professor Freek Vermeulen, in *Harvard Business Review*.[67] "A real strategy involves a clear set of choices that define what the firm is going to do and what it's *not* going to do. Many strategies fail to get implemented, despite the ample efforts of hard-working people, because they do not represent a set of clear choices."

He adds that "Many so-called strategies are in fact goals." He gave the example of a strategy, Freek cited the case of a British toy maker who faced bankruptcy. The new CEO established a new strategy for their train toys: "(1) To make perfect scale models (rather than toys); (2) for adult collectors (rather than for children); (3) that appealed to a sense of nostalgia (because it reminded adults of their childhoods." Goal: to increase Hornby's share price from £35 to £250 over just five years.

Freek explains that it was a strategy because "it represented a clear set of just three choices, which fit together to form a clear strategic direction for the company."

What separates "goal" from strategy? The statement "we want to be number one in our key target market" is simply a goal, not a strategy. How would you turn this statement into a strategy? Try Freek's rule of three choices. In this example, Freek modified the goal this way: "We want to increase operational efficiency; we will target Europe, the Middle East, and Africa; and we will divest business X."

L.I.F.T. Strategic Exercise

Go back to the case study in this chapter. Look at all the elements of the case study and write out the "strategy" as a statement—as demonstrated by Professor Freek. Now, list the tactical goals as a separate list. As an alternate exercise, do the same thing with your current situation in your current company.

1. Strategy _____

_____

_____

2. Goals _____

_____

_____

Strategy is about vision; tactics are about activities in service of vision

This is the easiest way to separate these two. They are befuddled in business in even the largest of companies. It is not strictly correct to try to separate strategy and tactics by timeline, as many people do: strategy is long-term; tactic is short-term. If tactics tend to be mostly short term in timeline it is because they are action-oriented in service of strategy. If strategy appears to be long term, it's about vision.

By vision, I do not mean it's only aspirational. It's not wishes and hopes. You have to plan the path to achieving the vision. Strategic plans contain tactics. Tactics should serve the strategy. I know, it's common sense, right? But, somehow, in companies around the world, the two are misunderstood, despite the fact that 2500 years ago, Chinese military strategies Sun Tzu wrote the go-to book for both business and warriors, the *Art of War*, where he wrote:

"Strategy without tactics is the slowest route to victory. Tactics without strategy is the noise before defeat."

So, let's be clear—pun intended. What is good strategy? What is a good tactic?

What is a good strategy?

The strategy is the foundation of all activities in your company or organization. Strategy is focus. Vision.

Vision requires context: history, competitors, markets data, performance metrics, SWOT (strengths, weaknesses, opportunities) analysis, scope.

Vision requires goals: what is the desired end result and timeline for the end result?

Vision requires core values. (See Chapter 1, Vision and Values.)

Example: in the case study of the toy company above by Professor Freek:

Vision requires context: company nearing bankruptcy, too diversified.

Vision requires goals: to make scale models targeted at adult collectors—rather than the legacy audience of children.

Vision requires core value: to position as the collector's choice for nostalgia products.

L.I.F.T. Exercise: Strategy as Vision

Take the case study in this chapter, and the results in your last exercise, and restate the strategy as the three separated vision statements:

Vision requires context (list all the context, history, and data from the case study): _____-

_____

_____

_____

Vision requires goals (list all the goals from the case study):

_____

_____

_____

Vision requires core values: (list all the core values from the case study):

_____

_____

_____

Repeat the exercise for your own company.

What is a good tactic?

A tactic has a goal/purpose, just like a strategy, so what is the key difference? Tactics are in service of activities that support the vision-strategy. By definition, a tactic usually includes goal, along with activities to achieve the goals and a timeline. The tactic is in service of the vision. So, for example, let's stick with the toy company in Professor Freek's example.

Their vision and strategy: ""(1) To make perfect scale models (rather than toys); (2) for adult collectors (rather than for children); (3) that appealed to a sense of nostalgia (because it reminded adults of their childhoods)." Goal to increase Hornby's share price from £35 to £250 over just five years."

In support of the vision, they might have deployed a number of tactics:

1. Extensively study the adult collectors of train models, determining, market scope, wants and desires, expectations, price points.

2. Determine costs to retool the factory for production of scale collector trains.

3. Develop a nostalgic brand to market to the collector.

The complete list of tactics, depending on granularity, can be quite long to accomplish a visionary goal.

Tactical distractions are thieves

Tactics are in service to the strategy, but it's easy to let the daily grind of business, the almost constant obstacles, delays and environmental distraction to disrupt execution. This is where prioritization becomes important. Make the priorities clear. This is where the combined Strategic Tactical L.I.F.T. Dashboard will help you out. Check in daily, weekly, monthly (no later than monthly) to monitor your gaps, your shortfalls and surpluses, your resources and funds. The dashboard helps you keep everything top-of-mind.

Here's a simple truth: numbers do not lie (assuming the numbers are accurate.) Whatever the numbers demonstrate—that's the story. It is by virtue of numbers we can distill an operational plan down to a single page dashboard.

Here's a number for you. There are five days in a week. You blew by one because of a client distraction. You felt it was important; the client is an A-list customer. What do we now know? You have four days left in the week to accomplish your weekly goals. What if, today, you get sick? Three days. The principal of your school needs to see you right away about your child's welfare. Two days.

Now, what about the other team in your company who relied on your deliverable? Their entire team is set back three days as well. The damage cascades and escalates.

Numbers are as much about time, as they are about dollars and percentages.

Think of the tactical distractions as nothing less than break-and-enter thieves. Dial 911 (metaphorically.)

Think strategically; act tactically

This is another way to separate the two. Strategy, as a vision, is a thinking and visualizing process, based on all available data and projections. Tactics are purely about activities or actions. Think strategically, act tactically.

Strategic Cognition

What constitutes the process of logic and thinking? The process of cognition is defined as "gaining knowledge and comprehension." The processes of cognition are no different to those of the Strategist-Visionary:

- Knowing

- Remembering

- Judging

- Problem-Solving

- Higher level functions: imagination, perception, planning.

   In other words, the strategies will undertake the cognitive stages:

   - **Knowing**: the analysis of available research and data, comprehension of product benefits and features, performance data, supporting services, competitive scenario

   - **Remembering**: understanding the history that led to the current situation.

   - **Judging**: Analysis of the product, market, pricing data.

   - **Problem-Solving**: Various forms of SWOT analysis: our strengths, our weaknesses, our opportunities, our threats

   - **Higher Level Functions**: creative brainstorming of solutions to the issues established under "problem solving", using data from "knowing" and "remembering"

We equate Strategic Planning to Cognition process to align it with the concept of: "Think Strategically" versus "Act Tactically."

The Three D's of L.I.F.T. Strategic Tactical Planning

A lot of business leaders lose site of the three D's of planning. Regardless of the scope of planning—marketing, business operations, divisional operations, product development—the careful L.I.F.T. Leader will always work through the three key stages of planning to implementation:

1. Defining Stage: History, Present Situation, SWOT and GAP analysis.

2. Development Stage: Blue-Sky brainstorming, analysis and planning implementation. (See Blue Sky brainstorming section.)

3. Determination Stage and Distilling: Conversion of the "big plan" into concise, actionable strategic-tactical dashboards ready for implementation. (See L.I.F.T. Dashboard.)

L.I.F.T. blue-sky thinking: cognition with optimism

One reason I settled on the acronym L.I.F.T. was it connoted a sense of optimism. The one lesson I learned after numerous turnarounds is—there is ALWAYS a solution. I put the word in caps deliberately. Always. ALWAYS.

To be a blue-sky thinker—defined as "brainstorming with no limits" you have to be an optimist. You never give up searching for the better way.

Not all great thinkers are optimists. You can be brilliant; you can master cognition: knowing, remembering, judging, problem-solving and all the higher-level functions; but many high thinkers are fatalists. L.I.F.T. Leaders are not. Analyzing and problem-solving may lead to inescapably dire conclusions—for example, as in my case study in this chapter. The fatalist problem-solver would just see a stormy sky and shut everything down. The blue-sky thinker finds a solution that not only achieves the vision, for the higher good of all, but does it with inspiration and enthusiasm—hence the "I" for Inspire in L.I.F.T.

I can't emphasize this enough.

What separates the L.I.F.T. Leader is inspiration. Brashness. Exploring all the crazy scenarios until you find the big opportunity. One way to hold on to the "blue sky" thinker is to remember your stakeholders. You, the Leader, are responsible to all.

Again, I'll fall back on my war-leader metaphor. In battles, decisions are made for the higher good. Sometimes, you send your soldiers to their demise. Yet, you do it with a vision of sunny, peaceful, prosperous days after the war ends. You have a vision. You instill the vision in your army. They fight with enthusiasm. You win. Some may perish for the greater good. Yet, this is still blue-sky thinking—as long as you hold to the greater good.

Blue-Sky Thinkers forge new paths

The key thing that separates Blue-Sky Thinkers from the rest is not the inspirational tone or optimism. It's the outcomes. Blue-Sky Thinkers almost always forge new paths. Find new niches and opportunities. "Brainstorm without limits." It's called blue sky, because the long-list of brainstorm ideas will seem whimsical, flighty, imaginative—until it isn't. Suddenly, that whacky idea is "the one."

The example I always cite is that of Peloton stationary bike. We already had a market saturated with bikes, stationary bikes, exercise equipment. We already had the "Spin" bike—in fact that's trademarked. Along comes the Blue-Sky thinking, the optimist, the "all ideas are on the table" process, and we end up with the Peloton—at $2000 (plus) for a stationary bike with a brilliant, immersive 22-inch LCD panel and thrilling software that makes you think you're actually biking in the Alps, with live virtual classes, a camera, joining frat groups, social interaction through friend requests, virtual high fives and more. Now, you can bike in your basement, alongside others who are biking in their basements—and all of you feel like you're racing together. I repeat—$2,000. For a stationary bike. Plus, subscription. Plus, accessories. And, well worth it.

What separated Peloton from other "Spin" solutions? Vision. Blue-Sky Thinking. They didn't want to compete in the market—they wanted to define the market.

How-to conduct your own "Blue Sky" Brainstorm Session

Before undertaking your team Blue Sky Brainstorm Session, remember to gather all the data relevant to the brainstorm.

"Brainstorming is a neurological deep dive into a sea of creativity that needs data and facts to create achievable ideas that are steeped in brilliance and innovation."

To make the most of a brainstorming session, invest first in real market insight and research that identifies all the strengths, weaknesses, opportunities, and threats. Engage market researchers to talk to your customers. Collect all available market data. Demographics. Psychographics. Pull all the data on your products and services—and just as importantly, the data on all your competitors and their products and services. Avoid at all costs drinking the organizational Kool-Aid of how things are done and who has what…facts not opinions matter more at this point.

You may jump-start the meeting with a high-level view of the data: strengths, weaknesses, opportunities, threats, but save those pages and pages of data for the challenge phase of the brainstorming—after all the ideas are up on the whiteboard.

The most outlandish idea first

The problem with group brainstorming is momentum. If you bog down a session with data slides, you'll lose them before they begin. Save the data for the post-brainstorm analysis.   What I find is the fastest way to loosen up the brain cells is to start with —

"The most outlandish idea possible."

You heard me. Put it up on the whiteboard. Allow a giggle or two to turn into a rumble of laughter.

Why do such an "out there" thing? Because, Blue Sky Thinking means "every idea is good." You put them all up. No parameters. No limits. No criticism. Just put them all up there on the virtual whiteboard.

What does this signal. In a group it tells them that there is "no bad idea." If you, the leader, are willing to be mocked for the crazy idea, then anything goes. This is exactly what you need. Later, you can laugh, and say, "I was just kidding about that, but seriously, there are no bad ideas here..."

Another way to trigger blue-sky thinking is a series of open-ended questions—or you can use these questions to guide your market research company in preparation for the brainstorm meeting to follow. In the brainstorm meeting format, remember, simply list all the answers without challenge or analysis—you want as many as possible, even the most ridiculous points. I have found, in past experience, that in the ridiculous, wisdom is found. Here are some prompts:

1. Even if we are doing things well, what can we do better, what capabilities can we add to enhance our product or service?

2. How else can our excellent products and services be leveraged, sold or distributed—with minimum investment—to maximize our existing capabilities.

3. Which products or services are not realizing a return on investment? Why? What can we do about it?

4. Putting aside objections and obstacles, what opportunities do we have that we have not yet pursued.

5. Assuming we had unlimited budgets and funding, what other opportunities turn up? Dream big on this one. (If someone hadn't bravely proposed a ridiculously expensive stationary bike, the Peloton stationary bike would never have seen market.)

6. Turn the question around: if your customers didn't care about budget, only about features and benefits, what would be their ideal product/service?

Word games

If you get stuck, try the old "ad agency" brainstorm approach of putting all the relevant keywords up on the board—then asking the group to free-associate with word-association. Tell the group to not even try to filter, just let it all flow.

In an article in Fast Company, called "Brainstorming Doesn't Work: Try This Technique Instead" they suggested Brainwriting instead. Basically, it's a similar free-association every-thing-goes process, but you ask each team member to do it on their own in writing. Then, you gather in your meeting, with a moderator, write the shortlists on the white board, and go to it.

Painting the picture—key to visionary strategic thinking

Whether you're working on a product strategy, service, company-wide strategic vision, or pitching a concept to investors, you need to be able to convey your vision. L.I.F.T. Leaders are visionaries. They can visualize. They can convey their visualization to others. They paint with words and numbers.

Blue-sky thinking is especially reliant on visualization. When you brainstorm, you are usually conceptualizing and innovating. To succeed you need to convey a picture. In engineering, we go through a similar process of cognition, leading ultimately to an "elevator pitch" description, an engineered-design process, then various "renderings" of the concept. What is the rendering for? To present to people who are not necessarily engineers. We need to be able to picture the solution.

L.I.F.T. Leaders do the same thing with their high-level visions. They paint a picture, a rendering in words and numbers.

The form manifests in an operational plan. And, like a good picture, that plan should be concise, clear, visualized. It should be designed around the idea of "action." Any engineer will tell you that the greatest idea in the world, even rendered, is nothing but imagination unless someone actually builds it. To visualize that end-result, requires the rendering.

The picture should illustrate all the critical eight points of a plan. (The eight points explained below.) It should be clear and concise, so it can be readily understood. It should be visionary: "This is what we will look like in 3 months, 6 months, 1 year..."

In planning, we have to go beyond visualizing—and show how we can attain the vision. That vision, ultimately, will include both strategy and tactics.

In L.I.F.T. Leadership, this takes the form of the one-page dashboard.

I advocate dashboard for everything actionable. The entire company would have a master-dashboard—the "one dashboard to rule them all" (see below)—containing, on one page, a complete picture of vision, goals, tactics, milestones, contingencies, and more.

Don't stop there. Each department needs a dashboard. They might take the overall vision down to a more granular level, focused on the vision, goals, tactics, milestones, contingencies, and more for their department. Then, take it down another level to the individual leaders. They should have their own dashboards—you guessed it—with vision, goals, tactics, milestones, contingencies, and more.

What makes the dashboard approach so valuable is that it not only serves as a "picture" or visualization document, but it's also a complete roadmap, a plan, and contains milestones. Just as you renew your dashboard monthly, you should renew progress to the milestones monthly with your team members. You have, in other words, a mechanism for accountability, and review.

How are you doing? Where are you going?

These questions are top-of-mind in companies that work with live dashboards. The metrics update constantly. At any given moment, if you take this approach, you can see:

Are we ahead or behind the goal?

What can we do to make up for the deficit in the goal?

How can we take advantage of the surplus over the goal?

How can we make it more efficient?

What did I do wrong this week or month?

What did I do right this month?

Speaking of doing right: compensation and performance

All your team members, anyone who merits their own "dashboard"—containing their own goals and tactics—also should have an open, defined path to reward. If they consistently meet their dashboard objectives, they deserve compensation. Of course, the reverse is equally true. If they consistently miss objectives, action is called for: modified tactics, revised goals, new resources, or possibly even repercussions in review.

One thing you don't need research to show you is that if you don't compensate your team for performance, there'll be no incentive to exceed the goal the next month or quarter. Exceptional performance deserves exceptional reward. Some of it can be tied to overall company performance, but you should still consider compensation if they personally exceed goals in the face of negative company performance.

If a team-member moves the dashboard needle in a meaningful way, the least they deserve is recognition. If they roar past all the obstacles and exceed goals, they deserve much more than just kudos. Material reward is not bribery—it's compensation. Money is a big motivator. It is equally a big de-motivator if it is withheld.

As much as the live dashboards are a way to track goals and progress, it is equally powerful in personnel reviews and compensation - reward decisions.

Tactical execution and the dashboard

There's no veil of obscurity in a company who uses public dashboards. Even private dashboards, if monitored by a team, are transparent. There's an energy behind this quasi-live dashboard approach to planning, objectives and metrics. Put it all in one place, accessible, and you'll see gains in tactical execution. Because tactics and milestones are updated regularly, there's no hiding behind the shield of "wait for the quarterly result, you'll see."

Tactical implementation is smoothly facilitated by dashboards. You'll find its as much a scorecard as a game plan—all on one page.

Multinational or multi-office companies will especially benefit from cloud-shared dashboards. Nothing instills discipline, accountability, action and traction more than the shared dashboard.

Traditional Unified Business Plan

There are numerous books on unified business planning, all good. I've listed some in the bibliography that I recommend. This chapter's focus on "one dashboard to rule them all" and other unique L.I.F.T. methods, does not mean you don't have a one-hundred page (or so) unified business plan. Inevitably, you will. As cumbersome as it is, before you can write a one-page plan for action, you need the bigger picture. You need to cover off all the tick boxes: Defining Stage, Development Stage, Determination Stage. Ultimately, action derives from the Determination Stage—which is why L.I.F.T. focuses extensively on this stage and the Dashboards.

You'll see in the illustration, these three stages, and their ultimate end-point of collection point. The Defining Stage ultimately distills into a GAP analysis. The Development Stage ultimately distills down to your Unified Business Plan. Because your Unified Business Plan is too cumbersome for daily activities, at the Determination Stage you'll distill the information down into our famous L.I.F.T. Dashboards.

All of these stages are fairly standard and typical. Mostly, in this chapter, we focus on the unique aspects of L.I.F.T. Leadership—especially distillation.

Determination Stage

At the **Determination Stage**, you'll explore your past, present and future possibilities:

- GAP analysis: what we know about our history, what we've learned, the GAP between where we want to be, and where we are.

- SWOT analysis: nothing replaces a good strengths, weaknesses, opportunities, threats analysis.

- Market research and data: our reputation, legacy, brand awareness, market share, competitors market share—all the insights that allow you to move on to the next stage, Development.

- **Distillation Point: GAP Analysis summary**

Development Stage

At the **Development Stage**, you'll meet separately with all your departments, working with them on their plans, and—ultimately—unifying their data, findings and tactics into a Unified Business Plan. This might include sessions, planning and final goals and tactics mapped out for:

- Sales and Marketing, including advertising

- Product Development

- Engineering and Research and Development

- Operations

- Logistics and Customer Services

- Financial and Accounting.

- Distillation Point: Unified Business Plan

Determination Stage

Most of this chapter focuses on this aspect of Strategic Tactical Planning, since this is unique to our approach—and it involves the ultimate in distillation. This involves taking all we know from the first two Distillations points—GAP Analysis and Unified Business Plan—and combining and distilling further into action dashboards. Not just a "master one-dashboard to rule them all" but a distilled dashboard for each department, each project with milestones, each executive. The rest of this chapter focuses on this vital method.

As team leader, or as CEO, you will love the fact that everyone on your core team has their own dashboard. Not only can they monitor themselves, you can monitor them. You can offer them assistance when they fall behind. Incentive to get them going. Extra resources. Compensation when they really knock it out of the park.

Nothing is more effective in managing a multi-team operation than this distilled, one-page dashboard for every core team member.

One Dashboard to Rule them All

In the Lord of the Rings, the quest revolves around destroying the one ring of power—"one ring to rule them all." In business, however, we seek that one ring—not as a matter of rulership, but as a driving force of the quest. In our case, the quest would be your visionary mission and your visionary strategy. In service of the vision are actionable tactics. To coordinate this quest, in L.I.F.T. terms, we recommend the one-page central L.I.F.T. dashboard—one dashboard to rule them all.

Having a central dashboard empowers the tactics, which serve the strategy, as defined in your goals. In other words, having all the important strategic goals and tactical goals and actions in one dashboard brings focus and amplifying power. Forget the long, windy business plan. By all means write one, but before you present to your stakeholders, distill, then distill further, then some more, until you have a one-page dashboard.

Focus. Clarity. Precision. The one-page business plan.

The first thing to know about the one-page business or operations plan is, it contains all the same information as a full business plan. The key points, goals, tactics are all there. You just eliminate the pretty, the wordy, and the unnecessary.

The second thing to know about the one-page business plan is—it is not an executive summary. It's a full action plan. An at-a-glance Game Plan containing all the needed plays, broken down into timed milestones. The coach doesn't flip out a manual and read the details, he flips over the clipboard with the game plan and after all the collective work of the team, everyone knows the background and uses the collective knowledge to precisely determine the next step on the board.

The third thing to know is—no cheating. To make your plan one-page does not mean you can use 3-point typefaces that requires a magnifying glass.

It's a discipline. Full 11- or 12-point typeface, one page. Say all that's important. In other words:

Be concise. Be precise. Be clear.

It's akin to, although more difficult, to the "rule of fives" for Presentations. (No, this rule of fives isn't a L.I.F.T. rule.) That rule laid down harsh rules for a successful presentation: no more than five words per line, five lines per slide. Say it that concisely, or you fail. There are good reasons for this rule. I've seen executives puzzle over the presentation for weeks to get their presentations sharpened to this level of focus.

Here, the discipline is similar. Focus. Clarity. Precision.

There are some tips, or questions you can ask yourself in the process of "trimming":

1. What are my goals, stated clearly and measurably?

2. What tactics can deliver on my goals?

3. What is the shortest possible way to express those tactics and goals?

4. What are the milestones?

5. What can I leave out?

Remember, you'll be a team working on this plan. You'll have opportunities to brainstorm solutions to tactical issues, to develop contingencies, and to implement. You'll miss some milestones but make it up in other ways.

All of this is why one-page works. If everyone is on the same page, they know that if a milestone is missed, they have to develop a remedial action or contingency action. If your plan, on the other hand, is fifty pages long, and has an exhaustive list of all contingencies possible, will you achieve any momentum in your plan? Move the constancies and parallel operations to their own plans. Overall operations may have one master plan, on one page. Logistics may have another one-page plan they develop to accomplish the milestones established in the operations plan. Customer service teams may have their own one-page plan with goals and milestones and their tactics needed to fulfill their part of the master over-all plan. The key point is, everything is precise, concise, and focused.

L.I.F.T. Out-take: One Thousand Words or Ten Thousand?

"A picture is worth ten-thousand words" is often cited as a Chinese Proverb—although it was never verified. Some more recent quotes, include:

- "One fact well understood by observation, and well guided development, is worth a thousand times more than a thousand words" - *The American Journal of Education*, 1858.[68]

- In 1862, Ivan S Turgenev wrote: "The drawing shows me at one glance what might be spread over ten pages in a book."

The eight key points of the one-page plan

Here's something that might surprise you: your one-page business plan must have the same eight points covered in the more-traditional multi-page plans:

1. Problem

2. Solution

3. Model

4. Target

5. Advantage

6. Team

7. Financial Summary

8. Funding Required.

In other words, everything an investor, manager or stakeholder on your team needs to know is there. At a glance. In one L.I.F.T. Dashboard.

I doubt the average reader of this book needs a breakdown of these eight points; they're part of every good business plan. In the event you need a quick review:

1. Problem

What problem does this plan attempt to solve, and any data that supports the problem?

2. Solution

In what ways does your product/service solve these problems?

3. Model

How exactly, precisely, concisely, will you make money? Highlight the key costs of production and selling and the price customers are expected to pay.

4. Target

Who is your customer? What do you know about them that is relevant to the mission (remembering, one-page limit!)?

Try to include TAM, SAM and SOM. Don't know what this means? No problem, but you'll need to keep these solidly in mind:

TAM—Total Addressable Market—everyone in the world who "could" buy your product (doesn't factor in conditions, just total scale.)

SAM—Serviceable Available Market—that portion of the market you can acquire with your tactics. For example, you decide to focus tactically on North America. That's your SAM, plus or minus other conditional variables.

SOM—Service Obtainable Market—the portion of SAM that you realistically can target with your particular offering.

Don't be wordy. Just state the facts, and footnote citations if required.

5. Advantage

This is your competitive advantage. You have one, right? If not, this should be part of your tactical one-page plan—how to attain a meaningful advantage. Remember the word meaningful. It's one thing to differentiate, but if no one cares, no one buys.

6. Team

Focus on your management and implementation teams. If you're writing an overall one-page business plan, you highlight key executives. If you're writing a project implementation plan, your implementation experts.

7. Financial Summary

All the critical things we covered in previous chapters—go back if you don't remember—although in concise form. This includes profit/ loss cash flow, balance sheet, sales forecasts. This is the most difficult section to make concise, so use a tabbed consistent format where possible.

8. Funding

Regardless of your plan, there's always a need for funds. What is the source and why is it needed? If an investor ever says to you, after reading one of your plans—"Great, but why do you need my money?"—then, you haven't been clear.

To review: **Focus, Clarity, Precision.**

The *L.I.F.T. Dashboard* in the next section is not only an "exercise," it makes a perfect one-page template.

L.I.F.T. exercise: L.I.F.T. Dashboard of Fives

In the age of information, it is easy to get overloaded by data, spreadsheets, presentations, business plans, budgets, evaluation tools, and reams of documents to describe a company and its market. One of the biggest productivity obstacles is too much paper.

I suggest you run through this exercise with your leadership team. The work that goes into distilling the data to these few important highlights is a good way to hone the skills of your team. I find that the act of cutting/distilling is one of the most creative processes you can adopt as a leader. "Please get to the point," should be a business mantra. One characteristic I look for in my leadership team members is the ability to embrace focus, clarity, and precision. Clarity and precision are characterized by concise presentation of ideas and plans.

In the spirit of "getting to the point," try out this dashboard template—you can download a version from the www.randydewey.com website—and really dig in an analyze-distill your true position. This exercise will force you to grapple with your weaknesses and vulnerabilities, which is essential to developing your ultimate strategic plan and respective financial budgets.

Once all the work is done, the most important and meaningful step is to distill and crystalize on a one-page dashboard—which can be readily updated—to track these powerful metrics, actions, responsibilities and governing values. The one-page dashboard puts everyone on the same, single, at-a-glance page. It makes presenting your ideas focused, clear and precise.

The LIFT dashboard format is simple, yet clear, and presents all the information your team needs to know in a one-page strategic framework: where they are going, what's important to the company, and how they are being measured as a group. It puts on one-page all the concepts and data points and personal accountabilities for everyone to be on the same page.

Structure of the L.I.F.T. Dashboard—More Fives!

The LIFT Dashboard can, and should, be filled in quickly. The eight points I mentioned above are here, distilled down into a simpler format that still contains the essence of the key points.

Section One is your **Five Core Values** which are the **5 Values** you and the team have crystallized from the exercise in Chapter One. It is paramount these values are on this page—even though you went through that exercise previously in chapter one—because it crystalizes the expectation and keeps it in a "live dashboard" for your teams' daily interaction.

Section Two is the **Charitable Efforts** you and the team have decided embodies your company and is the way you want to give back. (Refer more about this in Chapter 13.)

Section Three is your **3-year Target** numbers and where you are attempting to drive the business.

Section Four is the **Target** for this year, which are the most important metrics that track your company's financial performance, which is part of your budgeting process, but this is expanded in Chapter 8.

Section Five is the **Key "90-day" Performance Indicators**, as you breakdown your business and budget into four legs of a year. There are five key metrics, as we discussed in chapter 5 "The Five Essential Metrics", but we've included Adjust EBITDA, not because it's one of the essential five—simply because everyone always expects it. It is important that you review the numbers on a frequent basis, (informally weekly) formally quarterly, to decide if you are behind or ahead—you'll find the four quarters indicated on the template—so that you can dynamically adjust and learn in each period. You can plan how to make up a deficit or carry the surplus and surpass your target.

Section Six are the **Five Quarterly Priorities**—specific to whoever is acting on the plan, such as a specific key executive on your team. For example, if you're customizing this dashboard for a single executive, and you have accepted their business plan for their area, with their key deliverables and goals, then you would write these priorities on their next 90 day dashboard. Create a customized dashboard for each team and team-leader—anyone who has business goals and deliverables.

Section Seven are the **Key Customers** for this year. Use this to note actionable key customers. For example, if you are trying to reduce customer concentration, where a customer represents a large percentage of overall contribution to revenue, indicate their importance here.

Section 8 is arguably the most important—the **Top 20 Most Important Deliverables** in the first half of the year. (It's pointless to try to make this a list of five – detailed, precise deliverables are important.)

Here, in Section Eight, spend some time making sure you have what's needed. You will work on these lists for each key team leader—they'll each have at least 20. Then, it's a good idea to have a "master" one-page operations plan, where you'll take the 20 most important deliverables.

The 20 deliverables should be a distillation of all the things the entire executive team have agreed on that summarizes across all disciplines what everyone is doing and who is responsible to deliver this accomplishment.

Remember, although this is a one-page template, you should always feel free to append specific actionable data or details. For example, on your two key customers, you might append some notes. The point is to make sure your plan has information on all the important points. Be sure to label the appendix information, though, to make it clear the main plan is on one page.

Company Name			LIFT Dashboard

Core Values / Beliefs	Charitable Effort	Target (3 years)	Target (this year)
1)	What are we going to do that makes a difference?	Year _____	By December _____
		Revenue $_____	Revenue
		EBITDA $ _____	EBITDA Goal
		Gross Margin _____ %	Gross Margin
2)		FCF Margin _____ %	FCF Margin
	Key "90 Day" Performance Indicators		Current Ratio
	Revenue	Q1 / Q2 / Q3 / Q4	Quick Ratio
	Adjusted EBITDA	Q1 / Q2 / Q3 / Q4	Return on Assets
3)	Net Cash at close	Q1 / Q2 / Q3 / Q4	Operating Profit Margin
	Gross Margin	Q1 / Q2 / Q3 / Q4	Return on Equity
	OPEX Spend	Q1 / Q2 / Q3 / Q4	Fixed Assets/net worth
4)	Stress Test Goal	Q1 / Q2 / Q3 / Q4	Debt to Equity
	Quarterly Priorities for Key Executive/Leader		Asset Turnover
	Executive Name:	John D	Inventory Turnover
	Top 5 Agreed Priorities for the next 90 Days		Days Sales Turnover
5)	1)		Return on Inv Capital
	2)		Stress Test Goal
	3)		Key Customers for this year
	4)		1)
	5)		2)

Top 20 Most Important Deliverables in H1			
Key Accomplishment		Executive Assigned	Expected Date Absolute Deadline
1)			
2)			
3)			
4)			
5)			
6)			
7)			
8)			
9)			
10			
11)			
12)			
13)			
14)			
15)			
16)			
17)			
18)			
19)			
20)			

Reflections from the Conqueror

Mehmed II honed his "conqueror" leader skills in small skirmishes and territorial battles, leading up to the Fall of Constantinople.

An early test for Mehmed was an invasion attempt by John Hunyadi and the Hungarians. Mehmed's father, Murad II, assisted his young son with this campaign. His father demonstrated the strategy of "overwhelming response"—sending crushing military force that literally flattened the invaders. It also resulted in an end to a 20-year schism.

Mehmed also learned valuable lessons from his father on how to hit your enemy's vulnerable points when the Hungarians crossed the Danube river. He met them in Varna, a tactically advantageous topography in east Bulgaria. He focused on killing their leader.

These years in skirmishes and defence prepared Mehmed for his ultimate goal—to conquer Constantinople. Mehmed learned the importance of detailed strategies. He learned that in battle, decisions must be quick, and commands must be concise.

Mehmed did not rush his attempt to breach the famous Theodosian walls of the city. He carefully prepared and planned, in the muddy field of battle. He brought together military leaders with ideas. They developed innovative naval strategies such as the use of a great cast iron chain to help them contain the port. In the words of Alexander the Great, "There is nothing impossible to him who will try."

Mehmed II knew he needed to have a thoughtful tactical strategy, immense determination, inspired troops, and tight focus.

Why this is so important in business

Strategic planning is a purposeful and methodical effort to produce foundational truths and actions that shape the course of one's future.

It is essential to *paint the picture* of the destination, determine your current position and chart the course to arrive at that place. As always, every journey has challenges you didn't anticipate but the more you understand the destination, your strengths and weaknesses and raw capabilities as an organization the better prepared you are to course correct and move with the changing tides. We must strategically prepare and drive forward with boldness and determination.

Strategy and execution to a company are like air and blood to a body, they flow through every member of the body and without either you cannot survive. Although they feel complex, they can easily be defined and clearly captured for everyone's understanding.

12

L.I.F.T. PERSONAL POWER: FORTUNE FAVORS THE BOLD

Bold Leadership is essential in a world full of uncertainties. Failure is not an option and the tone must be set at the top—in psychology we call this the "dynamic transference." To be a leader that your team is willing to follow you must convey traits they admire: I call this the Brave Heart.

"I am not afraid of an army of lions led by a sheep; I am afraid of an army of sheep led by a lion".
Alexander the Great.

In this chapter

- Why the Brave Heart is indispensable – and how courage can be developed as an indispensable skill.

- Using the "Power of Transference" to create a team of "eager followers."

- Developing the Brave Heart: exploit your strengths, remedy your weaknesses

- Set the bar high and go for "all or nothing"

- Never admit defeat – there's never a good time to surrender

Important Take-away

- "Leaders, quite rightly, are the heroes of the corporate epic (a few leader-villains notwithstanding). They motivate us to go places that we would never otherwise go. They are needed both to change organizations and to produce results. In any business climate, good leadership is perhaps the most important competitive advantage a company can have."—*Harvard Business Review* quote, Michael Maccoby

Reflections from The Conqueror

- The executive "conqueror" leader's mantra should be "Fortune favours the bold"—from the Latin proverb *audentes Fortuna iuvat*. These three words appear as the motto on numerous countries, armed forces, or organizational logos for a reason: you cannot prevail, if you are afraid to fight.

The Values of L.I.F.T.

The Brave Heart—boldness—goes to the heart of all aspects of L.I.F.T.

Lead: Leaders must have followers to be effective. To have followers, you have to demonstrate admirable traits—such as boldness, honesty, loyalty—to employ the proven method of "dynamic transference."

Inspire: These same traits that bond you to your team are proven to increase productivity in your followers. Your inspirational example is more than just an aspirational template of behavior.

Focus: What characterizes a focused leader who can inspire results from a team? Bold, incisive, gutsy leadership. For a team to focus, you have to remove all doubts.

Transform: Transforming through transference—in the same way parents transfer their wisdom, discipline, morals and compassion to their children, you, the leader, transfers the transformative power of your conduct to your action team.

Leaders are not brave, insightful, and tenacious for the sake of being brave, insightful and tenacious. Although we may not calculate it in this way, the truth is this: we are brave, insightful and tenacious—with some other hopefully admirable traits—because we have to inspire followers. What is the value of great leadership, if no one follows? What's the point of great followers, if the leader is mired in doubts and fears?

In psychology, the "follow the leader" phenomenon is known as "dynamic transference"—a term invented by Freud. In business we define it differently, but the essence remains. What Freud learned is that people "transfer" past experiences on to their present and future situations. The very Freudian example—this is the "reason" that so many of us choose spouses similar to our parents.

Developing the Brave Heart

The point is, similar principles apply to business teams. I call it the developing the Brave Heart, after the movie of the same name. We tend to shape our expectations of our leaders from our past experience with other leaders. Who do we follow? We follow the leaders with the **Brave Heart**—not just boldness, but compassion, cause, courage, the three "c's" of the Brave Heart.

Today, especially, it is more and more difficult to earn followers. Whether in business, politics, charitable fundraising or any other "cause" the cynicism of potential team-members is the first obstacle. Psychology tells us that we follow for many reasons, grouped under two types of motivators: rational and irrational. Politicians, for example, are masters at stirring up the irrational motivators. In business, we tend to focus on the more rational triggers.

Before we dive into the importance of bravery, boldness and tenacity—and ultimately dig into dynamic transference—I'll illustrate with an early case study. It was this situation that shaped my future thinking as a leader. I call it "last man standing."

Real-life L.I.F.T Values Case Study—"Last man standing around the boardroom table."

In the 1990s I was a fast corporate-ladder climber. I received an offer to take on a leadership role of a company. The only problem was—they were two months out from filing Chapter 11. They must have sensed my youthful courage, since the company was very up front about their situation. They asked me to join—but made it clear I would have to accept the risk.

Why did I agree? Most executives would blanch at the peril. On one hand it was a chance to shine—to turn around a company on the brink. On the other, potential oblivion (or at least a negative entry on the resumé.)

I decided to have faith in my abilities—that I could indeed turn the situation. It was worth the risk; if successful, it moved me into a senior operational role in a key industry. Although I knew pending Chapter 11 was high risk, I also knew it would be a learning experience—leading in a high-pressure crisis.

All leaders have to be willing to face crisis—it's part of the job. Any leader not willing to assume risk or deal with catastrophe is not suited to the role.

With full understanding of the risks, I jumped into the job aggressively. I pushed hard, and in six weeks we developed our strategic plan. I worked closely with the president and the entire team—all new to me. In record time, for a plan of this scope, it was complete—and every member contributed whole-heartedly. We made sure the tactical details were precise, actionable, and clear.

The best way to describe the ride is—standing up on a roller coaster at full speed. Many executives would have dreaded this scenario. I had walked into it willingly. To me, it was an amazing experience.

As planned, over the next four weeks, the company filed Chapter 11. A private equity group provided the DIP (Debtor in Possession) financing, and our owners gave us the green light to implement our plan with the stipulation that we had 18 months to complete all the work and swing the financial performance from -$27M EBITDA to positive profitability.

As the saying goes, the die was cast, for both the company, and my future.

The outrageous walkout

What I hadn't prepared for, was the outrageous walkout of every single member of the executive strategy team. Every single executive leader left, starting with the President, and right down through the leadership—"leaving to pursue other opportunities." Courage in the face of the reality of Chapter 11 had failed the team.

I was the last man standing around the board room table. Literally.

I was flabbergasted.

The owners were in a panic and they flew in from New York. They asked me—the "rescue executive" they had only hired weeks ago—to step into the lead role, defacto President so to speak, keep the wheels on and do my best to keep the strategy moving forward. They promised to replace the members of the leadership team.

Did my courage wane? Did I lose hope? It would be glib to say, no, I charged on without reservation. The truth is, we all have these moments when fear rises. I've always lived by the proverb "Fortune favours the bold"—from the Latin proverb "*audentes Fortuna iuvat*"

In modern times, Nelson Mandela said it perfectly:

"I learned that courage was not the absence of fear, but the triumph over it. The brave man is not he who does not feel afraid, but he who conquers his fear."—Nelson Mandela

---

I viewed this as my moment to conquer fear—and to seize a truly great opportunity to be the defacto President—remembering that "fortune favours the bold".

I erupted into action—erupt is the best way to describe it—energized by the challenge. I executed—with precision—every detail on the strategic plan. I communicated clearly with New York and completely restructured the entire company. The one thing you must know, as leader, is not only do you need bravery, you need fortitude. There will be countless sleepless nights on the road to victory. If you aren't willing to march the road, your only course is the one charted by the executives who left the company.

One-by-one, we hired people to replace those we lost. Interestingly, the board did not recruit a new President. Ultimately, I became that leader.

In 18 months, we emerged from bankruptcy, moved all the costs out of the business and were on a path to make over $30M that following 12 months. We sold the company for 9 figures the following year.

I was asked by the Private Equity owners to move to another troubled company and that began a 15-year run of turning around companies in difficulty to success. It wasn't a career choice, but it was the path of courage, and it was one of the most exciting periods of my career. The experience I gained was priceless. It was in this period that the principles and methodologies of **L**ead, **I**nspire, **F**ocus and **T**ransform were born.

Leaders must be the example

I learned one very big lesson, too, out of this amazingly turbulent time—you, as leader must embrace that bold tenacious spirit of the Conqueror. You must set the example to your leadership team, leading the charge personally, to show that we can, and will prevail.

"Example is not the main thing in influencing others, it's the only thing."
Albert Schweitzer

Albert Schweitzer coined it perfectly, bold leaders set the example that others will follow. If every single leader had "deserted the sinking ship" in my case study, including myself, it's likely the ship would have sunk. As long as one leader is willing to stand up and start bailing, everyone will join in.

The view from top, I have learned, is a precarious, adrenalin-producing view. I think one skill leaders should aspire to is skydiving. To jump from a plane, facing your fears—it's not different from being a leader in a company.

For me, if I had to choose one characteristic of the L.I.F.T. Leader—even though I know there are many important qualities—the one distinguishing factor I look for in my leadership team is boldness. Courage. Not only does Fortune favor the bold, I do as well.

It was this courage and persistence in those 15 turbulent years that empowered my team to stand with me to overcome our adversities and guide the ship to crest the waves, endure the storm, and, ultimately, unfurl the sails—and sales—in triumph.

Military examples work

And this is why I persist in quoting ancient conquerors such as Mehmed and Alexander the Great. Think of Alexander the Great. He took the throne at 20 and lived to 32 years of age (only 12 years as a Conqueror), yet in that time he built the largest empire in the ancient world—rampaging through history in his march across western Asia and northeast Africa. Yes, he was a genius, but above all, he was brave. (Of course, it helped that he had great mentors and teachers, including Aristotle.)

Today, the brave Conquerors are in the business world. Steve Jobs had the same guts and youthful vigour as Alexander the Great—building an unprecedented empire known as Apple.

Top of mind business conquerors, who certainly enshrine the idea "Fortune favours the bold"—regardless of whether we like them or not—not only built empires, they changed the world as we know it:

- Henry Ford

- Jeff Bezos

- Bill Gates

- Elon Musk

- Warren Buffet

- John D. Rockefeller (America's first billionaire)

- P.T. Barnum

- Andrew Carnegie.

Did these leaders really embrace the values of courage and other characteristics of the leader, such as "distillation" teambuilding, simplicity and tenacity? You don't have to hunt long to find quotes attributed to many of them:

P.T. Barnum

"Fortune always favors the brave, and never helps a man who does not help himself."

John D. Rockerfeller
"Singleness of purpose is one of the chief essentials for success in life, no matter what may be one's aim."

Steve Jobs
"That's been one of my mantras—focus and simplicity. Simple can be harder than complex; you have to work hard to get your thinking clean to make it simple."

Henry Ford
"Coming together is a beginning; keeping together is progress; working together is success."

Andrew Carnegie
"People who are unable to motivate themselves must be content with mediocrity, no matter how impressive their other talents."

Sakichi Toyoda
"Before you say you can't do something, try it."

Being a super-hero

If you ask a six-year-old what they want to be when they grow up, many will answer "I want to be a superhero, or a firefighter." Why? Superheroes and firefighters idealistically characterize both bravery, and compassion—two characteristics of leaders.

If you ask the same question of college students, you'd probably hear "entrepreneur, CEO, business leader"—and if you asked them to characterize that leader they'd likely say something like "a bold leader, filled with heartfelt compassion for his or her employees."

Who are the super-heroes in real life? The larger-than-life business leaders tend to be a top-of-mind answer.

To be a growth leader you need to adopt some of that super-hero persona.

What are the characteristics of a great leader? Here, I'll quote retired four-star general, and Commander of U.S. and NATO Coalition Forces in Afghanistan, General Stanley McChrystal: "People need to be led, not directed. They need to follow an inspirational, charismatic, *courageous* leader."

Whichever historical or living example of leadership you choose to emulate, you almost certainly aligned with an iconic character who exemplified boldness and compassion.

Brave Heart defines the great leader— and how courage can be learned

The Brave Heart of a leader is more than just a heart of courage. The three c's of the Brave Heart, at least in my experience, are: compassion, cause, and courage. We've discussed compassion and ethics and cause at length. What about courage. You're either brave or you're not, right? What if you're a quivering mess, who quakes at any conflict or obstacle? If fearlessness does not come naturally, remember that courage is a skill. It's also a matter of life or death. If you are unable to embrace courage, you cannot undertake heroic deeds—and make no mistake, leaders have to be heroes. Imagine a firefighter who was afraid to enter the blaze to save the family. Without doubt, that firefighter feels fear. But he learns to overcome natural fears. Courage is empowering—it overcomes fears. It doesn't replace them. That firefighter charges into the flames empowered by courage.

Where does the firefighter learn courage? Through skills. He or she learns how to save lives, how to put out fires, where to cut the roof, where to place the ladder, how to avoid the smoke. He practices endlessly in drills. This is training. Firefighter training is among the most difficult and dangerous career training paths available.

Corporate leadership is no less dangerous, fraught with risk and peril and unexpected hotspots. Corporate leaders, no less than firefighters, must train in courage. Make no mistake, when you fall behind in your quarter, panic sets in. When you face an economic downturn, it feels no less dangerous than facing the burning house. We train for the worst, hope for the best. I'll show you some of the ways you can prepare in this chapter. In the end though, there will come that moment when you, alone, must face your own crisis. You, as leader, must bring your team of warriors through it.

What does it take? The Brave Heart.

Having the Brave Heart

I really spark with the phrase "Brave Heart." That's exactly what defines a great leader. In the epic historical film, *Braveheart*, the icon of courageous leader is exemplified. The 1996 Oscar winner for Best Picture engaged audiences with a perfectly crafted and inspiring leader archetype. Audiences left theatres shell-shocked but inspired by the real-life leadership example of William Wallace of Scotland. The movie was so electrifying, we felt as if we had been transported back to 13th century Scotland. We almost felt we were marching along valiantly into battle with him.

Why did we care. Most of us probably didn't even know the story of William Wallace. Many of us have low interest in Scotland's history. The draw of the film was the perfect portrayal of the bold, genuine, courageous leader—Wallace. It didn't matter that we knew nothing of Scotland's history. We responded to the leader—a leader in an apparently hopeless cause, who stirred up his people with purpose and passion.

While the film was an embellished account of the farmer-turned-warrior, Wallace's character was real, as were the battles. And those rag-tag followers? In the movie they are depicted as zealous followers of the hero of the story – so much so that they risked their lives for him—and for their freedom. Was that movie artifice? Clearly it was, yet the emotions generated were very real. Why would they put their lives at stake to march against the Royal Army of tyrannical King Edward I of England? Because

Wallace, the leader, found a way to connect with them emotionally and personally. He was one of them. He fought with them. He would die with them. He had no formal training, just a heart filled with purpose, boldness, and an ability to connect people to view his cause and the vision of success.

Reaching farther back in time to 336 B.C., we see another remarkable leader; Alexander the Great, ascended to the throne at age 20. Although he would die only a decade or so later, in that time, he conquered much of the known world. Though a king, he was a humble, inspiring, determined, risk-taking leader. He led his armies to conquer more of the world than anyone else before him. Although we can't know, we can surmise from the reports and histories that his main draw was a charismatic and compassionate leadership style that attracted thousands to fight with and for him. He led well—and inspired many. By remaining precision-focused on his tasks ahead, he and his men transformed the ancient world.

His small army defeated the mighty Persian Empire, which had been an age-old enemy of Greece. By the time Alexander turned 30, he ruled 50 million people – or about one-third of the known world's population. His empire spanned 3,000 miles—an extraordinary feat—considering this was the era before modern weapons. The men traveled on foot, or if they were lucky, they rode atop an elephant. Like Wallace, Alexander the Great fought alongside his brave warriors.

The defining characteristic of all great leaders—from Alexander the Great to Wallace to Henry Ford—is boldness and bravery.

How tenacity is the equal partner to bravery – how to create the habit

Another inspiring and courageous hero-leader was General George Washington who faced his own herculean task: winning against the British Empire. Washington was tenacious, and certainly brave. Like all great commanders, he was willing to march with his troops. The British Empire had the best trained army and navy on the planet at that time.

Washington's troops were volunteers, poorly fed, ragtag—not career soldiers. Washington didn't sit back in the command encampment and send battle commands to the troops. He marched with them. The sight of him on his horse, in the midst of the battlefield, not flinching even against canon fire, inspired his troops.

Valley Forge—and courage

It was December 23, 1776, at Valley Forge. Washington's men were malnourished and barefoot. Some used hats as shoes and others wrapped rags around their feet. Great tactics and strategy alone cannot win the battle—not without grit. Washington knew the British soldiers camped at Trenton, NJ—and would not be expecting an attack. As a strategist and tactical genius, he knew he must attack when no one expected it—on Christmas eve. During a blizzard, when the enemy would be huddled around fires, shivering.

Tactics are one thing, but to lead a virtually barefooted army in a dangerous crossing of the icy Delaware River was near madness. It was their chance, and he knew it. He even convinced his poor, shivering commanders. But no commander can face these decisions, life and death decisions, without pure courage. His men would not cross alone.

"Sir, the River is Half Frozen"

To any ordinary person, the orders would sound like a death march. Yet, his troops knew him. He had fought alongside them, in the trenches, on the ground, in the mud. They knew he wasn't going to ask them to do something he wasn't prepared to do; he was just as invested as they were.

While their victory may not seem like a particularly significant triumph, from a strategic point of view, Washington's initiative raised the spirits of the American colonists. Previously, the British seemed invulnerable. Now, men who previously feared the enemy knew they could prevail. They knew their general was with them in battle, sharing the risk. They knew he was an inspired leader. In the following five years, these men morphed into a fighting force that unseated a superpower.

Your own "George Washington" moment

Big or small, if you are a business leader, you will have your own "George Washington" moments—where you must draw on courage, overcoming your fears, going beyond your expectations. I gave the example of one of my "George Washington" moments in the chapter case study. My "frozen river crossing" moment was accepting a job at a company facing Chapter 11. Talk about sink or swim! In hindsight, I sometimes wonder where that courage came from. The mother of courage, your courage, George Washington's courage—is necessity. To get ahead requires risk. "Crossing the Delaware" in my case, was joining a Chapter 11 company. We find the courage when we need it.

When you face one of your George Washington moments—if you are a business leader, you will, trust me—you will find that courage, just as George Washington did. If you don't, you will perish in the icy waters. Courage is required, not optional. That doesn't mean you won't be afraid; but you will find that courage. Sink or swim. And, once the decision is made, like the great general, you will stand shoulder-to-shoulder with your team to fight for your vital goals—sloshing through the metaphorical icy Delaware.

A word of "Braveheart" advice

In life and leadership, the only way to gain a tenacious and brave heart is to face your adversities head on. Regardless of your fears. Regardless of the nay-sayers and down players and their empty words full of fear. If you've researched the problem, analyzed the strengths, weaknesses, opportunities and threats, come to a strategy and specific tactics that can win the battle—then charge, shoulder to shoulder with your troops.

Another word of "Braveheart" advice. Neither William Wallace, nor George Washington, nor Stephen Jobs, nor Henry Ford won every battle. They lost more than they won. One aspect of courage is determination and faith. Faith in your troops (team.) Faith in your strategies and tactics. Once a decision is made, have faith. If you lose one battle, analyze why, learn the lessons, and plan the next skirmish.

Create the life habit of fighting in the metaphorical trenches. In business, work with your teams, roll up your sleeves, pull the all-nighters in the virtual trenches, listen to your team's suggestions, provide guidance and resources—and together you march to victory.

Above all—as leader—demonstrate tenacity and bravery, even if you're shivering, sweating and wailing inside. Do you really think William Wallace and George Washington had no fear? They certainly had their doubts and fears. But outwardly they remain steadfast and courageous. So must you.

Bravery in the C-Suite: it's also life or death

Let's pivot now to the C-Suite. You may think that we modern-day executives don't face life and death decisions. We will never come close to sloshing through the icy Delaware river, right? Wrong. Your decisions in the C-Suite determine the lives of your team: their careers, families, well-being, your investor's money, the economic consequences. Michael Macoby, in Harvard Business Review[69], put it this way:

> *"Leaders, quite rightly, are the heroes of the corporate epic (a few leader-villains notwithstanding.) They motivate us to go places we would not otherwise go. They are needed both to change organizations and to produce results. In any business climate, good leadership is perhaps the most important competitive advantage a company can have."*

We may not fight with swords or muskets, but we face a fight every day in the C-Suite. The enemy might be competitors—and, like Washington we face natural obstacles, economic factors rather than rivers—but the stakes are high. If you can't deliver, you can't provide a livelihood for your team. It's literally life or death for your team.

In my case study, why did that Private Equity firm of the company facing Chapter 11 back me as leader—without experience as a President—to lead a half-billion dollar-revenue company in its worst hour? Was it desperation?

No. It was more heroic than that. They saw this lone executive, only hired weeks ago—the sole leader courageous enough to not cut and run when the going got tough. This isn't a play for ego on my part.

They saw courage. People follow courageous people. No one follows the coward.

Businesses will constantly face daily, weekly, monthly and annual skirmishes, struggles, battles. Business is competitive. Our competitors are no less ruthless than enemies on a battlefield. Since, in business, conflict is never far off, we come to rely—we need to rely—on leaders with courage. Humans have real psychological need, and real leaders can connect with them on many of these levels.

We, as leaders, must recognize our strengths, and our weaknesses. Even if we're afraid, we push through.

Natural versus learned strengths

Before you throw up your hands, convinced I've lost it, try this little exercise. Inventory your strengths. Your natural capacities. Beside them, list your weaknesses. Now go back through the weaknesses and write down all the ways you can train to overcome it. Something like this:

Strengths	Weaknesses	Remedy
Details-oriented		
	Trouble communicating	Write-out all plans as presentations and rehearse presenting your ideas
Written planning		
	Oral presentations (fear)	Try speech skills seminars?
Willing to take risks	Not good at analyzing risks	For important projects enlist skilled analysts

And so on.

The point is simply that we all have strengths and natural capacities—usually different ones from other team members. Combine your various skills, supplementing areas where you are weak with people who exemplify what you're missing. There's no such thing as the perfect leader—but there can be the perfect team.

The vast majority of people never take the time to understand their strengths and weaknesses.

In this chapter, I hope to demonstrate through a couple of exercises, how you can develop a personal plan of action—to continue "remedying" those areas you identified as weaknesses. The other thing to remember is that previously trained skills can be lost with lack of use.

The *L.I.F.T. Exercise: Measuring your leadership and bravery quotient* will help you understand your strengths and weaknesses as a leader and provide insight into how you exploit those innate strengths—and how to remedy your weaknesses.

Courage and creativity: the partnership of heroes

What distinguishes the courageous leader from the irresolute wannabe? Creativity. Creativity is certainly part of the language of great strategists and tacticians, but it's not found in the dictionary definition of "courage." This is despite a history of great military leaders throughout history exemplifying creative solutions:

- Washington, daring to cross the uncrossable river to surprise attack the British.

- Plucky Admiral Nelson taking on a massive fleet with never-before-tried tactics—cutting the massive French naval line into three parts. (Yes, he died a courageous man at Trafalgar, but they prevailed.)

- Mehmed—with his astonishingly creative concept hauling his ships over a hill to bypass the chain barrier of Constantinople's port. Achievement is a creative process. It's no secret that personal gurus such as Anthony Robbins ask you to "visualize" success to achieve it. (That's overly simplified. I'm just highlighting the creative aspect of bravery.)

- The Allies in World War II using master illusionist Jasper Maskelyne to use mirrors, lights and reflectors to hide the Suez Canal from bombardment.

- Julius Caesar's "reverse wall"—where he built walls in front and behind the enemy to prevent two larger forces from joining. Although out-numbered 4-to1 through this creative tactic, and bravery, Caesar prevailed.

- WWII's Ghost Army. And who thought of the brilliant "Ghost Army" of make-up artists, actors, sound technicians and photographers who created a phantom army to confuse the German' Armies with inflatable tanks and other decoys.

- Here's one that takes amazing courage: Wen Ping (in China) opened the gates to the fortress—using reverse Trojan Horse psychology. He bravely double bluffed the enemy, who thought that inside the gates was an ambush. Not daring to risk the ambush, the enemy retreated. Imagine the courage and creativity of this ancient leader.

There are countless other examples. This is why I encourage business leaders to study military history in their "spare time."

Creativity is often spawned in the face of a great challenge. What distinguishes the creative courageous leader? Visualization. Wen Ping visualized a scenario where open gates would trick the enemy. Nelson visualized a way to cut the French flagship off from the rest of the fleet by daring to break his line-of-battle into three. I don't know who came up with the "Ghost Army" in WWII, but it exemplifies both courage and creativity (imagine you are the unnamed soldier who's responsibility is to guard a balloon tank—how brave is that?)—and some brilliant mind had to visualize it first.

Your L.I.F.T. Super Weapon: Visualization

Courageous leaders are distinguished by their ability to visualize success. Not just what it looks like, but how to achieve it. How do you visualize winning "against all odds" if you have no personal courage? You can't. Your visualization vocabulary wouldn't include ideas like "inflatable tanks" and "open gates." Instead, you'd visualize "slamming the gates closed" as your best option.

Impossible, is the secret to creativity. Mehmed engineered the impossible win by using "crazy wisdom"—an insight that led to literally carrying massive ships over terrain even soldiers hesitated to climb. Washington was told to his face, "Sir, the River is Half Frozen" and that it was impossible. He visualized achieving the impossible and won.

In other words, to visualize success—whether as an athlete in the last mile of a marathon, or a business leader facing a catastrophic natural disaster, or a military leader facing overwhelming odds—requires courage. A coward can't visualize prevailing against an army four times the size. On the other hand, history is full of brave leaders, who lost the battle. To win, you still need to embrace creative visualization to see how you can use your bravery to win. What does victory look like?

Think of the Olympic athlete—they have to visualize breaking through, pushing that last mile even if it puts him or them in the hospital. They see themselves winning. Visualization is the super-weapon of all great L.I.F.T. Leaders. Or the mountain climber, who takes on K2, despite the weather system moving in.

The price of visualizing the win and courage is sometimes failure—but the cost of not visualizing and not having courage is almost certainly defeat.

Once we have our vision, it's "all or nothing." Imagine the Chinese leader Wen Ping, suddenly changing his mind and slamming the gates closed. Immediately, the enemy would understand the subterfuge and attack. The day would be lost.

We must set an "all or nothing" bar once we have our vision. Changing direction in mid-stream always leads to defeat. Do you think Nelson would have triumphed at Trafalgar if he abruptly changed his mind and tried to reform the single line of battle? History would have changed.

Here's vision: George Washington had a clear vision—move the British Empire off our land at any or all cost.

The vision in business is no less high stakes. We, like Washington, must weigh the options with courage, fearlessly find the "unexpected" solution, set our vision, then charge.

There's never a good time to surrender

Regardless of your mission, you will face obstacles: competitors, lack of financing or resources, economic factors, or new technologies. The L.I.F.T. Leader "never surrenders" in the face of any adversity. This isn't a novel idea, in fact it's a famous proverb: "If you're not part of the solution, you're part of the problem." To which I'd add the unattributed saying:

"Impossible only means you haven't found the solution yet."

If you surrender, you won't have the opportunity to find that solution. Clearly, courage, along with creativity can lead to a solution. Surrender only leads to defeat. One saying I do not believe in is "When you find no solution to a problem, it's probably not a problem to be solved but rather a truth to be accepted." In my experience, this is never true. You may be wrong, or you may be misguided, but there is always a solution if you persist.

External problems are no different

L.I.F.T. Leadership is guided by this firm belief that there is always a solution, and there is never a good reason to surrender. External disasters are no different. They are still obstacles that have solutions.

If we rewind the past century, we see clearly how world events rocked the business world. Wars have been fought on several continents. More than once, financial meltdowns have sent global shockwaves through all the major stock markets, chiseling away profits and drying up revenue streams. Add political drama and the fear of contagious diseases, and it's a wonder that businesses can survive at all.

It isn't something you can predict—but in flash you're in the middle of that perfect storm.

COVID-19 caught the business world by surprise in early 2020; without a warning it brought seemingly insurmountable obstacles to every businesses plan. Do we lose our vision?

No—in fact, these battles distinguish and separate the true leaders.

"Be decisive in times of crisis. Be nimble. Find truth in trials and lessons in mistakes" Howard Schultz

---

L.I.F.T. Exercise: Measuring your individual leadership and bravery quotient

Are you ready to face every problem, without surrender? Do you consider yourself courageous? Do you panic in emergency situations, or excel?

Explore your own courage/creativity balance by auditing your own Leadership Strengths and Weaknesses.

This exercise has 10 key individual leadership characteristics. Rank yourself in the context of the descriptions below on a scale of 0-10. Don't expect to be a perfect 10 on most or all of these. Even the great leaders of history would not have scored a ten, including Washington, Alexander the Great, or Mehmed. The goal is to honestly inventory your strengths/ weaknesses in the context of courage and bravery; then to either remedy or recognize your weaknesses and exploit your strengths. Be as honest as you can with yourself—for example, when answer "how does your team feel..." Stop and think about it. Don't imagine the best out of pride or ego. You can't "fix" your weaknesses if you don't recognize them.

This survey is not entirely about courage. It seeks to inventory your trust and faith in your team—and their faith in you. After all, how can solve problems without the confidence of your team.

Circle the most appropriate

1 **How does your team view your degree of trust in them?** In other words, not: does your team trust you? The question is do they believe **you** trust them? Be brutal with yourself. Do they see you as a "hovering helicopter" monitoring everything they do? Do they understand that once you delegate, you walk away and trust them to complete the task?

Micromanager   Helicopter   Delegator

0--1--2--3--4--5--6--7--8--9--10

2 **What is your actual degree of trust in your team?** Do you constantly hover, or ask them to check in. Are you available around the clock, indicating you don't trust your team's judgment? Do you trust your team to come up with solutions once you assign them to work on a problem?

24/7 available   Often there   Full Autonomy

0--1--2--3--4--5--6--7--8--9--10

3 **Are you an Authentic leader with a humble, yet genuine and empathetic manner?** Be honest with yourself here. You might be courageous, but does that translate into arrogance? Remember, courageous heroes are almost always defined by authenticity and convictions.

Autocratic/Unpredictable   Authentic/Genuine

0--1--2--3--4--5--6--7--8--9--10

4 **Are you approachable and accountable to your people?** Mysterious leaders in corner offices, who convey an atmosphere of untouchability—and are rarely heroes. Courage is exemplified through openness, transparency, and accountability and willingness to expose your responsibilities to the broader stakeholders.

Mysterious/Inaccessible   Open/Available

0--1--2--3--4--5--6--7--8--9--10

5 **Are you clear on the expectations and objectives?** Heroes and triumphant leaders are always clear on vision, strategy and tactics—and communicating goals, deliverables and milestones. Do you play the blame game? Do your people know what they should do? Are they clear on what success is, and understanding of the importance of their responsibilities?

Murky/Disjointed   Clear/Unified

0--1--2--3--4--5--6--7--8--9--10

6 **Do you create an atmosphere of continuous personal development both for you and the people?** Heroes lead heroic troops. Leaders always look for other leaders in their team. Leaders encourage development and training.

Never   Somewhat   Always

0--1--2--3--4--5--6--7--8--9--10

7 **Do you view your relationship with your work colleagues as a priority? Or are you all business?** We literally spend more time with our work colleagues than with some members of our family. Ask yourself honestly, do you have time for your team, or is it an annoyance? Do you make a "huge effort" to engage with your team?

I'm Too Busy   Yes/No   Huge Effort

0--1--2--3--4--5--6--7--8--9--10

8 **Are your words and actions consistent?** Do you find you have to explain yourself, over and over? Do your teams and stakeholders tell you that you're not consistent? Is your persona at work an honest one?

Inconsistent   Mediocre   Pure Harmony

0--1--2--3--4--5--6--7--8--9--10

9 **Do you feel confident in your vision—and your ability to achieve the goal? Do you inspire others?** There's a difference between having faith in your actions, strategies and action, and conveying that courage outwardly. Do you genuinely believe? Do your teams believe you when you give them goals?

Struggle with it   To some degree   Totally

0--1--2--3--4--5--6--7--8--9--10

10 **Do you take team input and recommendations? Are you decisive? Do you listen and adjust the course readily?** Putting aside right and wrong solutions, how decisive are you? Confident-and-humble is more important than confident-but-arrogant. Are you brave and humble enough to admit you got something wrong and make the change? The courageous leader just rise above the need to be right.

Too autocratic   Waffle a lot   Decisive

0--1--2--3--4--5--6--7--8--9--10

TOTAL SCORE

The most important part of this exercise is not the total score but the process of honest reflection itself. It may seem like few of these questions related to courage—although clearly, they focused on leadership. In fact, all ten of these areas are factors in how your team views you as a leader.

Take a moment and write down the things that struck you for each question—and what you plan to do about improving in that area.

1 _____

2 _____

3 _____

4 _____

5 _____

6 _____

7 _____

8 _____

9 _____

10 _____

Reflections from the Conqueror

Mehmed the Conqueror's bravery is unquestioned. In history, many of his tactics were considered "crazy" in his day—and took courage. Convincing his army and engineers to hall massive ships over the hills to the harbour is one famous example. Would his army have followed if they didn't believe in their leader? Perhaps, under penalty of death, but clearly, the combined leadership displayed in historical accounts, portrayed him as a leader his army would follow into death.

Where did he excel? Not all of the strategies were his own. He was willing to listen to his empowered team-members. He listened to the concept of the "super canons". He sought the opinions of engineers, not just military experts. He excelled at connecting with his people.

One factor in charisma is courage. Another is a willingness to listen. Equally, the leader must either be creative enough to develop solutions—or trust his team to find those solutions.

It was for all of these reasons that Mehmed's people followed him—and it is the reason I've used him as my metaphorical example in L.I.F.T.

Mehmed listened—to his mother, his vicars, his generals, engineers—and, he fostered relationships with people at all levels.

As with all great leaders, he had mentors. Notably, he learned post-humously at the feet of Alexander the Great. He learned humbleness at a very young age, as the son of a slave in the royal palace.

Why did Mehmed succeed to his throne, despite all the disadvantages? Mehmed connected with his people in ways most kings in his time did not.

For example, his opponent, Emperor Constantine XI, rejected Urban's concept of a great cannon—and how they could decisively win the battle. Constantine dismissed Urban, ignored the advice of others. He even hired a mercenary, Giustiniani.

Mehmed, his opposite number, listened to Urban—giving the go ahead for the mighty canons. It was those great cannons that finally breached the impenetrable walls and pushed the Roman Empire out of existence.

Mehmed had the courage to embrace new ideas. He encouraged new ideas and solutions.

The Top Ten Attributes of L.I.F.T. Leaders

"Fortune favors the bold" should be the "mantra" of all business leaders. In addition to courage itself, there are other traits, related to bold-ness, featured in this chapter's L.I.F.T exercise.

It's worth reviewing the top ten key attributes of the "bold" leader that Fortuna favors:

The 10 Key Attributes of Bold Leaders

1. Strategic—yet highly action-oriented and tactical.

2. Genuine, authentic and charismatic.

3. Purpose-driven and focused.

4. Resilient and self-disciplined.

5. Listens and adapts.

6. Believes relationships are vital in business.

7. Believes in two-way communication.

8. Understands accountability starts with them—but extends to all.

9. Embraces calculated, courageous risks based on listening well, gathering all the facts, and understanding every problem has a solution.

10. Shares in the reward and glory with the team.

Strategy and the role of the leader on the tactical battlefield

"Strategy" is from a Greek word, defined as pre-battle arrangement of fighting forces. One critical point to re-emphasize, in closing this chapter on "boldness":

Strategic leaders should never abdicate their responsibility—letting tacticians and internal teams handle the field of battle. You, the strategic leader, must march into battle with your armies.

Do you think Alexander the Great, Mehmed, or—in modern times, the likes of Steve Jobs— walked off the field of battle and let the team fight? No, Steve Jobs rolled up his sleeves, a tough leader, but courageous.

He wasn't always well liked, but he was well-respected by his teams. He led his company to many break-through innovations that still impact the world years later. We can imagine Alexander the Great, and Mehmed were similar leaders—tough, uncompromising and ruthless at times, but reliable and loyal to their "teams." What unites these visionaries? Courage. Confidence. Faith in their soldiers. Faith in the cause. Boldness.

Alexander was a genius on the battlefield, especially deep inside enemy territory. One spectacular way he displayed his strategy was during the pivotal Battle at Issus. His 40,000-strong army was deep inside enemy territory and was outmatched and outnumbered – by at least two to one, perhaps more.

Genuine / Authentic and Charismatic

Don't mistake charisma for likeability. The well-loved leader is not always the authentic leader. Although it certainly doesn't hurt to be loved, the key thing is to be respected as the bold and creative leader.

The Greeks defined "Charisma" as a gift of grace. Many experts agree that charisma can be acquired as a learned behavior—in the same way we can learn courage.

Do you remember Princess Diana? Publicly, she carried herself with unrivaled poise. Her mere presence and dazzling smile fed an insatiable media. She exuded charisma and boldness.

In memorializing her life, *Time* magazine writer, Tara John, captured her essence: "The extraordinary life of the Princess of Wales, not only humanized the British monarchy, but captured the world's attention. And she harnessed that media frenzy to raise awareness of a number of pro-gressive philanthropic causes." Her mission was, in fact, these causes. She used her charisma and boldness to raise awareness.

Later, after she understood the astonishing power of her influence, the activist advocated for HIV/Aids, and she championed landmine removal and youth homelessness. Was she successful? She was instrumental in a 1997 international treaty which outlawed the landmines.

Diana displayed a great degree of selflessness—and courage. This was displayed clearly when she walked across a field littered with explosive mines.

Iconic leaders are defined by courage and boldness. Purpose-driven activists who believe in making the world a better place or who taking a courageous stand, exemplify leadership, greats such as Mother Teresa, Nelson Mandela and Martin Luther King, Jr.

Courage goes hand-in-hand with authenticity, which at its core, emphasizes L.I.F.T. Leadership virtues such as: justice, fortitude, honesty, fairness and simply doing the right thing.

13

PERSONAL MANIFESTO – 80-20 AND YOUR PERSONAL PIVOT TO SUCCESS

Only eight percent of people achieve their goals. Condition yourself for success and pivot to align to your life plan. Having solid focus in your personal life, reinforces the discipline that you will bring into your leadership style. L.I.F.T. Leaders have success in their personal lives.

L.I.F.T. Facts

- Only eight percent of people achieve their goals in life.[70]

- 80 percent of effects come from 20 percent of causes.—the Pareto principle

In this chapter

- Leadership starts with your personal life. Develop your own Personal Manifesto and life plan.

- The importance of releasing the past—to remove the self-imposed limits to success.

- Condition yourself for success and pivot to align to your life plan.

- Analyze your weaknesses and develop a self-help improvement plan.

Important Take-away

- **"A man is a product of his thoughts; what he thinks he becomes" Gandhi**

The Values of L.I.F.T.

The Personal Pivot to Success is a vital part of the L.I.F.T. Leadership system.

Lead: To lead in the corporate world, it is helpful to exemplify leadership characteristics in your personal life. Leadership must be genuine, not rehearsed staging.

Inspire: Inspiring our self, will help you inspire others. You do this by defining your own personal dreams, articulating our vision, defining our mission, and creating awe-inspiring actions to that will create lasting change—just as you do in your corporate life.

Focus: To focus on our purpose, remain steadfast to our personal cause and achieve amazing results.

Transform: To transform a company into a success requires us to forge the path of personal success first.

I began this chapter with an alarming statistic. 92 percent of people don't achieve their goals; only eight percent do achieve them—labeled in the study as "goal-achievers."[71] You know where I'm going with this by now—if you're not among the eight percent you're not L.I.F.T. Leadership material. There's nothing elitist in that statement. The fact is, anyone can achieve their goals. It comes down to your own self-discipline, your personal manifesto, and what I call your Personal Pivot.

Given the Pareto Principle—which has remained a guiding force in business, investment, and personal transformation since 1896—the pivot is an inevitability. In *Cours d'économie politique,* Pareto showed that 80 percent of the land in Italy was owned by 20 percent of the population. What does this have to do with Personal Pivots?

Causation. Investors, executives, entrepreneurs all know the 80-20 rule. Before you dismiss this as an "axiom" rather than a statistic, in the decades since, this rule has been shown to be a force in economics, wealth distribution, investing, and—you guessed it—personal development and wealth. The first thing you need to decide is to become part of that 20 percent.

L.I.F.T. Leaders flip this concept on its head: they look for the 20 percent to impact the 80 percent. In business—what can we do to create that 20 percent force that changes everything? In personal life, rather than waiting for the economic or life forces to carry us irresistibly along, we can embody that irresistible force—becoming a "compassionate force for positive change" for many.

In other words, L.I.F.T. leaders, even in their personal lives, don't wait for things to happen to them—they happen to others, in a positive way. I call it the L.I.F.T. Personal Pivot.

If you're a pragmatist, a "I only want the nuts and bolts of leadership" type reader, you may feel the urge to skip this chapter. I encourage you to try to stick with it. The goal is empowerment, not personal intrusiveness.

In this chapter, I get more personal—but don't mistake that as a non-pragmatic discussion. I'm sure the 92% that don't accomplish their goals in life would skip this chapter, don't be that person. The bottom line is avoid being a victim of the Pareto Principle. This is about being the 20 percent impacting the 80 percent. This is about finding that 20 percent—the changes that will translate into the biggest tangible impacts in your life as a leader and avoiding the waste of spending any time at all on the 80 percent.

To do this, most of us will engage in major Personal Pivots. The majority of people engage in a form of this every year, at New Year's with their resolutions. Unfortunately, 92 percent don't accomplish their resolutions. You're not one of these, are you? If you are, this chapter should help—because it's not optional in L.I.F.T. You need personal success in your life to achieve in business.

To illustrate this more clearly, I can think of no better example than my first internship in college. I grabbed on to a 20 percent opportunity, one summer evening in 1991...

Real-life L.I.F.T Case Study— "Personal Pivot to Success"

Mehmed the Conqueror and I differ completely in our religious and moral beliefs, but in terms of leadership style, we're not dissimilar. How can that be?

We both sat at the feet of the greats of our respective eras and applied the personal success approach we learned from leaders who exemplified the ideals of:

- Lead

- Inspire

- Focus

- Transform

In life, where dreamers differ from visionary leaders is activity. We must transform our dreams and visions into concrete steps.

In my first job as an intern during college I had moved away from Sarnia to a small northern town called Espanola. I was hired and taken in by two great mentors: Dennis Sheptika and Ted Priddle.

I was a rough apprentice with hard edges and a lot to learn, but Ted saw something in me that I didn't see—perhaps, a mirror of himself ten years prior.

He focused on my development with extra coaching—much more than any first year co-op student could have ever asked for. My first internship was nine months and I'll never forget those days with Ted. He revealed to me a view of the world and business that I never imagined—as idealistic as I was in those days. He didn't just show me, he exemplified leadership and integrity, and how you can achieve whatever you set your mind to.

I changed. Not overnight, to be sure, but by the end of the nine months he had pulled out my hidden leader persona—traits I wasn't even aware of myself. I was honoured and delighted when he invited me back for my final internship. Later, when I graduated, he offered me a full-time position. Ted gave me the hand on the ladder I needed. Why? He saw potential leadership qualities and he fostered that in me.

Leaders don't rely on fate—we create our own path to success—but we are able to seize opportunities.

Serendipity favours the bold.

One warm summer night in 1991, I headed home by foot at the end of my shift, and crossed paths with the President Alan W. To say I was nervous is an understatement, but courage is not measured by fear—but by how we handle it. Not knowing what to expect, I greeted him and asked how he was doing, trying to sound calm. I wasn't sure it was the right thing to do, but I walked alongside my President without being invited. It was a lovely evening, and we were both headed home by foot. I knew this opportunity was precious. I mustered up my courage, and literally bombarded him with business questions—every thing I could think. It could have gone wrong, but he responded to my boldness and graciously answered all my queries about our pulp and paper company. This was the early 90s, a tough time in the pulp and paper industry.

We ultimately parted ways at a corner, and, although he was stoic in nature, I seen a side of him that was vastly generous.

I also realized, even as a starry-eyed youth, that a CEO is also just a human being, just like me. I knew, in that moment, that—if I applied myself—I could achieve the same things. I understood the role of President was not out of reach in my lifetime. His genuine and kind answers and lessons that day made it clear that I could achieve the same, with focus, determination, education, courage, and experience. That short conversation changed me.

I came away from the evening with the lifetime aspiration of becoming not just a CEO—but the CEO of rapid-growing companies. I now had a real and concrete vision, and nothing would stop me from achieving it. Through the years I mentored with greats. Everyone became my teacher. I turned to the wisdom and sages of the day in modern business and leadership: the likes of Tony Robbins, Jack Welch, Dale Carnegie, Stephen Covey, Peter Drucker, and W. Edwards Deming.

I literally consumed every personal development process and methodology that I could find. I listened to tapes, read books, created plans, worked through programs. I accomplished two more business degrees online and continued to refine my approach.

Did I ever stop being the student? No, not really. Nor, should you. For thirty years since, I've learned from dozens of teachers and mentors.

I achieved my dream. As is the nature of dreams, I visualized new goals, new dreams. Never stop dreaming.

Personal Pivot to Success

Can anyone be a leader? Of course. Anyone can learn from mentors, teachers, and books like this one. If you feel you're not born with a particular set of talents, you can learn them. Innate talent is not a requirement, it's only a bonus.

Before you aspire to be a CEO or C-Suite level leader, though, you'll likely need to take a few "pivots" in your own personal lives. In my experience, anyone can learn to be a leader—but it starts with the personal pivot and the 80-20 rule. To manage a pivot, you prioritize your own life the way you would in business. You ask:

"What are the 20 percent options in my life that will carry me to my goals?

"Who are the people in my life who can contribute to that 20 percent solution?"

"Where am I wasting my energy—the 80 percent?

"What changes can I make in my life that will drive me to my goals quickly?"

You have goals, clearly, or you wouldn't be reading this book. What it takes beyond goals is activities to accomplish those goals—ideally those 20 percent of activities that bring 80 percent results into your life. I'll cover the secrets of goal-achievers in the next section.

"The path to success is to take massive, determined action."
Tony Robbins.

My grandfather's personal pivot

My grandfather, at the age of 40, is the perfect example of the personal pivot. He didn't escape the invading German army in southern Holland during the war. These occupiers destroyed hope and created an untenable situation that lasted for years. 5 long years. As the war drew to a close, the Canadian forces liberated his small town. He knew his war-devastated country would take decades to rebuild and wanted more for his kids and grandchildren.

He had a vision. He acted on the vision. This is the essence of the personal pivot.

Though they barely had food, my grandfather packed up the whole family and scraped together barely enough for four tickets to North America. His vision—make a new life in the country that set them free, Canada. His action—set sail to this new world. He manifested his vision with boldness. It takes guts to sail to Canada, after enduring years of war, with empty pockets, clinging only to a dream.

They had the clothes on their back, and a clear mental vision in his head of success in Canada. There was no certainty—but, in his mind, he was making them a life in this strange new country.

Grandfather didn't even know English. Using my mother—who was 7 years old at the time—as his interpreter, he navigated the strange new world. Slowly, they began to build the dream.

He spent the next four decades creating a platform of success for us—his family. North America is certainly the land of opportunity—but it must be earned through hard work. Can you imagine a greater personal pivot than moving to a new country, penniless, not speaking the language—and your assets are a dream and a willingness to work hard?

He imagined it. I'm here because he imagined it.

The four steps in the Personal Pivot

The four steps in the Personal Pivot to Success Approach is a slight modification of L.I.F.T. to emphasized slightly different points:

- **L**eave it all behind—if you're not willing to let go of the past, you have no future.

- **I**nspirational Visioning—if you can't visualize your goal, you can't achieve it.

- **F**ulcrum—to pivot requires a fulcrum, a pivot point. What is your turning point?

- **T**actics and Taking stock—how are you going to achieve your vision? What are you willing to sacrifice to achieve it?

This is a linear progression. Like my Grandfather you have to be willing to leave it all behind to make a new life—in his case, Holland. Then, you have to have a vision. He dreamed of Canada. With his dream, and his turning point, he planned the journey, working until he had enough money to bring the family to his new country.

L.I.F.T. Five: secrets to achieving goals

Before I dive into the details of managing your own Personal Pivot, let's deal with that eight percent success-against-goals statistic. Of course, I'm going to make it a list of five ways "secrets" to achieving your goals (They're not really secrets, they should be common sense.) I'm assuming you want to be in the elite category of those who achieve their goals each year.

You can apply these secrets—principals are perhaps a better word—to both your personal life and your leadership career.

1. Mind—it's not a cliche: mind matters

Mind over matter? Mindfulness in business. Set your mind. Pick your cliché. Like most tired sayings, theres a core truth. If you can't manage your mind, you can't manage your life or your company, it's as simple as that. Setting goals is an activity of the mind. Visualizing goals is no less important. Here's a tip for working with mind, which sounds contrary: write everything down.

Try a pen and paper and journal—it's statistically proven to improve memory and intake of ideas and improve cognition. The citations on this are endless, elite publications such as *Psychology Today* to *Trends in Neuroscience*.

It is also proven to improve conceptualities. Handwriting allows the mind to process, rather than just "take notes." I have one more cliché for you—the pen is mightier than the sword, despite all my military metaphors.

2. Set lofty goals: no mediocre challenges

Moderate, achievable goals is mediocrity. Our own minds parse it this way. We shrug, don't care, move on. Lofty challenges bring out our competitive spirit—the challenge drives our mental charge and our physical adrenalin. Skip "realistic" and go for glory.

3. The hated to-do list and procrastination

I'm sorry about this, and nothing new here, but you *need to recognize when you are procrastinating.* You do need your to-do lists (hand-written?). You do need to work back from your deadlines. My best tip—break everything down into achievable chunks. Multi-tasking may be amazing, but it's also the reason people don't accomplish much, which leads to procrastination. (Call that tip 3b.)

4. Learn from athletes: practice the 50-20 Rule

Interval training is a big thing today because it's proven to "break through" in training for professional athletes. You're professional and elite, right? Our muscle of choice is our brains. The athlete version, as suggested by Brad Stulberg in his book *Peak Performance*, is more precise than I'll recommend—52 minutes training, 17 minutes rest. I use 50/20, since I don't regulate with a stopwatch. The key is plenty of interval breaks but keep pushing through until you accomplish your goals. Avoid the long breaks. With this rule, you will find the mental breaks—take a walk, catch up on the news, have a coffee—will refresh your brain cells in a tangible way. You'll also find your physical stamina improving. In mental interval training, try 50 minutes at your desk, 20 minutes on your stationary bike (or exercise alternate.)

5. Build your support network— anchor your life in compassion.

You'll see in my case studies how I've gravitated towards high performers all my life. also gravitate towards compassionate people. If you want to achieve, network with achievers, both at work and in your personal lives. If you want to achieve meaningfully, you'll likely already undertake philanthropic, spiritual or other important personal missions. Compassion is an important characteristic in L.I.F.T. Leadership. Exemplify it at work—and live it at home. Be a volunteer, join networks of like-minded people, pursue what resonates with your life. You have aspirations beyond the office, right? Make them count. Surround yourself with wonderful achievers, and like-minded people who inspire you.

First—Leaving it all behind— and the 100 percent rule

The first step of the L.I.F.T. Personal Pivot to Success is "Leaving It All Behind." We have to start from the important premise, because baggage and past trauma are inhibiting chains to L.I.F.T. Leaders. To break these chains, remember: no one owes you anything. Not even your parents. Even if you have supportive parents and partners, you still need to take 100 percent responsibility for your life. Not 80 or 90 percent. All of it is on you.

As we grow, learning lessons in life, we develop baggage. Bullies in school. Bullies in the workplace. Bad relationships. Hard times. Angry partners. If you live in the past, you cannot embrace your future; you live in virtual chains. You can learn from the past but stop living in it.

There's an old Zen proverb: "The past is already gone."

Avoid the three Rs: resentment, revenge, reprisals

Resentments, revenge and reprisals. The three Rs of a stalled life—and career. The one thing I've learned in decades in business: you can learn from the past, but you cannot change it. You don't have a time machine, so just put the past away. If you focus your energy on resentment, revenge, reprisals, or any other negative emotions—or any baggage from the past —you will not progress to the next stage in the personal success pivot.

Once my grandfather and family arrived in Canada, he could have sunk into despair and depression, remembering the war, family and friends lost, dire poverty and starvation, watching his children waste away—or, the traumatic beatings from the German soldiers in jail. He could have dwelled on all that and acted like a victim the rest of his life.

Instead, he moved to a land he didn't know, with a language he couldn't speak, and worked tirelessly to change the outcome of his life. Our response to life's events is what determines the outcome. Instead of despair, he used the events to inspire visionary action.

L.I.F.T. Fives: Five things our mind controls

Everything we experience today is the outcome of the choices we have made in the face of the events of the past. We all have the ability to control five things in our mind:

1. What we focus and dwell upon,

2. What we visualize and picture,

3. How we feel about what we experience,

4. The response and actions we choose to take.

5. Our habits and clinging attachments.

Winners respond to the past as lessons and inspiration. Losers sink into despair.

It is often said that we are a product of our environment. I would slightly modify this concept: we are a product of our responses to our environment.

If we keep on doing what we have always done and expect a different outcome that will never happen.

Luck is not a force of change we can count on.

Even if our situation is not as dire as my Grandfather's, we have to take 100 percent responsibility for our life—even in the face of environmental or societal forces—and shift our thoughts, habits, visions, dreams and actions to achieve personal success. The war wasn't my Grandfather's fault, but it was his unavoidable situation. He overcame with discipline and mind.

If you are a L.I.F.T. Leader you are bold and brave (see chapter 12) and willing to embrace change (the pivot)—then you will see great positive progress begin in your life.

Are you a person that blames others and deflects responsibility? Blame is very disempowering; yes, it is a defense mechanism, but it's totally "uncool" for a leader. Middle managers may play the blame game, but C-Suite are above all that, right?

Blame is a natural re-active response. But, as you've no doubt picked up in previous chapters, reactivity is not a virtue of leaders. Proactivity is a leadership attribute, not reactivity. Blame, let's face it, is nothing but a primitive reaction. C-Suite leaders are above all disciplined, proactive people.

Even if your reactivity, including blame, is instinctive and impulsive, take a metaphorical deep breath, stop yourself from reacting publicly—and damaging your all-important leader persona—and logically deduce that guilt, hurt, disgrace, sorrow, dissatisfaction or insufficiency are unproductive.

Blame is a vortex. It gains momentum. It sucks in others into the stormy maelstrom of vindictiveness and bitterness. There is not one positive, redeeming aspect of the three Rs: resentment, revenge, reprisals. Instead, adopt the positive three Rs:

- **Replace Resentment with Reduction**—reduce the problem to logical, deductive lessons learned. Take that wisdom and respond positively.

- **Replace Revenge with Responsive Empathy**—understand the cycle of revenge is damaging and the cycle of empathy is growth. Forgiveness is the biggest springboard you'll ever find.

- **Replace Reprisals with Replacement Activities**—earn back what was lost and demonstrate you have risen above primitive reprisals. Remember ultimately the best reprisal is success.

L.I.F.T. Exercise: Taking stock of the past as lessons

The first step in releasing the past, is activity. Form new habits out of new actions that re-wire our thinking.

Albert Einstein once said, "Nothing happens until something moves". There is a cause and effect in life, and we must choose to cause good and create good effects.

Start by making a personal inventory—including past experiences you might be supressing—and list all of the things that you have either witnessed, experienced, or endured that has shaped your life. It can be positive or negative, or even traumatic. List as many as you can in either column.

Positive Events/Experiences	Negative Events/Experiences

1.	1.
2.	2.
3.	3.
4.	4.
5.	5.
6.	6.
7.	7.
8.	8.
9.	9.
10.	10.

Once you have exhausted your memories and written this list, take the pro-active analytic step of breaking down the impact these moments had on your life:

Positive Events/ Experiences	Actions/Responses (Thoughts, mental images, things you did, beliefs you took on)	Outcomes
1.		
2.		
3.		
4.		

5.

6.

7.

8.

9.

10.

The next step is more difficult and may require time and careful consideration. It is important to recognize the things that have ***robbed you of past success in your life***. It can be anything: your childhood, neighbours, friends, parents, schools, coworkers, health, jobs, spouse, world events, financial impact, or anything you have historically "blamed" in your life.

Negative Events/ Experiences	Actions/Responses (Thoughts, mental images, things you did, beliefs you took on)	Outcomes
1.		
2.		
3.		
4.		
5.		
6.		
7.		
8.		
9.		
10.		

Taking this step to write down the things that have shaped your life—whether it is positive or negative—is, in itself, an act of personal courage, and a step towards the realizing and resolving past issues that negatively impacted your life.

The next step in "Leaving It All Behind" is to create an action plan to release the past. Fill out the following:

Attitude of Gratitude Plan	
The Top 5 Things I am Most Grateful for?	What am I going to do to show my appreciation for this or ways to give back?
1.	1.
2.	2.
3.	3.
4.	4.
5.	5.

L.I.F.T. Fives: Five Facts About Gratitude

We need to recognize the people in our life, the things that have happened that positively shaped our life. It is important to be purposeful in expressing our appreciation for the impact it has had on our life. This is not about being inspirational. Gratitude is pragmatic. Here are some scientifically recognized benefits of gratitude (with citations in footnotes):

1. Gratitude creates opportunities for more relationships

A 2014 study indicated that people who demonstrate gratitude have more positive associates. In business, what is more important than positive associates? [72]

2. Gratitude improves physical and psychological health

Separate studies (too numerous to cite individually) directly link gratitude to both physical and psychological health. As any C-Suite leader can tell you, both types of health are critical to performance, creativity, and stamina, especially during crisis.[73]

3. Gratitude is the secret to better sleep

A study in *Applied Psychology: Health and Well-Being* indicates direct benefits between gratitude and sound sleep. As any stressed executive can attest, sleep is critical to performance.

4. Gratitude increases mental resilience and strength

Yes, you read that right. Our list in the exercise above is all about listing those traumas that hold us back. A 2003 study in *Journal of Personality and Social Psychology* "found that gratitude was a major contributor to resilience following the terrorist attacks on September 11." This is a major trauma, similar to the one faced by my Grandfather in WWII. Being "thankful"—to God, to people, the nation, your team, your Church, your sports team, choose your label—is proven to help us rise above major trauma—and minor stresses as well.

On September 13th 2001, I sat at the corner of Broadway and Fulton street in Manhattan staring at the 30' concrete pile once known at the World Trade Center. I was aghast at the site, watching First Responders risking their lives, seeing family members walking the streets with pictures of their loved ones in search of them. I sat at the footstool of this moment and fear wasn't my first thought, but rather gratitude and inspiration as I witnessed the most courageous spirit within these people. As that scene plays back in my mind at times, it puts many things in perspective for me, and gratitude for my life, circumstances, family, experiences, adversities, victories, and everything else is usually the place my mind goes. I am grateful for everything I've been blessed with, endured, and for the road that lies ahead, no matter how short or long. Life is precious and those around you are important, be grateful.

5. Gratitude increases self-esteem

Gratitude increases self-esteem—which is critical to the L.I.F.T. Leader. This is another reason to engage in these exercises towards the personal pivot. In a 2014 study in the *Journal of Applied Sport Psychology* "found that gratitude increased athlete's self-esteem." It was determined to be a critical factor in athletic performance. In separate studies it showed that "gratitude reduces social comparisons."[74] As I've indicated in previous chapters, high-performing athletes face the same mental challenges as C-Suite executives.

The L.I.F.T. leader must have an attitude of gratitude in all that we do each and every day. When was the last time you expressed your gratitude to your family members? To your team at work? To your suppliers? To your investors? To your old classmate from school?

Work on manifesting gratitude. Make a list of people you have neglected—or didn't appreciate until now. (It doesn't matter that you felt gratitude—the question is, did you express it?)

Balancing the books

Start balancing the books now. If you haven't expressed your gratitude, like Scrooge in the Dicken's novel *A Christmas Carol*, wake up from the nightmare and start spreading the goodwill. Make up for negative past issues by volunteering to help others.

The point is simply to stop unproductive negativity and find opportunities for productive positivity. You'll immediately start benefiting from the five benefits of Gratitude.

Shifting the Future Outcomes

I recommend an additional step: prior to planning your persona pivot. Take your Negative Events/Experience Chart (above) and think through different ways to view the situation. I call this third-party analysis. Try to put aside your own point-of-view, and sit-in on your list as if you're an interesting third-party.

Now, work through the "Shifting Outcomes" exercise. The key word in this exercise is "stop!" Stopping the blame. Stopping the wasted energy. Stopping the negative emotions. Healing and moving on. Take your time with this:

Shifting the Future Outcomes by Changing my Response to the Past	
What person, event, situation, or experience am I still holding on to?	What am I going to do to heal this hurt? What effort will I make to change my thinking about this situation? I must commit to stopping the blame for this!!
1.	1.
2.	2.
3.	3.
4.	4.
5.	5.

You have taken a very important step—the first step to the pivot.

Second—Inspirational Visioning

The second step of the Personal Pivot to Success is **Inspirational Visioning**. This is the step I suggest you undertake in retreat. You don't have to escape to the mountain cabin or cave. You do need a quiet surrounding—with a clear head and heart (which was the purpose of the above exercises!)—and now ready to dream big. Where you want to be in six months, one year, two years? What you want to accomplish? Who do you want to impress? Who do you want to help? How are you going to achieve it?

In the previous exercises we defined the unproductive past. Now's the time for a reset.

A reset usually starts with—what is your life's purpose? Nothing big.

Obviously, this is a life-changing or affirming aspiration. Many people never stop to consider it—but L.I.F.T. Leaders certainly do. You don't need to make it spiritual or religious—but you do need to have purpose.

Coaches of athletes embrace this. First responders who face life-death situations embrace it. Religious leaders live it. Business leaders exemplify it. If you don't have a life purpose, ask yourself what motivates you? What resonates? What makes you feel grateful. It doesn't have to be grand, although it certainly can be. It should include an element of gratitude for reasons previously discussed.

The purpose could be things such as:

A) Coach the next generation of athletes to first be great people as well as great athletes,

B) Humbly serve the poor and less fortunate.

C) Invest in my employees to become high functioning leaders in their life and for those around them.

D) Give the world amazing music to appreciate and to inspire them.

E) Teach others how to be great parents, or teach kids leadership, etc.

It doesn't matter what your purpose is—but rather that your purpose makes you feel fulfilled and satisfied. How do you know you have it? If you could spend countless hours working on this mission—paid or unpaid—you've nailed it.

Don't despair if the answer doesn't pop into your head on your first "retreat." As J.R.R. Tolkien once wrote, "Not all who wander are lost." You may need time because you've never really asked yourself this question. Take the time to really answer this question. Leave it as an open "to do" if you can't resolve it now. But try, here, to at least write out a working life purpose:

What is my life's purpose? _____

_____

_____

Values to embody your purpose

Next, consider the values that reinforce your life mission. Start with what you believe now. Your values probably grew organically, a distillation of your past experiences, your parents, mentors, teachers and society and peer guidance. Now, ask yourself if your current values match up well with your life purpose. If not, ask yourself why.

We often talk about the importance of values in a company—if you need a review, back to basics, see chapter one. But we must consider our life values. Do they match up with our professional values? Why not?

None of these exercises are designed to change you, or to diminish you—on the contrary. The one thing that defines a L.I.F.T. Leader above all else is—willingness to change.

No one is perfect, but we strive to become better people. Values are our guidepost. Do you need a "business" reason—rather than a moral one—for values? Then, it's as simple as "accountability."

Values that exemplify life missions

Since vision is a perspective, I'll illustrate values linked to vision with corporations. I do this, here, in the personal values section to illustrate concise vision and values. Corporate values may be formulaic, but they're short and precise.

Challenge yourself. Can you match up this values/vision statements with their companies?

1. To create a better everyday life for many people.

2. To empower every person and organization on the planet to achieve more.

3. To make people happy.

4. To accelerate the world's transition to sustainable energy.

5. To give people the power to share and make the world more open and connected.

I won't hold you in suspense. These, in excellent examples of concise vision embodying values are: 1. Ikea; 2. Microsoft. 3. Disney 4. Tesla and 5. Facebook.

Now, do the same thing for yourself. Take your life mission above, and translate that into a one-sentence values/vision statement:

With your life mission, and your values/vision statements, you're ready to really drill down to your core values. Be authentic.

You should pick five core values that you want to exemplify and demonstrate in your life. You can be as basic as: authenticity (be true to yourself in every occasion you are the same, what you see is what you get), truthfulness/integrity (being honest and forthright in all your dealings), joyful/loving (you want to be known for your compassion and positive energy), kindness, patience, forgiving, courageous, respectful, ethical,

self-confident, fair/decisive, trustworthy, perseverant, resilient, faithful…..
the list goes on and on.

Remember, though, this is about your five core values. Distill down to
the five that are central to you. What are they?

The Top 5 Core Values most important to me

1.
2.
3.
4.
5.

Removing limiting beliefs—and your bucket list

Now that you have your life's purpose—and your five core values—ask
yourself nothing less than the 10 things you want to accomplish in life. In
other words, your bucket list.   Inspirational vision requires us to think
without limiting beliefs. Personal success is very individual. You define it—
no one else.

Make this an "all or nothing" exercise. If you removed the barriers of
time and money—but not the barriers of physics —what are the absolute
"must achieves" in your short lifetime? Climb mount Everest? Build five
companies? Sail Solo across the pacific? Run a marathon? Save the lives of
200 people? (No joke, some people keep logs.) Whatever you have always
wanted to do and finish in life is the right answer. What are those 10 things
on your life accomplishment list?

The 10 Things I want to accomplish in my life!

1.   6.
2.   7.
3.   8.
4.   9.
5.   10.

Visualize your lifestyle

The next step is determining in your aspirational lifestyle—what is your future state? It requires a degree of visualization of the things you would want in life. For example; relationships with God, relationship with your spouse, find a spouse, physical weight and physique, accumulating a certain amount of money, doing charitable things, travel, have a certain car, giving back to society in a certain way, living in a different place or environment.

Dream big but keep it meaningful. This is about finding your central destination—but remembering it's a shared destination. What represents fulfillment, personal satisfaction and reward—that is meaningful to you and others you will share it with.

Everyone enjoys reward for their hard work and effort—there's no shame in aspiring to personal reward or fulfilment, especially if you share those blessings with others.

For example, one of my personal beliefs/values is "sharing reward with others." By definition, we are being rewarded, but we include others in our dream. Remember the power of gratitude and compassion.

The greater responsibility we have in this world is to use our talents to benefit as many as we can. We have a duty of compassion and sharing. Anne Frank wrote in her diary, "No one has ever become poor by giving".

As a kid when people would ask me what I wanted to be when I grew up, I would tell them a Philanthropist. I wanted to seek and promote the welfare of many and use the riches I can amass to make the biggest difference in the lives of people. I am still on that journey.

Now, ask yourself, in this context, "What are the top 10 things you want in life?"

The 10 Things I want in life!	
1.	6.
2.	7.
3.	8.
4.	9.
5.	10.

Your Personal Manifesto in one page

As with all things L.I.F.T., I recommend distillation. Take all of your hard work in this chapter and transform it into a single page, concise Personal Manifesto. Frame it. Put it on your desk. Remember it. Don't let it gather dust.

We need to distill the words from the previous exercises: Life's Purpose: Five Core Values: attitude of gratitude reminders; shifting the future by dissolving the past; the list of the 10 things I want to accomplish; and the 10 things I want in life. Make it all fit on one page—crystallizing these declarations into a call to action.

Personal Manifesto

Date: _____   Top 5 Core Values

My life's purpose? _____   _____

_____   _____

_____   _____

_____   _____

_____   _____

Attitude of Gratitude Plan

The Top 5 Things I am Most Grateful for?	What am I going to do to show my appreciation for this or ways to give back?
1.	1.
2.	2.
3.	3.
4.	4.
5.	5.

Shifting the Future Outcomes by Changing my Response to the Past

What person, event, situation, or experience am I still holding on to?	What am I going to do to heal this hurt? What effort will I make to change my thinking about this situation? I must commit to stopping the blame for this!!
1.	1.
2.	2.
3.	3.
4.	4.
5.	5.

The 10 Things I want to accomplish in my life!	The 10 Things I want in life!
1.	1.
2.	2.
3.	3.
4.	4.
5.	5.
6.	6.
7.	7.
8.	8.
9.	9.
10	10.

Third—the Personal Pivot Fulcrum

The third step of the Personal Pivot to Success is the Fulcrum. Contemplation doesn't manifest without activity.

Now that all of your mission, values and aspirations are stated, in one page, you have reached the critical stage—the fulcrum of the pivot process.

"Whatever the mind can conceive and believe, it can achieve".
—*Think and Grow Rich by Napoleon Hill*

Belief is a choice

""Man is what he believes" Anton Chekhov. Beliefs are basically the guiding principles in life that provide direction and meaning in life. Beliefs are the pre-set, organized filters to our perceptions of the world (external and internal). Beliefs are like 'Internal commands' to the brain as to how to represent what is happening, when we congruently believe something to be true. In the absence of beliefs or inability to tap into them, people feel disempowered."[75]

This is from a paper published by the National Institute of Health in the US, from the publication *The Biochemistry of Belief*, written by T.S. Sathyanarayana Rao.

This is fundamentally true—if you set honest goals, and if you believe they are achievable, and you are determined you will achieve them—you have programmed yourself to succeed. Doubt is a limiting belief: "In the absence of beliefs…people feel disempowered". What helps you overcome doubt? The inventory process we engaged in above is helpful. An audit of your strengths and weaknesses will clarify. What do you believe? Work with that.

Visualizing the win—athletes' corner

Another way to overcome doubts, and to push past self-limitations is visualization. Sports visualization is actually an area of coaching specialty. It's considered a vital skill. It's sometimes known as "Mental Game Coaching." Michael Phelps, holder of the all-time record for medals in a single Olympic game—22 gold medals!—credits visualization with his success. His sports visualization coach, Bob Bowman, actually urged Phelps to film himself in winning moments and to play, and replay these moments:

> We figured it [imagery] was best to concentrate on these tiny moments of success and build them into mental triggers... It's more like his habits had taken over. The actual race was just another step in a pattern that started earlier that day and was nothing but victories. Winning became a natural extension. "[76]

Jack Nicklaus and Tiger Woods were strong advocates of the power of visualization and the mental practice in their golf training. Jackie Burke Jr followed in their footsteps and famously remarked "You can't do what you can't see." Tiger Woods often described how he mentally practiced with every shot—visualizing it in his mind. His skills in manifesting from visualization are legend. Surgeons often prepare for critical surgery, first be studying all the imaging, then by closing their eyes and visualizing the surgery.

Visionary leaders dream big, see the future in their minds, and drive forward to their goal—they do not drive forward while looking in the rearview mirror.

The pivot comes with the belief you can do it.

A simple visualization can help—for example, when preparing for a job interview, or an annual general meeting, or any other high-pressure, pivot point. I have gone into job interviews, speeches in front of large audiences, or an important game, that is a win or go home moment, and I have used these emotional moves to drive myself into a peak state. It works. You can do it in the bathroom before you walk in, or at home before you leave. The goal is to prepare your mind for the win:

1) Stand with a straight back and breath in through your nose and out forcefully through your mouth.

2) Focus on your facial expression and deliberately transform it into one of confidence and focus. Repeat affirmative words several times such as: I can, I can, I can, and I will!

3) Visualize the outcome you want. See yourself in the win. Visualize it as clearly as you can. Run the movie, until it seems real.

4) Seal the visualization with something symbolic, like a chest thump, arm gesture of strength, or a victory pose that proclaims what you're truly after.

Fourth—Tactics and taking stock

The fourth step of the Personal Pivot to Success is Tactics and taking stock. We have to shift from planning, thinking, emotional pivoting, to tactical plans and taking stock of our progress. There's no difference here, in steps, to the problem solving we undertook in chapter three. The difference here is personal context.

In our previous exercises in this chapter—resulting in our one-page manifesto—we defined what we needed to "Leave behind in our life;" then in step two we focused on what success should look like. We looked at what is possible and what you truly want to accomplish in your life, what is your purpose, and what are the things you want in life—your bucket list. Finally, we moved into the "examine" phase of problem solving—reflecting on the things that are holding us back, how we can break through the limiting beliefs, and what we really desire down deep inside. In step three we moved to the fulcrum and decided what we needed to do to pivot our lives. The problem-solving cycle is half finished.

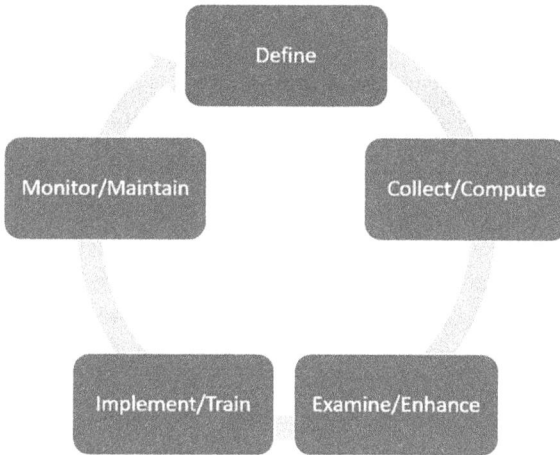

If we continue through the problem-solving cycle the final two categories implement/train and monitor/maintain are at the heart of tactics and taking stock.

Tactics map to short-term plans that address immediate actions supporting a course of action to accomplish a longer-term strategic plan. Tactical plans align with work we need to do that directly or indirectly produces assets or gaining information to capitalize and build an incremental step towards the strategic plan.

Our Personal Manifesto has a lot of complexities—similar to those we undertook in chapter three for our companies and brands—and it requires us to decide those steps and milestones we need to achieve that type of success. As in chapter three, with our business planning, we need milestones to keep ourselves accountable.

The first step is to separate your strategic goals and define your tactical needs. Take the two lists you developed—the "10 Things I want to accomplish in my life" and the "10 Things I want in life"—and distill down to five things which you consider top priorities. Remember, L.I.F.T. is a distilling process. What are the most important in the shorter term?

These five will be the most pressing and important initial goals you want to accomplish—in your personal life. You can always add more—accelerate and accomplish more things in parallel—as you get good at multi-tasking these efforts. For now, decide the top five goals from those two lists.

Top 5 Goals
1.
2
3.
4.
5.

The top 5 goals move forward into the next step of tactical decision making. We need to take each of these strategic goals and decide on the three or more actions required and what define completion or rather the goal. These could also have a key performance indicator that helps us track progress. Ultimately, we must put a deadline on this in order to push ourselves to complete this step. We have to take this imperative step as it puts a framework around what we envision as progress and assists with personal accountability.

Top 5 Goals	Three Tactical Steps / Actions Required	Goal/KPI	Due Date
1.	a)		
	b)		
_____	c)		
2	a)		
	b)		
_____	c)		
3.	a)		
	b)		

_____ c)

4.   a)

                b)

_____ c)

5.   a)

                b)

                c)

Take this as seriously as you did the business planning in previous chapters. You're setting concrete actions, tactics milestones, KPIs, due dates, to your previously visualized life goals, bucket list, and values. Use all the same methods and discipline here that you would use in your company as a C-Suite leader.

Making transformation a habit

This is about transformation, transition, and forming of new habits.

One new habit that is helpful is a "fifteen minute" taking stock break. Go back to your personal plan once a day and check your progress. Re-visualize your goals. Analyze the obstacles. Solve the problems.

Find a quiet place without distraction (phones on airplane mode)—usually in the morning—and take the time to reflect and think about your progress and your next step. The daily morning fifteen minutes of solitude and planning will produce momentum, brings clarity, boosts creativity, enhanced time management and improves your overall productivity. The five daily steps are:

1) Exercise and plan your meals and other healthy daily habits. It is important to spend time investing in your own personal health, spiritual and mental development.

2) Read the Personal Manifesto one-page plan and review to keep it fresh in our mind. Reflect on your "Attitude of Gratitude" and take the time to reflect on those things you are grateful for in your life.

3) Review the "Top 5 goals and tactical plan" with Top 5 and focus on what you've achieved—actions, goal/KPIs and due dates. Consider enhancements, further actions, roadblocks, lack of knowledge or additional steps needed to accomplish those goals. It is a moment to contemplate your progress and ponder what else you need to do.

4) Make a list of a minimum of three to four things you will do that very day to take steps of progress to accomplish that interim tactical goal.

5) Determine the relationship investments you will be making today and how you will schedule time for those that matter most: family time, kid time, spouse time, relatives, friends, advisors, colleagues, employees, and others.

A day planner or a journal that has a lot of space for notes and areas for writing. I encourage you to write with pen and paper in a good old-fashioned journal. This is pragmatic. As I indicated previously, research reinforces improved creative capabilities, internalization of data and cognitive benefits. A good day planner and a pen provides you a lot of value: helping cognize and internalize as you write and read, brainstorm, contemplate, and decide on actions and steps. An iPad, iPhone or computer does not have these benefits—I'd argue even the ones with digital pens.

A checklist and a refresher through the day adds tremendous value to help you accomplish more things—rather than relying on your memory.

The act of having a planning session with yourself—and writing things down—will:

- boost your personal creativity

- enhance productivity

- allow you to focus and articulate clearly

- heighten your memory

- enhance absorption of concepts

- reduce stress

- squeeze more from your time

- be more organized

- and create a written record of achievement which will bolster your confidence and help you track your progress.

There is power in the written word and the act of writing it.

"We write to taste life twice, in the moment and in retrospect."
—*Anaïs Nin*

"Either write something worth reading or do something worth writing."
—*Benjamin Franklin*

"I can shake off everything as I write;
my sorrows disappear, my courage is reborn."
—*Anne Frank*

Reflections from the Conqueror

The boy Mehmed, born to disadvantage—his mother was a slave—dreamed of being a king. His brother was already lined up to be king. To be a king in those days, was a bloody affair. But he had a vision. He saw himself as king.

He developed a plan, a personal manifesto. A major pivot would be needed to take him from "son of a slave" to future king.

To accomplish it, he set the goal of becoming a master strategist and war leader. He studied the wisdom of past masters—the teachings of

Aristotle, Alexander the Great, Julius Caesar, Attila the Hun, Timur, his father Murad II, and his great grandfather Suleiman the Magnificent.

The future King Mehmed II studied these ancients and their approach to leadership and the methods they employed in their life. His values and morals are not in line with what we would today call "values"—but he knew what his life stood for. Personal success, to Mehmed, meant domination.

14

L.I.F.T. LEADING WITH THE FIVES

We're trained to think in "top fives"—on average, humans have an eight-second attention span. The top five things to remember about L.I.F.T. is: leadership is distilling the essence; inspiration is about communicating the essence; focus is about clarifying the essence; transformation is about acting on the essence.

L.I.F.T. Facts

- The average human has an eight-second attention span, according to a study by Microsoft (2018 data)—down from twelve seconds in the year 2000.[77]

- Concentration timespan, if highly interested and engaged, maxes out at 20-35 minutes.[78]

In this chapter

- To distill the concepts of a L.I.F.T. Leader to five essential points, focus on: vision/values; networking and relationships; strategy and feedback; working with the five essential metrics and reward; fortune favors the bold.

Important Take-away

- A marketplace always has room for a company that serves it well, creates value, and answers the need, and, ideally, predicts the needs. But—there is only room for one leader. To be that leader, we need to find a way to serve that separates us from our competent competitors.

Thinking like a L.I.F.T. Leader

Lead: Leaders think in "loglines"—or well-defined niches that you can describe in one sentence. The smaller, the better. The Leader asks, "What can I own?" The follower asks, "what can I do well?" Ownership cuts out the competition, simplifies your message, and helps you build a unique team-culture.

Inspire: Think Hollywood! Yes, movies. Producers have perfected the art of the one-line pitch—known as a "logline"—and so should you. (See chapter 9.) The clarity of the pitch will inspire not only your customers, but all of your stakeholders: investors, internal teams, suppliers, and influencers.

Focus: Defining your central theme—your own logline—and building all of your strategies around your unique position will bring value clarity to all audiences.

Transform: To transform a company requires confidence in where you fit in the market, and the humble pride your company telegraphs to all stakeholders.

As a L.I.F.T. Leader, you champion this confident, well-defined message to all your stakeholders. I've distilled the L.I.F.T. Leadership system into a few short chapters. In many of these, I refined the essence to L.I.F.T. Fives. As epilogue or summary, I'll leave you with the most essential "L.I.F.T. Fives" from these chapters. If you focus only on these, you'll see the all-important Leadership transformation.

L.I.F.T. Five: Five ways to bond with your team over Principles

1. Transparency and communication

Before you assume you are both transparent and communicative, remember the statistics:

- only 15 percent of employees are satisfied with the quality of communications in their companies

- only 15 percent believe their managers give them "highly valuable feedback.

2. Opportunities and incentives

Your team is motivated by the same things you are—opportunities to advance or be recognized, and incentives to perform.

3. Life outside of work

Taking an interest in your team's personal life isn't about intrusion or stripping away your team members privacy. It's about showing interest and engaging your team—without being invasive.

4. Support and help

Every day is filled with teaching moments. Setting goals and priorities—then achieving them—reinforces these moments and helps your team feel genuinely rewarded in their career.

5. Appreciation—say thanks!

We all want appreciation and gratitude, not only from family, friends, and significant others but also from our managers. It costs nothing to say thank-you.

L.I.F.T. Fives: Five Keys to Great Decisions

In L.I.F.T., we outline five keys to making great decisions in business:

Key 1—Layered Thinking

Layered thinking means digging deep into that evidence and viewing that collected data from all perspectives. Don't make conclusions yet. If you do, you may miss an opportunity buried in those facts.

Key 2—The Right Data for the Right Decisions

As a C-suite leader (or aspiring leader), you already know the difference between information and data. Data guides decisions. Information can obscure decisions.

Data is vital, and numbers run businesses, but it's essential to have the right data and metrics. The more time you spend with data that matters, the sharper your instincts will become.

Key 3—Parallel thinking

Only the most skilled of L.I.F.T. Leaders tend to develop this nuanced skill. The key is to remain open, seek the input of many, listen to all the involved stakeholders, ask questions from all angles of the situation, and gather the information. All scenarios, all suspects, all sides are equal—until they're not. It will soon become evident which one is the real suspect or the viable scenario.

Key 4—Listening to the soft voices

Leaders listen. You learn more "walking the line and talking to the soldiers"—as Mehmed did—and listening to the soft voices.

Key 5—Four steps to decisions and mental processing

Distill, distill, distill, distill ...

The Top Five Pain Points— Feedback Without Pain

Frequent feedback loops make everything less painful. At first glance, it seems like more work, but you'll find it amounts to less work. The clarity will drive enthusiasm and momentum. The frequency will eliminate the need for expensive "course corrections"—which can be as costly as lost business or as significant as replacing a team-member who has gone too far off the path. Here are the top five pain points, regularly cited by H.R. Managers, stated from the point-of-view of the employee team-members:

Pain Point 1—I'm not valued

It's easy for team members to feel undervalued, especially if you're not recognizing them in small ways, in near real-time, and, at a minimum, every 90 days.

Pain Point 2—My ideas aren't heard

Frequent feedback loops also feed the "agile" workplace. In today's pace of business, a rigid, inflexible workplace results in declining returns on every investment. Not only that, feedback loops mean you'll have real-time feedback on your performance as a leader and be able to improve yourself. Finally, you'll create a dynamic, agile workplace that fosters creativity and ideas.

Pain Point 3—My workplace feels poisonous

Lack of morale and the "poisonous" workplace are real phenomena. You may not be able to remove stress from the workplace. It's the nature of business to thrive in a stressful environment. But, you can remove much of the inter-team stress by being more dynamically watchful and interactive.

Pain Point 4—My team expects the impossible

Lack of recognition destroys the motivation to better the team. In turn, this feeds the momentum cycle of failure. Failure leads to lowered expectations and results. To improve morale and exceed goals takes real-time leadership, not annual goal setting, and merit reviews.

Pain Point 5—No one trains me

One of the most often cited complaints in H.R. is "lack of training." No matter how senior the hire, and regardless of their past experience, each workplace requires training in how you want things done. Without training, it is unreasonable to demand performance.

L.I.F.T. Fives: The Five Essential Metrics

Every business has its own set of essential metrics. L.I.F.T. Metrics is all about customizing Metrics and Key Performance Indicators (KPIs) to your business goals. If your goal is gross sales above all else, you'll have different plans to a company focused on reputational goals—and you'll focus on a different set of metrics.

Business Leaders, certainly L.I.F.T. Leaders, will keep four categories of metrics in front of them at all times—and one "wild card" metric, I call the *L.I.F.T. Stress Test*.

Usually, these four categories are indicated by 13 performance indicators. To the four main categories, we've added a dynamic real-time metric, we call the *L.I.F.T. Stress Test*, arguably the most important of all.

We discussed customized metrics in chapter 6, in the section True North Metrics. Regardless of the customized metrics you land on as critical to your business, all business will have at least five essential metrics. If you group the most common 13 performance indicators, you'll end up with four categories of metrics:

- Liquidity

- Profitability

- Leverage

- Efficiency

- To this, we add the *L.I.F.T. Stress Test*. If you only measure one thing, this is the one to spend your time on—in real-time—since crisis and stress are fluid and dynamic.

L.I.F.T. Fives: Your Five Provable Points

What are your top five provable points? In chapter 9, I asked you to make a list of your top five. If you didn't do it, now's the time. To market your business—not just for customers, but for any stakeholder, including team-members and shareholders—you need to hold these "five provable points" in mind.

L.I.F.T. Fives: Predator Rule of Five

Leaders are clever, primal Apex predators—top of the food chain. We discussed this extensively in chapter 10. To review, here are the predator guidelines for almost any market you sell to—from consumer products to business to consumables to services:

1. Positive brand image offsets most price differences.

This is about being the Apex predator. Top of the food chain. In marketing terms, that means a positive brand image. Without a strong brand, you have to "hunt" with clumsy weapons such as "discounts." Be diligent in building your reputation, like the lion protecting the pride.

2. Educate prospects

Apex sellers educate. The companies and sales teams willing to invest in educating the prospect will close most of the three-percent of buyers ready to buy in any given cycle. (See chapter 10 for details on this statistic.)

3. "Cult of the Expert."

You, as the expert, listen twice as much as you speak. You ask questions. You invite questions. You answer their questions.

If you're not an expert in your product or service, you're in the wrong market. You, as a leader, should be an expert. The people you recruit should be experts. Prospects buy from experts who know more than they do.

4. Camouflage and Stillness

Does a hunter tell his prey, "Hey, hunter over here, watch out!" Since terms like "sales representative" have initial negative impressions—and since first impressions can make or break a pitch—why advertise you're a hunter?

Instead, focus your sales team on their function as experts, representatives, informers, and communicators.

5. Confidence of the Predator

The confidence of an Apex Predator does not arise from being "faster" or "better." The critical thing to remember is that hunters strike when they're sure of the kill. If your audience is in the 97 percent phase—not ready to buy—you watch, make friends, convey expertise, warmly invite them to return at a later time when they are ready. Hunters are precise, careful, and intelligent, and strike only when they are confident of success.

L.I.F.T. Five: Secrets to Achieving Goals

Achieving goals is a matter of focus, prioritization, and discipline. There are five things that characterize a great leader:

1. Mind—it's not a cliche: mind matters

Mind over matter? Mindfulness in business. Set your mind. If you can't manage your mind, you can't control your life or your company. It's as simple as that. Setting and visualizing goals is an activity of the mind.

2. Set lofty goals: no mediocre challenges

Moderate, achievable goals are mediocrity. Our minds parse it this way. We shrug, don't care, move on. Lofty challenges bring out our competitive spirit—the challenge drives our mental charge and our physical adrenalin. Skip "realistic" and go for glory.

3. The hated to-do list and procrastination

I'm sorry about this, and nothing new here, but you *need to recognize when you are procrastinating.* You do need to work back from your deadlines. My best tip—break everything down into achievable chunks. Multi-tasking may be impressive, but it's also the reason people don't accomplish much, which leads to procrastination.

4. Learn from athletes: practice the 50 -20 Rule

Our muscle of choice is our brains. Like any "athlete", our minds can benefit from "interval" training. I use 50 minutes of work, 20-minute break rule. The key is plenty of interval breaks, but keep pushing through until you accomplish your goals.

5. Build your support network— anchor your life in compassion.

If you want to achieve, network with achievers, both at work and in your personal lives. If you're going to achieve meaningfully, you'll likely already undertake philanthropic, spiritual, or other critical personal missions. Compassion is an important characteristic of L.I.F.T. Leadership. Exemplify it at work—and live it at home. Be a volunteer, join networks of like-minded people, pursue what resonates with your life. You have aspirations beyond the office, right? Make them count. Surround yourself with wonderful achievers and like-minded people who inspire you.

15

100 DAYS—HOW TO PIVOT A COMPANY IN FOUR STAGES

Every company will face a necessary pivot—not "if" but "when." The good news is it can be a science. The better news is you can do it—in fact you must do it—in 100 Days. To take longer is to diminish the return on your pivot investment. In this final chapter, I show you how you can do it.

L.I.F.T. Facts

- According to a post-mortem of 247 businesses, "approximately 10 percent of failed startup entrepreneurs surveyed attributed their failure at least partially to a "pivot gone bad," while 7 percent attributed it partially to a failure to pivot." [79]

- Venture Capitalist Fred Wilson reported, "Of the 26 companies that I consider realized or effectively realized in my personal track record, 17 of them made complete transformations or partial transformations of their businesses between the time we invested and the time we sold."[80]

In this chapter

- To improve is to change.

- The first 100 days of any pivot—in four phases.

- Time is the enemy.

- The top 10 tenets of pivot leadership.

- How To: Day 1 - 30: data gathering and evaluation.

- How to: Day 31 - 60: analysis, offsites and plan creation.

- How to: Day 61-100: strategy, re-org and communication.

- How to: Day 101 and on: execute and pivot!

Important Take-away

- The pivot may seem like "wrestling a gorilla"—but it is not a matter of "if" but "when. The secret to success is, in the words of Walt Disney "quit talking and begin doing." The hard truth of the pivot is that "time is your only enemy"—it never gives you a second chance. Don't aim for 100 days. Make it happen! My L.I.F.T. mantra is: "Never surrender to time."

To Improve is to Change

The science of the Pivot in business is not an occasional necessity for C-Suite executives. The scale of the Pivot may change, but pivots in business are ongoing and desirable. The best "Pivot" business advice I can cite came from a famous change leader Sir Winston Churchill, who rallied a small island in World War II against unimaginable odds in one of the most extreme historical pivots:

"To improve is to change; to be perfect is to change often."

As Winston Churchill understood, change must be rapid and meaningful to win a war—including business battles. I'll show you how to engineer a significant business pivot in 100 days and four stages. I choose the word "engineer" and "science" deliberately. Although there are creative and "art" aspects to the business Pivot, decades of hands-on implementation demonstrate the reliable outcomes of these "100-day methods," regardless of the artistry of the leadership team. As Guy Kawasaki wrote: "Ideas are easy. Implementation is hard." This chapter is a 100-Day map for Pivot implementation to make the hard part easier.

The First 100 Days of Any Pivot

The first 100 days of any pivot is critical for momentum—and those 100 days should manifest as action. There are countless reasons for a pivot, some pre-emptive and some reactive:

- economic setbacks necessitating a pivot (reactive)

- company takeovers (pre-emptive or reactive)

- competition-driven scenarios forcing change (reactive)

- new product launch (pre-emptive or reactive)

- capturing a new market position (pre-emptive or reactive)

- a market-driven major pivot (pre-emptive or reactive)

- a fortifying pivot, where the market leader changes to retain dominance (pre-emptive)

- the deliberate re-invigoration of the company (pre-emptive.)

Once you get past the brainstorming and discussing phase, the first thing to know is that action and activity are the lifeblood of change.

You can't find better advice on this than from Walt Disney, who was famous for "change" in his many businesses:

"The way to get started is to quit talking and begin doing."

Declaring change is not enough. You, the C-suite leader, need a purposeful plan and activity map for the first 100-days—with the momentum and full focus and attention of the organization. No plan and activity map will succeed without the C-Suite's inspirational leadership, acting as motivating coaches.

Wrestling the Gorilla and the Goal of Change

The goal of a 100 Day Pivot is nothing less than a fundamental change to the company's course—and the ultimate improvement of the financial performance. I like to think of it as "wrestling the gorilla." Robert Stauss wrote:

"Success is a little like wrestling a gorilla. You don't quit when you're tired, you quit when the gorilla is tired."

To make the gorilla tired, to wrestle King Kong, requires a fulcrum to succeed. Once you commit your force to the Pivot, there is no surrender (or the Gorilla will break your legs). Whether the Pivot is pre-emptive or reactive, the stakes are nothing less than "Victory or death!" (William Barret Travis.)

Victory or Death may sound extreme, but it's important to remember that the Pivot analogy describes you as the Pivot fulcrum, enabling the exertion of force to create overwhelming momentum. If you stop to rest, if you pause the exertion of force on one side of the Pivot, the lever swings back.

Without the Pivot fulcrum, force is neutral. With the Pivot fulcrum, the force—you and your planned activities —develop irresistible momentum.

You commit to victory—and assuming you exert tremendous force around a Pivot point, you should win—just as Winston Churchill did when he Pivoted an entire country into a World War II war engine. He exerted the irresistible force of a unified mission for victory, despite a seemingly unconquerable aggressor. Every person, factory, and resource in Britain became part of that engine.

The Fulcrum of the Pivot

As a leader, you, your team, and your plan are the fulcrum point of the Pivot that enables rapid, effective change. Regardless of the scope of the Pivot—a turnaround, or preparation for growth, or attempting to bulletproof your company—there comes a moment in time that all the weight comes to bear on that one spot. With this momentum, you can shift unimaginable weight.

That fulcrum point firmly rests on your shoulders. There is no glory in being the fulcrum leader other than as an instrument of victory. As Lao Tzu wrote, "If you don't assume importance, you can never lose it." You lose momentum if you concern yourself with taking credit for the change. You lose sight of the fact that it is a collective effort. You may be the critical fulcrum point, but the momentum requires the weight of the team.

Time is the Enemy: Four Phases of the Pivot

In every Pivot situation—whether you're a long-term executive needing to ignite a change, or you are walking through the door on your first day—the first 100 days is, no pun intended, a "Pivotal moment." As Steve Douglas explained:

"Time is your only enemy, it disappears very quickly and never gives you a second chance."

To accomplish meaningful yet rapid change, there are three essential foundation phases to achieve within the first 100 days—with the fourth phase carrying the momentum forward:

1) Day 1-30: Phase 1 – Data Gathering and Evaluation – 30 Days

2) Day 31-60: Phase 2 – Analysis, Offsites, and Plan Design – 30 Days

3) Day 61-100: Phase 3 – Strategy, Re-Organization and Communication – 40 Days

4) Day 101 and on: Implementation: Phase 4 – Execute and Pivot

Pivot change is time-sensitive—since one of the forces we exert on the Pivot is urgency—so, it is critical to keep to ambitious timelines. Remember, Pivot change is a parallel rather than linear process. You can—and should—implement multiple initiatives in parallel, although there are dependencies, and for this reason, I've mapped these as Foundation Phases 1-3. However, your fundamental goal should be to fast-track the activities and execution required to generate the needed momentum and drive a sense of urgency from the team. You don't wait until the 101st day to implement initiatives that are clear and pressing.

Mitigation and Analysis Paralysis

There is no time for analysis paralysis—or attempting to mitigate every single risk identified. You can count on things surfacing that you never anticipated. Yes, plan for readiness, flexibility, and agility, but don't waste time trying to anticipate every single contingency.

The mediation and "cure" for "analysis paralysis" is preparation. Don't plan every scenario, but build a team that can handle every situation. Equip and educate your team well, and they will have the weapons needed to address the twists and turns. As leaders, we cannot, and will not, anticipate everything. In particular, you should not spend time planning for every outside force: economic, competitive, or client variables. Instead, plan dexterity and skills into your implementation team to handle the inevitable bumps in the road. In other words, before an analogous road trip, invest in a good GPS map and maintenance on your car, choose the best route, but then be prepared to detour for bad weather, construction, or road closures.

Never Surrender to Time

In decades of implementing the 100-Day Pivot Implementation, one hard and fast rule I've learned—the one rule to rule them all—is:

"Never surrender to time."—Randy Dewey

I am not advocating a lack of proper planning and analysis—quite the opposite —, but we must balance mitigation planning against the more pressing "power of urgency." Momentum cannot be underestimated.

It is critical, as a leader, to never signal that delays are acceptable. Instead, reinforce the power of urgency. Build "problem-solving" of unexpected issues into your 100 days, and keep hard and fast to the 30/30/40 Foundational Phases. In doing so, you signal the vital importance of timely Implementation.

In inevitable crisis moments, instead of accepting a delay, telegraph urgency with "how can we solve this problem—but without delay? What additional resources do you need?" Never surrender to time. You may need other resources to overcome obstacles, but never give up time.

Pivot Declaration Day

From the moment you declare the Pivot is underway—let's call it "Pivot Declaration Day"—embrace the ten fundamental tenets essential to your leadership, in addition to the cardinal rule of "never surrender to time."

There's no difference if your Pivot initiative is for a new company and team or an existing team seeking refresh. Either way, from the Pivot Declaration Day, you start fresh.

All other aspects being equal, the Pivot is manifestly more difficult for mature teams, especially if you have worked alongside them for years. You must overcome preconceptions, history (including failures), performance habits, and resistance to change with mature teams.

You must now prove, through your actions, from Pivot Declaration Day onwards—with every action and word—that there is real change, without compromise, and that you want the team to hold you accountable, just as you will with them.

The Genius Leader is a Listener

The genius leader is the listener who relies on the team for ideas and feedback. A solid, guiding principle is the wise words of Elon Musk (SpaceX, Tesla), one of the world's leading entrepreneurial giants—a man who relies entirely on ideas and feedback from his team. His genius is steering a group of intellectuals equal to himself. He wrote:

"Constantly seek criticism. A well thought out critique of what you're doing is as valuable as gold."

Elon Musk was not referring to "giving" criticism. He was wide-open and enthusiastic as the recipient of all constructive feedback, in his words, he seeks criticism—constantly. Scan through the "Ten Key Tenets of Successful Pivot Leadership" below, and you'll notice that this advice can be applied to all of them.

Top 10 Tenets of Pivot Leadership

Regardless of your situation, the top 10 tenets of Pivot Leadership are:

1. The Pivot Leader Asks—and Listens as if lives depended on it.

Don't underestimate the degree of intimidation people feel when a CEO/C-suite person asks them a question. Depending on your leadership style, and the team member's personality, there is a tendency to answer you what you want to hear—and make sure the reply "sounds" smart.

Good leaders put the team-members at ease, giving them time to formulate an honest, helpful answer, encouraging (but not leading) with helpful follow-up questions. Don't assume they know that our purest intention is to truly understand their perspective and experience. Instead, make impartial, engaged interest your goal. Consciously park your biases and preconceptions—and listen to their full response without criticism. Probing deeper and follow-up queries are good, provided your questions are open-ended—and in no way lead them towards an expected reply.

2. The Pivot Leader Honors team dignity—and builds trust.

It is human nature to become defensive about negative past developments. It's critical for you, as a leader, to recognize that systems and processes evolve for many different reasons, most of which don't exist any longer. You, and the team, know that this system or process is no longer valid.

The purpose of the "Pivot" is to change what doesn't work. When you, as a leader, initiate a Pivot, you're putting everything on the table. You are challenging the past, underlying assumptions to catapult the business forward and alter the course of the company. You can't do this alone. You need an enthusiastic team, fully committed, especially at the leadership level.

Be sensitive to the fact that some will feel threatened—and possibly insulted—because their old systems and processes are in review. Reassure them that these past methods were valid in their time but that they are no longer efficient to the reality of the "now."

Destroy bad habits with positive reinforcement, logic, support, and a team approach (more on this in 3. below.) Great C-Suite leaders are diplomats, careful never to demean, insult and offend. We must accomplish the "Pivot" with three guiding principles kept top-of-mind:

- Speed, depth, and momentum of the Pivot implementation may never be compromised,

- Engage the team in addressing the problem without recriminations or blame.

- Preserve everyone's dignity and build a relationship that helps everyone see this win as a victory for all.

3. The Pivot Leader understands the dangerous psychology of habit, assumptions, and opinions.

Never accept the dangerous answer, "it's always been done that way." Risk assessment in business is a matter of facts, never of assumptions. These assumptions are usually a matter of habit, not malice.

According to Psychology Today, "40 percent of your actions are not conscious decisions but habits."[81]

These habits are dangerous in the face of a necessary Pivot. According to the same experts, "It's hard to shake off a habit since it takes an average of 66 days before a new habit takes root in our brain." Since a Pivot inevitably requires "new habits"—which takes up to 66 additional days—we can only rely on hard facts and data.

We must be truth vigilantes, diligent in presenting only options that are based on data and fact. Entrenched "accepted truths" are common in well-established teams or companies. In business, where the stakes are high, you should avoid language like "belief." There is no "orthodoxy" or "canon" in business. If it's "always done that way," it is suspect.

Only current facts and data should guide your path. When you ask for feedback, be clear that you are seeking "what we know" rather than "what we think we know." If we don't know, ask, "how can we find out?" What lens do you want to look through when planning a fundamental pivot: the past or the truth of the "now." If the facts don't support our strategy or tactics, it's time to rethink the plan.

Remember, it's not necessarily deliberate when people fall back on "accepted truths" or suppositions. It's part of our human psyche. Habit and method are helpful for efficiency—but it undercuts the power of the Pivot. When it's time to change, it's time to form new habits. Bear in mind the 66-Day Rule. It will take your team 66 days to build new "neural pathways" forming the needed new "habit." As a leader, you must support this period of Pivot transition—and your best tools are facts and data.

The problem with facts and data is that it's easy to "spin doctor" the information—especially when feeling defensive. As C-Suite leaders, faced with board criticism, we may ourselves feel tempted to present only the supporting facts. Likewise, your team might unconsciously reinforce their entrenched position with selective or spun facts. Positive reinforcement, steering everyone back to unbiased data, is your best weapon.

In the same way that social media, for example, influences the news—the so-called "fake news" phenomenon—you may find there are team members who are "influencers." Take extra care to involve them in the facts and data to ensure the influence they exert on the team is a positive one. Remember, there's a difference between deliberate "disinformation" and misguided fact spin.

As a CEO/C-suite executive driving a major business pivot, we have to be ready to counter opinions and biases—allowing for unbiased and thorough dialogue, including dissenting opinions, new views, and possibilities—while keeping a healthy and respectful team bond.

4. The Pivot Leader is the Fulcrum of the Pivot—creating momentum in the team.

The most important principle of the Pivot is the fulcrum. Without a fulcrum, the Pivot lacks momentum. This fulcrum—that single point upon which the pivot balances—is you, the leader. Your team, supported by facts and resources, exert their collected weight on one side of the Pivot, propelling irresistible force through the leader's fulcrum to achieve the needed Pivot or change.

You may be the fulcrum in this situation, but the collective energy to push the load over the distance to come to bear on the Pivot as it sways to the other side is not something you can do alone. We need the full engagement and motivated, collective energy of the entire company—work in unison to accomplish a critical, monumental change in a short period.

You, as a leader, must take the team forward with confidence. Remember the words of Henry Ford as you rally your team:

"Whether you think you can or you can't, you're right."

Your collective success as a team—or failure—rests on your ability to create purpose, inspire faith in the mission. We need willing, enthusiastic recruits, not drafted, reluctant soldiers. A leader cannot force loyalty and commitment. You, as a leader, should inspire action and vigorous change. Forced, dictated change will only inspire resistance, defensiveness, or even moderate rebellion or outright insurrection. Leaders inspire, educate, challenge, foster team-building, listen to opinions—and then make decisions.

When your team sees you are open to their feedback yet decisive, they will "think you can." If you lay down the law, shut down communication or punish constructive criticism, they will think, "you can't." The balance needed to manage quick and crucial change—in 100 days—while preserving your people's dignity, inspiring commitment, and resolve is the test of a true leader. An inspiring leader is the fulcrum of the Pivot. A leader always makes it clear that he or she "thinks you can."

5. The Pivot Leader always has a sense of fearless urgency—and the tenacity to drive essential change.

Urgency doesn't mean panic, stress, or loss of control. The Pivot Leader fosters a culture of speed and transparency but drives change through excitement and confidence—not fear. Model your leadership after the successful professional team sports coach. Team coaches who drive big wins from their team inspire them to perform, win, and succeed. Yes, they call out the bad plays and the mistakes, but they inspire with a new game plan. Despair and fear have no role to play in team sports—or in business. Fear drives mistakes. The urgency to win from an inspired game plan drives cup wins. You can't do better than to follow the advice of basketball coach Bobby "The General" Knight:

"To be as good as it can be, a team has to buy into what you as the coach are doing. They have to feel you're a part of them, and they're a part of you."

We all want to be part of a winning culture, whether it's business or sports. Winners use fearless urgency on the field, inspiring the team with tastes of victory but driving relentlessly until the final buzzer sounds.

6. The Pivot leader rewards quick wins and celebrates milestones.

How do you overcome this "fear" side-effect of urgency? Let your team taste of victory. The adrenalin of an even small win pushes fear aside. In the beginning, help the team visualize the win. Later, as the team scores a few, reinforce the success. Never left that sense of urgency, no matter how many wins you make.

How do you, as a leader, engineer step-by-step wins? Create small, achievable milestones that move you towards the ultimate goals. Move from smaller wins to increasingly critical "fixes."

Identify mission-critical situations and assign your best people to fix them. Ensure the success of your best people with the right resources. Then, celebrate each turning point.

There is nothing more satisfying for an organization than to see problems resolved, step-by-step—then to turn a significant problem, one that squandered the company's precious capital or resources, into a solution. A win. Then, another win. The energy and enthusiasm gained from a major quick win are exciting and cause for celebration.

7. The Pivot Leader reinforces and restores confidence—and the right attitude.

Confidence is not just a "belief in yourself." Confidence has real power. Likewise, lack of confidence robs us of power. More than a century ago, William James wisely wrote:

"Most people live in a restricted circle of potential."

Many scientific and psychological studies have reinforced this statement. The Pivot Leader must know how to build the confidence of the team to break the restriction circle. In Pivot situations, we likely have a history of failures—which drives the need for a Pivot. In the face of crisis, how does the leader build team self-assurance? There is no doubt it's up to the leader. Positive reinforcement from the C-suite is the only real way to restore or build confidence. Instead of "we failed," the leader inspires with "we know where this went wrong, and I know you can turn this around." Be watchful of incidents or setbacks that rob the team of confidence.

Remember, as we discussed in the psychology of habit (3, above), that lack of confidence is just another habit. As a leader, you need to demonstrate your confidence and instill it in every member of the team. Even transforming critical team members with confidence creates an irresistible avalanche of energy—a feeling of being unstoppable. It's worth remembering that when a pivot is needed, there is inevitably a problem with confidence and the team's collective will. As a leader, your goal is to restore that confidence—helping them visualize and generate good outcomes — and ensuring you have the right people with the right attitudes to drive success.

8. The Pivot Leader prioritizes and manages productive meetings.

"Meetings should be like salt—a spice sprinkled carefully to enhance a dish," wrote Basecamp founder and CEO, Jason Fried. "Too much salt destroys a dish. Too many meetings destroy morale and motivation."

The Pivot Leader knows how to organize and manage concise, compelling, productive meetings. Nothing robs a team of success faster than unnecessary meetings. Ruthlessly kill time-wasting meetings. At the same time, re-energize the necessary sessions with concise formats and precision. Don't call reactive meetings in response to urgent situations unless you have a tight action-agenda. Aside from lost productivity, remember the other costs of unnecessary meetings. The average American worker, according to statistics, spends 9.1 hours a week preparing for and attending meetings—each and every week, one full day lost to productivity.

We all complain about time-wasting meetings. At the same time, discussions are undoubtedly necessary for any team environment. Instead of canceling appointments, learn to re-organize them more effectively. First, ask yourself if the meeting is required to accomplish or review a milestone, and if it is, determine if there is a more efficient process. Can a quick catch-up call replace the need for a meeting with five team members?

Review at least the following in deciding to proceed with a necessary meeting:

- Specific agenda and goals.

- Who really needs to attend?

- Background research required to act on the agenda

- Does the meeting contribute to productivity and morale—the sense that things are changing?

One way to signal a transformation in a Pivot situation is to change some communication protocols—most notably meetings. As a general guideline, consider canceling, altering, or shortening every single routine appointment in the company. When a meeting is required, invite only the necessary team-members.

Finally, remember that you don't need to cover items that are on track, only the items that need course corrections.

9. The Pivot Leader knows how to manage the three fears.

A fearless leader is not enough. The team members must likewise overcome fears that rob them of confidence and productivity. It's important to remember three overwhelming fears rob us of confidence in the Pivot situation:

- Fear of change.

- Fear of failure.

- Fear of uncertainty.

Most other business fears arise from a variation of these three: fear of taking risks, fear you don't know enough, fear of costs, fear of disappointing others (which can lead to defensiveness), fear of discomfort (such as public speaking, or fear of work overload), and fear of being wrong.

Fear generally arises from a lack of information. We fear change because we don't "know." We fear failure because we don't have all the facts. Fear can be overcome with intellectual rationalization. If you are about to jump off a bridge tied to a bungee cord, fear naturally arises; but if you understand it's statistically safe, you make the leap.

Fear manifests in two main dangerous ways:

- Leaders who use fear to manipulate or manage a team.

- Team-members who are gripped by it.

Either form can be a mortally dangerous scenario in a team environment.

Leaders who lead with fear damage people's confidence, inspire gang-like mentalities and squash the truth. You may create discipline, but you lose loyalty, trust, productivity, and transparent engagement. You also lose free-flowing ideas that are the lifeblood of any enterprise. Often leaders don't know their team fears them. Sometimes it only manifests with failures, since fearful people are good at hiding their anxiety. Remember, though, that trust is rarely unrecoverable. If you discover your team is afraid of you, have the courage to humbly change and take the time needed to repair damaged relationships.

The second manifestation of fear is the leader or team member who is averse to risk and is unwilling to face it. Even if you know the bungee cord is 99.99999% safe (National Center for Health Statistics,) fear-averse people still struggle to step off the bridge.

The third manifestation of fear is uncertainty. Though tied closely to the first in fear of failure and change, it differs in that it causes people to dig—and dig further—for data or justification. The result is, there is never going to be enough support, and we have to go with our instincts. The fear of uncertainty would have stopped every pilgrim from venturing to a new land, but the reward of opportunity and a better life led them to face it. We need to keep our eye on the prize, more than grappling for the last piece of evidence.

As a leader, you guide by example. If you are trying to inspire a fearful team-member or correct your own fearfulness, you must first recognize it. It will manifest in an unwillingness to face conflict. Or not wanting to move outside the zone of comfort. It is evident when we get emotional over criticisms or want to be liked by our colleagues and subordinates or get anxious about the outcomes and potential failures.

Your own fear as a leader and the fear of your team-members is manageable. Typically, our safety net is information. If we have followed through on our research, analysis, brainstorming, and plan, we know we have the right course. Armed with that knowledge, step off the bridge.

10. The Pivot Leader always demonstrate gratitude—and reward team members.

No business or team can grow without motivated team-members. As humans, the need for recognition—to be appreciated and rewarded—is universal:

> "People are pulled toward behaviors that offer positive incentives and pushed away from behaviors associated with negative incentives."—D.A. Bernstein, Essentials of Psychology

The Pivot Leader doesn't engage in meaningless platitudes, however. Gratitude must be genuine and tangible in the form of positive recognition and financial enrichment. Leaders must treat people well, remembering that trust is earned from a consistent appreciation of performance.

We often lose sight of the fact that people in companies make personal sacrifices to help accomplish significant milestones. Never take it for granted. They might be onboarding considerable stress, working over-time, or sacrificing time with the family to finish the project. At the same time, every achievement doesn't always need a financial incentive. Consistent positive affirmations, open or public recognition, or thoughtful notes with specifics—from you as a leader—can be just as meaningful as financial bonuses. Personalizing the reward to their lives can be more significant than a generic reward: a surprise company-paid trip; or allowing a spouse to come along on a business trip—with the return four days later, or a gift card to their favorite store.

Gratitude and recognition come in a thousand forms, but it takes a diligent effort from you, the leader, to regularly and reliably reward team-members.

Appreciation makes you a better leader. It improves your own personal psychological well-being, physical health, joy, and social relationships. It does much more to boost the team member. There is an absolute joy in being part of a company that values the people for both leaders and team members. This type of celebratory culture also attracts new team-members.

The tone is set at the top. Make sure that attitude is one of gratitude and appreciation.

100 Days to Pivot Requires Consistency

To engineer a significant pivot in 100 days, as laid out in *The First 100 Days*, it's critical to consistently apply the 10 Tenets of a Pivot Leader.

You only have 100 days to make a monumental shift. You will need the team's collective momentum and energy to facilitate this enormous transformation in a relatively short period.

You won't necessarily be able to implement all 10 Tenets from day one. Remember you have to overcome history and habits, which can take up to 66 days (according to Psychology Today). Not everyone will believe right away. Not everyone will notice your commitment to apply all 10 Tenets. Consistency and transparency are required. Your habits may take 66 days to change. The transformation will occur naturally in your 100-Day Pivot, assuming you remain disciplined.

You may want to print these 10 Tenets and make them the new motto for the executive team—or use it as an accountability piece for the group. We need to take these 10 Tenets seriously and make it part of our modus operandi through the four phases outlined below—and beyond. If we are genuinely looking to create lasting, meaningful change in a company, demonstrate it with a sincere commitment to the 10 Tenets.

Pivot in 100 Days—in Four Phases

Although some fluidity may be required based on the situation, you can count on the four phases of the 100-Day Pivot method as reliable timelines. Never allow them to drift longer than necessary, and be careful of losing momentum when things take too long. Remember, if one team-member slips, it impacts the entire team. Instead of allowing unnecessary shifts, jump in with any assistance or resources needed to keep everything on track. Instead of "how much more time do you need?" ask "what do you need from the team or me to make your deadline happen?" Too much slippage in time commitments results in loss of momentum and return to harmful habits.

We must keep the pressure on—never accepting mediocrity—yet be respectful of people's limits. Be unwaveringly persistent for the team's sake and the goal—and, if needed, deal with office politics head-on.

As a leader, as the fulcrum in this change, you cannot make this happen without the company's collective effort. To do that, you must manifest the environment that drives change and momentum from the people. By definition, in a Pivot, we are moving an enormous burden. It requires the team's combined effort and a consistent leader as the fulcrum to make it happen.

Since Pivot's and change are about nothing less than transformation, process and commitment are essential to success. We've covered aspects in the 10 Tenets of Pivot Leadership. Now that you and the team are ready, it's time to proceed with the Pivot in 100 Days—in Four Phases.

Day 1-30 – Data Gathering and Evaluation: Phase 1 in 30 days

The first 30 days are about gathering reliable and current intel, information, and data necessary to plan for the needed change. Don't short-change this vital step—but don't stretch it either. It's easy to fall into the trap of analysis paralysis. Allow yourself no more, and no less, than 30 days to diligently collect and analyze facts and data. Ensure accuracy since the remaining forty days of the Pivot rely on this information.

In this phase, you are collecting needed transformational information and evaluating five different aspects of the company:

- Revenue cycle

- Operating cycle

- Financial cycle

- Metrics and analytics

- Human talent and Organizational Structure.

Revenue Cycle

The Revenue Cycle evaluation requires a thorough value stream mapping exercise of the sales process, including:

- Terms/conditions

- Customer credit reviews

- Commission structures

- Alignment of interests between the company and salespeople: i.e., pay when the company collects, commission on margin, not revenue, who pays freight/duties and is that deducted from commissions, etc.

- Product development: investments, ROIC, measures of success, scrutiny of resources committed and approvals, and alignment to the future evolution and desired markets.

- Customer support process and costs, and the overall marketing efforts and investments (i.e., Tradeshows, travel, entertainment, advertisement, social media, etc.).

We need to understand the full cycle of revenue thoroughly, the cost of adoption of a customer, and the investments required in each market that is aligned with the company's strategic direction. The review of this is arduous but essential. It is the front-end engine of the company. It cannot be left to sales to manage. It requires clear policies and complete alignment with the company's best interests and the strategic direction of the enterprise within its market.

Operating Cycle

The Operating Cycle evaluation starts with:

- Top 20 vendor relationships: credit, request for proposal process, number of alternatives, minimum order quantities, contracts, volume discounts, etc.

- Working capital management: inventory turns review including raw material management, WIP, and finished goods coupled with a thorough 3-year write-off history backed into the historical inventory turns and then measured.

- Value stream map of the entire operational flow, including: the operating time, yield, overall equipment efficiency, and working capital consumption measures.

- Top 20 customer relationships: accuracy of their forecasts, dependability on their commitments, credit risk review, payment terms and history, receivable insurances and costs, ways to move up stack and grab more value in what we build or provide customers, and vulnerabilities.

Financial Cycle

The Financial Cycle review organizes into the capital/debt structure and the operating performance of the company. A lot of the business pivot emphasis naturally focuses on profitability and the viability of specific markets—but you cannot ignore the company's capital structure and the risks that a levered balance sheet can pose to a company.

While it is challenging to change the company's capital structure and requires full shareholder support to complete, it's essential to evaluate. The key areas to be analyzed are:

- Absolute priorities within the debt stack.

- Capital and equity positions of shareholders.

- Historical performance for debt service coverage: fixed charge coverage, borrowing base, debt to assets, and interest coverage—any problems with lenders (i.e., demand penalties increase in interest for risk profile, new capital to pay down debt, increased collateral, or demand notices).

- Over/Under Capitalization reviews with a review of the competition. Determine if you are subject to penalties within a particular industry that could hamper your ability to properly leverage your assets, putting you at a competitive disadvantage (ie. Too high a debt leverage >3:1 in an industry with long R&D investment cycles—or Fortune 500 clients with extended payment terms. This could cause management to take short cycle work to keep their ratios aligned with the business moving towards a liquidity crisis. It could result in not creating long-term shareholder value through better contracts and too much dependence on too few customers).

- Gross Margin Management, SKU reduction, and overall internal control discipline. A company that pays attention to the various product lines' cash and contribution margins typically has better EBITDA margin performance and operating cash flow performance.

- Capital Expenditure Performance and measuring the actual return on these investments is essential to cash management and aligns the company with the need to be responsible with other people's money. CAPEX requires tight controls and structure.

Metrics and Analytics

The Metrics and Analytics used to monitor a business are critical. Are you a balance sheet manager or a P&L manager or focused on operating metrics? To succeed, we must be concerned with all the metrics within liquidity, profitability, leverage, and efficiency.

Measure every one of these sub-metrics within each of the four categories over time—with particular attention to the trends and norms. Goals should be in this range:

1. Liquidity

   a. Current ratio history with the goal of being over 1.5

   b. Quick Ratio history with the goal being over 1.0

   c. Net Working Capital % of Revenue history with the goal being <33%

   d. Cash at the end of the month as a % of Revenue being >33%

   e. Financial Stress Test being >18 months

2. Profitability

   f. Free Cash Flow Margin is over 50%

   g. Gross Margin is over 35%

   h. EBIT margin is over 15%

   i. Return on Assets with a minimum goal of 5%

   j. Return on Equity over 15%

   k. Contribution margin is over 12%

3. Leverage Ratios

l. Debt to Equity is less than 2:1

m. Debt to Assets is less than 0.4

n. Fixed Assets/tangible net worth is less than 0.5

o. Debt/net worth is less than 2:1

p. Debt Service Ratio is less than 2.75:1

4. Efficiency Ratios

q. Asset Turnover (highly industry-specific retail >1.75 and utilities >0.3)

r. Cash conversion cycle <60 days

s. You should breakdown the CCC into DII, DSO, and DPO and analyze them separately

t. Return on Invested Capital over 2.5%

u. EBITDA to FCF goal is greater than 80%.

The most crucial step is to take each one of these metrics in all four categories and calculate these back as many periods as you can—but at least eight quarters—to analyze the trend over time.

Human Talent and Organization Structure

The fifth evaluation phase is the Human Talent and Organizational Structure Element. HR resources are critical to any plan's success. This review is more about engineering the right structure, with the right people, properly aligned to the "Post-Pivot" company's needs. If needed, this review can be in parallel to Phase II (the next 30 days).

We need to understand several critical things—and time may be required to make that determination, for example, properly:

a. Hierarchy and decision-making complexities: are we lean and flat, or fat and layered?

b. Evolution of roles and those in them: were the jobs created for the person, or was the person hired for the job?

c. External and internal relationships: how can those be leveraged for greater benefit within the company? (For example, a VP Sales role is needed, but the apparent candidate has a lot of seniority but not the right relationships with the customer; or is great at the ground game of sales—versus the polish of a board room presentation).

d. People, talents, capabilities, desires, interests, energy, influence: It's important to inventory your team assets in these areas, going beyond resume and background. What is the intangible impact people have on one another? Based on their skills, do your best people appear aligned in the optimal roles? What happens if you "switch seats" and make changes that could have a lasting impact and create unbridled enthusiasm within the organization?

e. Willingness to change versus arrogant passive resistance. In a company, there are always positive and negative forces that cannot be ignored. The power of a long-tenured executive with an excellent pedigree is enormous, and their engagement can bring the rest of the team along. On the other hand, if that same executive has a destructive attitude with a narcissistic view of themselves, and that person's power to cast negativity across the entire company is costing you more than 10x their salary in damage to the company, it's time for a shakeup. In this case, the poor decisions, bad hires, neglection of certain duties—and the long shadow that executive casts—is damaging your team environment.

The organizational structure—with the right team and players—must be addressed during the 100 days because of the broad impact on culture and productivity. Any Pivot is dependent upon HR choices in the restructuring effort.

Day 31-60—Analysis, Offsites, and Plan Creation: Phase 2 in 30 days

In days 31-60, Phase 2, we advance to in-depth analysis and plan creation, building on what we know from our high-level evaluation in the first 30 days (Phase 1.) We gather in-depth, substantiating data to verify our findings from Phase I. The first step to a viable plan is the verification of data. Often, this is the time to bring in expert input, engaging third parties for any specific needs or skill gaps within the company. We are transitioning from data to the decisions needed for Phase 3.

The critical steps of Phase 2 include:

- thorough analysis

- true root cause investigation

- clarifying the most dangerous weaknesses and threats to the business.

Pareto's rule will likely apply—80% of the problems derive from 20% of the issues. In the course of this phase, we will work through the ten A's: Articulation, Assessment, and Appreciation, Analysis and Assignment, Adoption and Arrangement; Absolute Alignment, and Accountabilities.

Articulation

We need to articulate—or explain—what is driving the Pivot in clear terms. What is our crisis, stated with compelling conviction, that makes the Pivot necessary? This isn't about storytelling or spin. We must state, honestly and clearly, the vision and need for this inflection point. You must articulate it—and believe it with all your being—pitching your vision for the future with a compelling belief. In other words, what are we asking all of the stakeholders to support? Why do we need the transition? How will it make us succeed?

Assessment and Appreciation

In Phase 2, we assess the Phase 1 data critically. This is the time for debate and deliberation with your key people.

As you work through the findings, you'll notice assumptions, shortcomings in the information, and things you didn't previously appreciate. In this assessment, you may need to go back to review: gathering more information, calling in people with direct experience to shed more light, and taking the time required to precisely understand what the data is telling you. Brainstorming sessions, critical thinking reviews, and thorough assessments come in many forms, but the relentless pursuit of facts is the goal. Insufficient information leads to bad decisions. Ensuring your data and information are supported and verified will enhance your winning decision rate.

Analysis and Assignment

The shift to analysis and assignment is vital since analysis paralysis is an organizational problem that leads to momentum losses and endless second-guessing. Never compromise the timeline. Be decisive and confident in your choices and assign the resources, projects, priorities, processes to be improved, policies required, and organizational changes and roles.

Adoption and Arrangement

The plan needs to be formally created, all objectives clear, fundamental changes, and timelines determined. At this point, all concerns and hesitations are put on the table and worked through to their natural conclusion. Any last-minute changes are made, and the leadership team emerges clear on all the messaging and the vision for this crucial Pivotal moment.

Absolute Alignment and Accountabilities

Now, leadership and the teams need to align with a full understanding of—in written form—of:

- all the initiatives and tactics required for this Pivot

- supporting documentation for all the objectives

- one-page strategic plan

- projects tracker, project assignments, and every milestone, task, detail, and data point.

There is no room for ambiguity nor vagueness at this stage. No question should remain unanswered, and no potential problem should be ignored. It's decision time. Once we move into Phase 4, it's all about action and implementation—without any doubts or uncertainties.

Days 61-100 – Strategy, Re-Org and Communication - Phase 3

You have the vision, and you know what must be done. You've gathered facts, analyzed every variable and contingency with the 10 "A" s. Now is the time to act. The time for second-guessing is passed.

If you haven't already, formalize all the findings, decisions, ideas, and outcomes into a concise document summarizing Phase 2. Map out your milestones and project tracking system and determine the timing of the organization's changes and the communication strategy.

The actual strategy has four parts to it:

- organizational restructuring and role clarification

- business plan and vision

- operational improvement strategy

- financial improvement strategy.

All four aspects need to be thoroughly considered, clearly formulated, with timing chosen for parallel activities versus those in series with various gating items, plus the overall alignment to push this immense list of work and effort.

There's no turning back at this stage. You, the Pivot Leader, the fulcrum, will need to take the initiative to implement, make the necessary changes—and never look back.

The entire organization will align with you if you've done all the hard work leading up to this moment and communicated as a Pivot Leader.

The shift will come from the collective will of the organization. At this moment, you will see the best in your people, and their passion emerge. Your bold approach will be met with a courageous spirit from your people, matching your own.

Day 101 and on—Execute and Pivot: Phase 4

At this point, the Pivot is well underway. You're dealing with issues and problems with boldness and tenacity. The critical mindset you must instill is: "This is a marathon, not a sprint."

The first 100 days were about setting up the Pivot. The actual changes and tactical milestones will map out from Day 101 and on. The purpose of the 100 Days is to remove uncertainties, ensure success, and ready implementation.

Set up your milestones in your project tracker, designed to drive (and demonstrate) continuous improvements, day by day, task by task.

Keep in mind that Pivotal moments in a business are significant changes. Remember, the rule of 66—that it takes 66 days to form a new habit. Use monitoring, project management, task lists, and other tools to ensure those habits form.

Expect obstacles and new issues to arise that might not have been anticipated even with your extensive ten "As" assessments. Remain the strong pivot point, the fulcrum for your team, ensuring everyone stays on track. Your most significant role now is to ensure everyone stays committed to the cause—through any short-term pain you and the team may endure. With a Pivot, always remember that counterforce or counterweight can easily tip back the wrong way. It is your role, as the fulcrum, to ensure you apply sufficient force to keep the Pivot swinging on the plan.

Your prime mission must be to guard against any slips in progress—or people who might accidentally or deliberately sabotage the great work underway.

What if you think you're not ready to make that type of sacrifice to create such a pivot?

Understand that the personal cost and sacrifice it takes to make this type of monumental shift in a company is vital. Still, there are times in life when you are not in the best mental space. Always remain mindful of the mental health and personal well-being of the CEO/C-suite executives, leadership, and teams in this process.

This 100-Day Pivot requires the personal, professional, and business pivot of the leader. In other words, look after yourself. This is arduous, necessary, and do-able. Still, you cannot expect to take all that weight on that one spot (fulcrum) and pivot the entire company while dealing with significant personal issues, such as a divorce, kids drifting off into trouble, emotional leadership problems at work, or an underperforming team.

When there are significant personal issues that make you think you're not ready to sacrifice for the Pivot, it is best to re-schedule. Deal with the individual issues, get clear with the professional problems in your leadership style and get the right team behind you—before you attempt a major pivot.

You could consider an interim Chief Restructuring Officer or consultant to assist you with the effort, as they can take on a lot of the stress for you during such a difficult time. This is a good option either when you have personal issues distracting you or if you need additional support help in general.

Ideally, you need to be the center of this effort, but if you cannot deal with the situation—and assuming your business cannot wait for the Pivot due to circumstances—hiring support through an interim CRO or a professional executive coach that can help you through the tumult. In this case, it is well worth the investment. The cost of waiting versus the cost of an interim CRO or Executive Coach is small. An external consultant increases your resources and impartial analysis and can improve your chances of success.

A Pivot is Always Required

Every business comes to the point where a Pivot is required. Failure to recognize and act on these Pivot points lead to drifting down a road that could lead to the business's death. Turning points and change are necessary.

This 100-Day plan will help you manage these needed Pivots. Now, it is all about your willingness to recognize the need—and be committed to making the change. No company can avoid the Pivot. Even Nokia, one of the world's enduring companies, established in 1865, pivoted over the years to toilet paper, rubber tires, military radios, minicomputers, televisions, cellphones, set-top boxes, and telecom network equipment.

A company willing to accept change and create new and exciting opportunities—either within a sector or in a new sector—has the opportunity to succeed and grow. It all comes in their enthusiasm to adapt and change, accept the things they can change, and take action to make it happen.

> "Pivoting is not the end of the disruption process, but the beginning of the next leg of your journey."
>
> — Jay Samit, Disrupt You!: Master Personal Transformation, Seize Opportunity, and Thrive in the Era of Endless Innovation

A Last Word—all or nothing?

I'll leave you where we started. This book shows you how to L.I.F.T. your leadership. It's up to you to adapt these methods to your situation and leadership style. The one thing I can assure you is that top growth leaders always:

Lead with passion.

Inspire their people.

Focus on what makes lasting change.

Transform obstacles into opportunities for growth.

Worth Repeating

What I've learned in three decades of business turnarounds is that any crisis is an opportunity—and that transformation is only the beginning of the story.

I wish you every success in your journey as a passionate, inspiring, focused, transformative leader.

APPENDIX I

Mehmed II the Conqueror

In 1432 Mehmed II was born into the Ottoman royal family. He was the son of a Turkish slave girl from the royal harem. Moulded in the Christian way of life as most of the women in the harem came from Eastern Europe, but the religious culture around Mehmed II was Muslim. He was born second in line to the throne after his older brother Alaadin. Mehmed II was raised as royalty and was trained from an early age to be a leader. Upon the death of his older brother, in 1443, Mehmed II was the apparent successor to the throne, and at this time, thrust into a more aggressive training regime.

Stepmother Mara Brankovic, a Hungarian Princess, raised Mehmed as one of her own. She was given in marriage by her Father, King of Serbia, to the Ottoman King Murad II as a peace offering to avoid an Ottoman invasion. Mehmed II spent most of his formative years, 200 miles away in Manisa, an Aegean Province as Governor as was customary. Mehmed II was obsessed with Alexander the Great and all his conquests, battle plans and leadership tactics. He had a similar path and lead the Ottoman Empire into a world dynasty. Alexander the Great was part of the ancient Greek Empire, he individually led more conquests and took more land than any military leader before him. Alexander the Great was one of the most famous early conquerors that led his people with charisma and concern over the heart and soul of his people. Alexander sat at the feet of his teacher Aristotle. Mehmed II sat at the proverbial feet of Alexander the Great and wanted to model his leadership style and successes. Mehmed II viewed the conquering of Constantinople, as the pinnacle victory to begin his conquest. His forefathers coveted the great city and to start his reign from this location would cement his legacy. In Mehmed II's mind, there was no more fabulous prize.

Mehmed II spent countless hours studying all of the battles at Constantinople. All 12 failed attempts were well documented. The Royal teachers spent time training Mehmed on every military battle technique and studying the history of war. Mehmed II had a brilliant mind, and a fierce determination, and he knew by heart every battle at Constantinople, and the reasons each army failed and the plans they deployed and the shortcomings of every attempt. He was a leader with purpose and a vision that forged his youth.

Every Ottoman leader wanted to be the supreme world leader, and the golden jewel was to reign from the most strategic spot in the ancient world, and many before Mehmed held a similar view, Constantinople was the perfect place. The original vision came from the founder of the Ottoman Empire, Osman Ghazi. It was clear to the young leader, Osman, that an Empire needed a capital worthy of its role and Constantinople was, in every sense, the perfect location. Osman had started this obsession with Constantinople, and by 1280 he penned his dream.

"Suddenly, there arose a mighty wind, and turned the points of the sword-leaves towards the various cities of the world, but especially towards Constantinople. That city, placed at the junction of two seas and two continents, seemed like a diamond set between two sapphires and two emeralds, to form the most precious stone in a ring of universal empire." Osman's dream 1280

The two sapphires Osman is referring to is the Black Sea and the Mediterranean Sea, and the two emeralds are the continents of East Europe and Western Asia. The central point of trade and many Empires thought this was the epicentre of the ancient world. Its strategic location gave it a significant advantage in both the military and commercial sense as it was at the crossroads of the East and West.

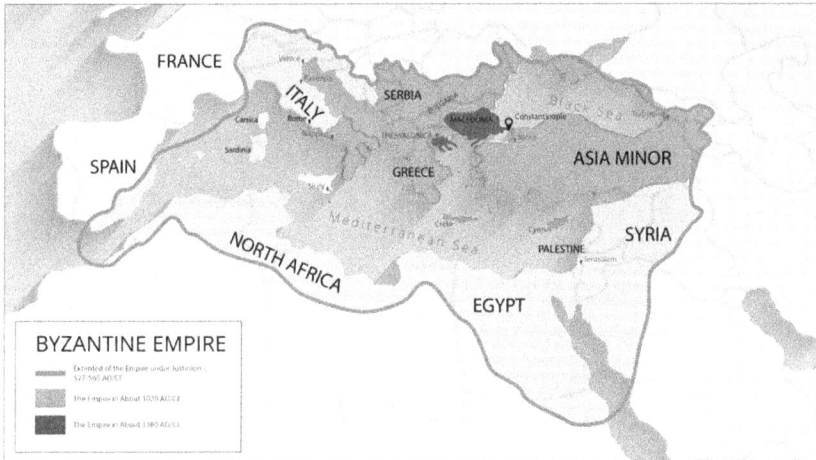

The Ottoman Empire sat on the border of the region of Constantinople. The fortified city sat as a beacon of Roman rule and dominance. Strategically located, Constantinople was also exceptionally positioned on a triangular peninsula extending out into the Sea of Marmara. It was surrounded on three sides by water and the land entrance had the most elaborate wall system built in the 5th century.

In 409AD, Emperor Theodosian embarked on an incredible 9-year project to construct the most elaborate barricading plan any city has ever known in the world at that time. He envisioned a complicated multi-layer wall system that would be 200 feet deep from the innermost wall to the outer most edge and the highest point of the inner wall, a towering 90 feet to the bottom grade of the exterior wall. These bastioned walls, coupled with an elaborate moot and two layers of killing fields, would leave any attacking army vulnerable and incapable of breaching the encased city. The engineered walls extended for a total of 23 kilometres with 96 towers, which acted as re-enforcement points and observation vantage points. The towers averaged in size 18m tall by 11m wide, with only three gates to the city by land; Golden Gate, Gate of Rhegion, and Gate of Charisius. The city walls, the moot, and a large fortified inner wall created an impenetrable barrier that stopped 12 invasion attempts over 1100-years.

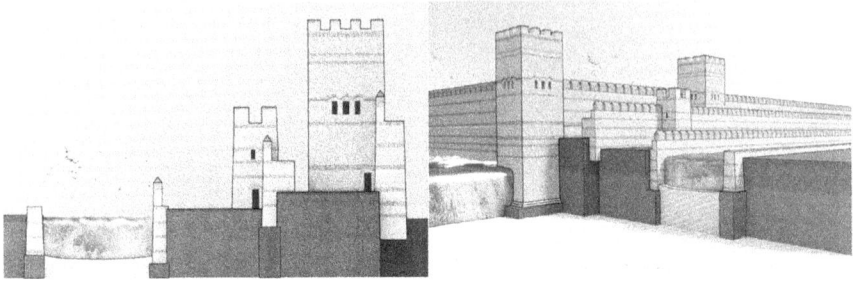

The death of Ottoman King Murad II in 1451 paved the way for young Mehmed II to rise to the throne. He was 19 years old and a very headstrong leader with a very determined plan. He was caught at the beginning of his reign with a threat from the Hungarians and most specifically, their leader, John Hunyadi. Mehmed II quickly and decisively defeated them, and this ended a 20-year schism between these two nations. It was a huge victory that pushed King Mehmed II into prominence as a young ruler.

In the early days of King Mehmed II's reign in 1451, the Byzantine Emperor Constantine XI was new in the role, appointed ruler in 1449 upon the death of his brother. In 1452 Constantine XI began making demands and provoking the new young Ottoman King. At one point, he threatened to send imprisoned royal Ottoman Prince Orhan back to Adrianople if his annual fees to hold the outcast royal were not tripled and paid immediately. Orhan posed a threat to Mehmed's throne as Orhan was a relative of Mehmed's Father, and without the law of primogeniture (firstborn right to succeed), it was considered an act of intimidation and an insult. Mehmed II, angered by this blackmail, he refused to answer the Emperor and contemplated his next move in the face of this insult.

Mehmed II decided to make his first strategic move by crossing the Bosphorous Strait on Byzantine land and construct an outpost opposite to his outpost. In effect, this would create a control point on the strait from both sides that could block access to the Black Sea or the Mediterranean Sea. It was considered an act of war by Mehmed II, but it was a calculated risk to measure the response from the other side. King Mehmed's advisors were very worried this act could cause a unification of the Pope with the greater Roman Empire, which were at odds with each other. King Mehmed believed the response would give them essential intelligence to the strength of the Byzantine Army and the degree of support they actually had in Rome.

Emperor Constantine XI realized the actions of King Mehmed, building this outpost on his land as an audacious act but was a result of his earlier actions. He decided on extending cooperative efforts, and he sent two Emissaries to Mehmed II to offer a truce and bring peace to the situation. Mehmed II responded barbarically by beheading the Emissaries and throwing their heads back in a box. The situation went quiet, and the Emperor did not respond in kind, but rather chose to heavily contemplate his next move. However, this lack of response was exactly what Mehmed II wanted to see to judge their vulnerability.

Emperor Constantine XI was arrogant and dismissive of the Ottoman threat and his apathetic attitude in the early days was his biggest failure. This egotistical mindset emboldened him, relying on a long history of Roman Empire dominance, back up and support in Constantinople, the 1100-year stronghold the city stood on, and the relative ease it was to defend the city and frustrate their enemies. The gross underestimation by Emperor Constantine XI was exasperated by giving away signs of his own fragility and susceptibility through these skirmishes and his weak response. At this time, the Emperor urgently sent messengers to Rome and the Vatican to get military support and protection. Mehmed took this opportunity to send a message of aggression and had the messengers beheaded and sent them back in a box. It was a clear act of war and it would have invoked the weakest of nations to respond with enmity.

The powerful Grand Duke, Loukas Notaras, of the Byzantine Empire, second in command to the Emperor, was growing frustrated with his rulers' feeble efforts. He was incensed by the beheadings and pushed the Emperor to act with aggression. However, most of the businessmen within the Emperor's ranks viewed the conflict as a threat to business in the Ottoman Empire, and they want more conciliatory efforts to bring peace and maintain harmony for trade. The rift within the Byzantine ranks grew, and the lack of leadership from the Emperor increased the divide. The Emperor's first mistake was ignoring the discontentment amongst his leaders. The second mistake the Emperor makes is depending on the re-enforcements from Pope Nicholas V and the Roman government, who gave at best, a very loose commitment to him for support with no specific timeline or description. The third mistake Emperor Constantine XI made was by turning and appointing Genoese Soldier of fortune Giovanni Giustiniani, to become the military leader over his army. He asked Giustiniani to lead his army in return for the beautiful Greek Island of Lemnos in the Aegean Sea. The appointment infuriated leadership, and they viewed Giustiniani as an Italian mercenary with no loyalty to Constantinople. Emperor Constantine XI had division on all sides of his camp. The fourth mistake was his rejection of Urban, the cannon maker that had presented a grand vision of building the biggest cannon that could fire ½ tonne cannon balls 1 mile and would be capable of destroying anything in its path. Urban wanted his support to construct the most massive cannon the world has ever seen. Emperor Constantine rejected the engineer's technology and sent him away and into the hands of his enemies.

Even though Emperor Constantine XI was outnumbered 10:1 with 9,000 troops, and 26 ships in his harbour, he had a tremendous advantage in the walled city and the infamous cast iron chain blocking entrance into the port. The city protected its inhabitants for a millennium, and a dozen failed sieges, enormous amount of Greek fire in his storehouse, and weapons at his disposal left the Emperor with a false sense of security.

King Mehmed II had a strategic advantage in that his years of planning and mental preparation bolstered his resolve. Alexander the Great never lost a battle, despite the odds, and his resolve, bold strategies, and unbelievable loyalty from his men gave him the edge in every action. Mehmed II endlessly studied Alexander the Great's approach and the importance he places on his plans, tactics, and how he inspired his people to do the impossible. Mehmed II excelled in his preparedness. He focused on 8 fundamental areas; clarity of vision, chain of command, the naval fleet, building Urban's cannon, controlling the flow of trade in the Bosphorous strait, building up his battlefield weaponry, information espionage, and augmenting his elite troops and mercenaries.

Mid-March 1453 King Mehmed II and his army of 120,000 soldiers, 7,000 oxen pulling 70 cannons, 125 navy vessels and thousands of horses set out for the ancient city of Constantinople on a 240-kilometre march. The entire contingent arrived on April 1, 1453. The Emperor Constantine XI and the whole population of Constantinople looked out over the high walls and seen a sea of soldiers and a navy 10x larger. A few days later, April 5, King Mehmed II sent Emperor Constantine XI his final offer for a truce. In this action, King Mehmed II was respecting the rules of battle and military engagement. However, the proposal went unanswered. The next day, April 6th, the first cannon shot was fired.

Urban's dream cannon he named Basilica was 8m long, walls 20 cm thick bronze, 100 oxen to drag it there (240 kilometres), 2.5-meter cannon-balls weighing 500kg. These massive cannons could only fire every 3 hours; Urban named the big cannons "the Bear," and the little cannons "the cubs." Mehmed II gave Urban his dream but imposed a 90-day deadline to complete the construction and prepare for war. These weapons were all deployed on the first day, and after six days of constant bombardment, the walls had suffered immense damage.

King Mehmed II's advisors continuously worried about the threats of the contingency coming from Pope Nicholas V, Rome, Emperor from Hungary, and even the Karamanids from the East. It looms with each day the battle drags on. The most ominous threat was the Venetian fleet being sent by the Pope from Rome.

After two weeks of intense bombardment, he decides to make his move with troops. Mehmed II is a great orator, and he compels his people to attack. He sends in the nimble Janissaries, and their archers and javelin throwers who were no match for the heavy plated Roman soldiers with their enormous swords. Mehmed II lost this first battle in the moot. Mehmed's first attempt to seize the city fails.

Like Alexander the Great, Mehmed II was masterful at intimidation, and he understood the psychological warfare and how to create an aura of strength and how to get the regular inhabitants of the city stirred up and creating anxiety and distraction for the Emperor. Mehmed II would light fires in front of the walls, he would have his men yell, Military bands playing loud music, even though they outnumbered the Byzantines by 10:1 they made that feel larger, and these tactics created a nervousness and a feeling of impending doom.

A few years before the siege, Mehmed asked his stepmother Mara if she would act as an informant, by returning to Hungary with her family because of her ties to the West and relationships she could be crucial for intelligence. She was originally from that region and the royal family, Mara Brankovic. Her husband, Murad II (Mehmed's Father), died a few years prior but stayed in the imperial harem as an Advisor to the new young King. He wanted a mole on the other side of the line, so he sent her back home two years before to gaining the trust of her family and establish lines of communication. He knew she was faithful to him and believed she could become an essential point of intelligence during his siege. He felt the Hungarians and other factions within the Roman Empire would align themselves against him, and they would provide military support to his enemy.

Week 3 into the battle, the walls had suffered enormous damage; Urban's cannons had made the most significant impact on those walls the city has ever seen. However, Mehmed II had suffered loss during his skirmishes outside the gates, and the battle efforts continue on many fronts.

Mehmed II knew from years of study of the previous attempts to siege the city that everyone lost the battle from the sea, and he believed he had to breach the harbour and gain access and launch an attack from that side. He began to deploy his naval strategy. He built up his Navy to a stunning 125 vessels, and he was determined to enter the Golden Horn. The first order of business was to sink or control the Emperor's 26 ships and take parts of the sea wall down through cannon fire. The biggest obstacle he faced was the 30-ton 1/2 half-mile long cast iron chain that reached from the southeastern corner of Constantinople to the other side of the horn's entrance where the Tower of Galata stood. The chain would lower for friendly ships but act as a barrier for enemy or unauthorized vessels. The chain was notorious and had sunk many ships before over the past seven centuries. The chain was a highly effective barrier that kept all back.

The threat of a Genoese fleet coming to the Emperor's aid left Mehmed II with some anxiety, and he believed they needed to stop any incoming support and controlling the harbour and unloading docks, was an essential step to choking the support for the Emperor. Baltaoglu Suleyman was Mehmed II's naval commander and senior advisor. Mehmed charged Baltaoglu to attack any threats from the sea and determine a way to breach the entrance to the port. On April 20th, four Genoese warships did arrive from the Pope Nicholas V. The four ships came from the Mediterranean Sea up the Sea of Marmara to Constantinople. Three of the vessels contained supplies, and one ship was full of military men to help bolster the Emperor's defences.

The Genoese ships were Galleons, and they stood 15 meters over the waterline, 50 meters long, with a mast rising 10 meters tall carrying six sails that created over a 1,000 square meters of sail allowing the ship to travel 7 knots. The Ottomans had more boats but much smaller boats; Galleys, large rowboats, and horse transport boats. The 31 Galleys were considered their assault vessel and were able to launch an attack on the 4 Genoese Galleons. The Galleys were powered by rowing with oars with a long narrow hull but were used by the Romans, Greeks, Illyrians, Phoenicians and the Ottomans on the Mediterranean for centuries. These ships were equipped with rams, catapults and cannons and were useful in open water battles. The primary military method was to blast your enemy as you got closer, creating a lot of strife while getting your vessel close to the enemy to board their ship with your men and enter hand-to-hand combat to overtake that ship. The Genoese Galleons stood 10 meters above the Ottoman Galleys, and it created a massive advantage as they killed the Ottomans as they tried climbing onboard. The Genoese commanders tied their ships together, which created a floating castle and the Roman Army on board the one ship spread to all four corners of this mass of ships and quickly defended the attack.

Despite casualties and burning sails, the wind picked up and blew the four boats past the Ottoman fleet towards the Golden Horn entry point. A 125-piece Ottoman navy could not stop four Genoese ships, and they got through the entry to the Golden Horn. It was a significant victory for the Emperor Constantine XI, and this renewed the spirits of the city and its inhabitants.

The land wall side of Constantinople was continuously being bombarded by cannon fire, while the battles at the moot appear to be at a stalemate. The naval attack was unsuccessful, and the loss of life began to mount for the young King. Mehmed II knew the walls were weak, but the cannon fire was taking long to breach the walls fully, and he enacted his next strategy to collapse the walls. Mehmed II had hired Serbian silver miners to dig tunnels from behind his battle line underground to the walls in an attempt to impair the understructure of the walls and eventually, the bombardment and a weakened foundation would collapse them. The miners make hasty progress and tunnelled their way past the enemy line. However, John Grant, a Scottish miner within the Emperor's Army, realizes Mehmed II's plan and cleverly discovers the exact location of the miners and instructs the men to dig to the tunnel. He successfully finds it, pours Greek fire and blows the shaft and kills many of the Serbian miners and thwarts Mehmed's plan. It appears at this point every project that Mehmed II has there is a response from the Emperor and they successfully push back the Ottomans.

In Hungary, Mara Brankovic is settled into her new life and winning the support and favour of her Father and family. She returned to Hungary at the time Mehmed II defeated the Hungarian invasion led by John Hunyadi. Although she returns because her husband King Murad II died, she comes from the Empire that just defeated their efforts to invade and comes back home with a shroud of concern. Mara Brankovic was a clever lady with much political prowess, and she spent two years before the attack on Constantinople winning the admiration of those around her in the Hungarian court. Three weeks into the battle at Constantinople Mehmed II's progress is notable, but his defeats are mounting, and his efforts so far not enough to win the war. Mara Brankovic begins secretly to send messages to Mehmed II about the contemplations of Rome and the discussions amongst the Serbian and Hungarian courts. The intelligence proves to be valuable as Mehmed II realizes Rome is disorganized, focused on other pressing issues, and the re-enforcements are likely weeks away.

Mehmed II contemplated his next step, and he will not allow these small defeats to stop him. He believed his destiny was the same as Alexander the Great, and that ultimate defeat was not an option and that he needed to find the way to victory and that it was at hand. He devises a new plan amid the battle, and though the odds were against him, and he could retreat with enough to show for that, it is the more magnificent victory that he is after. He doesn't allow compromise or the assuaging voices around him to fall short of the prize. He reflects on his progress, assesses the enemy's weak points, seeks the counsel of his commanders and makes a very bold move with his Navy. Mehmed II decides to secretly move a portion of his Navy overland around the notorious water chain and gain access to the harbour. An ingenious plan using cast iron wheels, metal tracks, wooden cradles, and carpenters. On April 22, Mehmed's Navy transported 70 ships with a team of oxen over the 200' embankment, behind the tower of Galata and slid the vessels down one by one into the port.

The harbour has a very narrow entrance with two towers on each side of the opening and the massive chain stretching from side to side, preventing anyone from entering the harbour without authorization. Mehmed II's idea is unorthodox and clever but requires speed and secrecy to enact in a location that has many spies and the inhabitants of Galata watching. Mehmed II gets support from the leader of Galata and heavily guards the site to keep out enemy spies and pushes his men to deploy his plan. It takes a few days for his men to create a land path by cutting down and hewn trees into a slide along with metal rails and cast-iron wheels. The pathway starts at the entrance to the Bosphorous Strait behind the Tower of Galata and down into the Gold Horn's inner harbour. It was a 1-kilometer stretch, and the Ottomans completed this engineering effort in a matter of days.

The craftiness and gutsiness of the move to bring those ships around at night was a huge victory, and it sent a wave of fear through the hearts of the Byzantine inhabitants of Constantinople. In 1100 years, that harbour has never been in control of another. The fact they are in the port pushes the Emperor now to put his limited resources along this 3.5-mile seawall and monitor Mehmed II's efforts.

Mehmed II knew the strength of the Emperor's army lies in the confidence they had with their leader Giovanni Giustiniani. The Italian mercenary had a pirate-like ambiance and a fierce resolve to protect the city in exchange for the island of Lemnos in the Mediterranean Sea. Mehmed II also realized it was financial gain that motivated Giustiniani and not the love of the country or Empire. Mehmed II sought to have a private meeting with Giustiniani and attempted to convince him to switch sides for a vast fortune and benefits that would have allowed him to prosper greatly. However, Giustiniani was a proud man and was as much concerned about his legacy as he was about prosperity. He chose the more noble direction of protecting the Roman Empire as opposed to turning his back on his Italian heritage. The attempt by Mehmed II did leave an impression on Giustiniani and the young King's tenacious spirit and resolve left Giustiniani with more concern. Mehmed II may not have convinced his adversary to join his side, but he continued his psychological war and kept planting seeds of doubt amongst his enemies.

Six weeks into the battle, the Emperor has renewed hope, even though the situation on the surface looks bleak, but new intelligence has arrived. A couple of informants watching the sea line for signs of help spotted a Venetian Armada of ships in the Mediterranean bound to be heading towards Constantinople. The Roman defenders seem to be willing to die for their city, and now their back-ups appear to be on the horizon. Mehmed II has a choice, and his advisers appear to be pushing for conciliatory efforts before those Venetian ships arrive. As news spread of the Armada, the spirits of the Byzantines rose. However, a few days past and these ships disappeared from the horizon, and the rise in optimism quickly faded with fear and concern the backups would never arrive, or at least in time.

On May 20th, a series of pivotal events transpired for the Ottomans. First, the nervous atmosphere amongst the inhabitant of Constantinople was mounting with the relentless mind games and the psychological warfare of Mehmed II pushing the balance. The great walls of protection for the Byzantines became a prison of their mind. The people longed to be far from that place and not trapped within its confines. A consuming fear struck the city as most dreaded their army was losing the battle and support from Rome was never coming. The Church officials felt they could renew the spirits of the city if they paraded the statute of Mary through the streets and pray along the walls at each spot, they knew the Ottoman's were targeting. The parade began, and the soldiers carrying the statue stumbled in front of all the people and Mary toppled off the platform. The people were stunned, and most believed it was a bad omen. Later that day, a lunar eclipse occurred, and a very pronounced blood-red moon sat in the sky, which created even more fear. The next morning the city was filled with a mysterious fog. This chain of events was like three harbingers that gave the local prophets and soothsayers angst and much to talk about. The Byzantine inhabitants and the Emperor were distressed. Mehmed II was trying to interpret these signs, and his advisors were troubled. However, the arrival of his Stepmother Mara Brankovic from Hungary with word these signs are predictions of victory was all the confirmation and shot of confidence Mehmed II needed. He gathered his troops and gave them the new frontal assault battle plan and told them to await his command.

Both Mehmed II and Constantine XI, during the evening of May 28th, gave rallying speeches to all their people. They wanted them to remember their ancestors, remember your God, your country and fight worthy of this moment. The moment for the Romans was stirring, but Constantine XI was attempting to inspire his people, but it was too late to rally such passions as he didn't lead his people well and left a great divide amongst his leadership that polarized his people. Where Mehmed II's troops were emboldened after weeks of wearing battle but with a leader with deep and passionate conviction to the cause, singularity in vision and purpose, it didn't take much to inspire his people for the final push. His last speech was riveting for the men and his certainty of victory apparent.

On May 29th, early in the morning, 1:30 am, Mehmed II gave the signal to attack. Mehmed II attacks with his first wave, which consisted of the mercenary soldiers, Bashi-Bazouks, fighters that were not well trained but determined. The attack lasted a few hours while his more elite troops rested. The first wave tired the Romans as they didn't have many soldiers and couldn't sustain too long a battle. The second wave of Ottoman Troops, Anatolian Turks, were far more trained and familiar with the battle. This wave was immense in numbers and presented a far more significant threat. Four hours into the battle and wave after wave of Ottoman attack. It appears the defenders may have the upper hand. It was at this point that Giovanni Giustiniani was defending a weak spot at the top of the wall when he was struck by lightning and fell near dead. He was carried off the battlefield leaving his men demoralized and defensive. Mehmed II seized this moment, like Alexander the Great, in many of his battles he led his men into the thick of the action. Mehmed II called his final wave, the Janissaries, his most talented men into the thick of battle. Mehmed II led the last wave himself, and they defeated the remaining defenders and forced their way through the St Romanus Gate. The first time the enemy ever breached the mighty walls.

Emperor Constantine XI turned to his commander and said his city is lost but he won't leave but will fight to the death. The Ottomans conquered the city, and Emperor Constantine XI perished.

May 29th Mehmed, at the age of 21, enters Constantinople and declares himself the new King of Rome. Constantinople renamed Istanbul, became Mehmed II's most famous victory. It was also the first major victory of cannons against a city. It marks the start of the three-hundred-year reign of the Ottoman empire that dominated most of East Europe, North Africa, the Middle East, and West Asia until World War I.

ABOUT THE AUTHOR

I grew up in Sarnia, Ontario, Canada, a beautiful border town mostly surrounded by water. There is a murky side to Sarnia—a shadow city of toxic chemical plants, and an underworld, fraught with trouble. I grew up on the proverbial rough side of the tracks, and saw relatives, friends, and neighbors drawn into Sarnia's dark side to either die or never recover.

This was my early turning point. Witnessing the damaging effects of life in Sarnia inspired me to get out of town—and, ultimately, to aspire to become a CEO.

By 29, I earned my way into a management position British Columbia. However, I wanted more. I brazenly booked a five-minute appointment with the company's CEO, and asked her one single question,

"I want your job, not today, but in 10 years. How do I get it?"

I hoped for a nugget or two of advice, but instead, she cleared her schedule and gave me three hours. Inspired, I spent the next 10 years, helping build five separate companies. I moved through the VP level to C-Suite to CEO in all stages – start-ups, turnaround, mature market, and growth acceleration.

I was still unprepared for what came next.

In August 2008, the Board of Directors of a newly licensed Canadian Bank asked me to act as the COO and senior most advisor to the CEO. I entered this position without any prior experience in banking. After getting up to speed, I developed a 100-day action plan.

A mere four weeks after I started, Lehman Brothers filed bankruptcy triggering the notorious, banking crisis that eroded $10 trillion from the market overnight, collapsing a total of 465 banks. Out the window went my 100-day plan.

Our executive team, myself included, worked around the clock, even sleeping in the boardroom, ready for the opening of the bell in London, Amsterdam, Frankfurt, Tokyo, Shanghai, and Hong Kong—fighting to keep our bank alive.

The Canadian Government watched our every move, hoping to stave off the failure of any Canadian banks. Around the world banks fell like dominoes.

And then the unthinkable happened...

Officials from the Government entered our building and removed our CEO from his position—gone without warning—for a questionable trade that could have led to the failure of the bank. We feared this would lead us to collapse.

At that moment, I became the defacto Bank President! It was a "battlefield promotion."

If I made a critical mistake, the Government would walk in and shut us down. They wouldn't let us fail. They would shut us down.

All the eyes were on me. I felt everyone's fear. Could I walk this company through the financial meltdown? Would we lose the bank license? Is the government going to just shut us down? It was the highest-pressure moment of my career.

They don't teach situations like this in business school or leadership books; you can only learn it through trial by fire. The next six months were a harrowing experience in leadership.

I relied on—and applied—everything I knew about business combined with my convictions about faith and belief. My team and I led the bank through the worst financial crisis in modern history, and all our employees kept their jobs.

The bank experience was a third turning point for me. Next, I lead, as either the Vice-Chairman or CEO, many organizations through turnarounds, financings, IPO, acquisitions, divestitures, carve-outs, growth initiatives, restructurings and capital expansions.

I'm driven to create real enduring value for shareholders and employees. I think great companies are like many-faceted diamonds. Every facet of a company matters—including, but not limited to, profit.

My passion is creating great companies that last—that are driven by the guidelines of ethical leadership and good business practices.

Nine of the ten companies I've turned around are still thriving today.

Today, with 30 years of leadership experience under my belt, I'm more passionate than ever about making the world a better place through business.

ENDNOTES AND CITATIONS

[1] U.S. Small Business Administration. Cited in Forbes. https://www.forbes.com/sites/forbes-personal-shopper/2020/07/02/best-4th-of-july-sales-happening-now/#109636a45789

[2] Jay Jakub, Senior Director of External Research Mars, Incorporated/Catalyst & Co-author, Completing Capitalism, quoted from ConsciousCapitalism.org.

[3] Quoted from: *Harvard Business Review*: *Companies that Practice "Conscious Capitalism" Perform 10x Better* by Tony Schwartz, CEO of The Energy Project

[4] Andrew Hewitt, Game Changers 500, quoted from Entrepreneur Magazine.

[5] *The Four Principles of 'Conscious Capitalism' Entrepreneur Magazine*, by R. Michael Anderson, founder The Executive Joy Institute.

[6] Gallup State of the American Manager: Analytics and Advice for Leader" report 2015.

[7] 2017 Cone Communications CSR Study, reported in SustainableBrands.com

[8] From a three-year study by Kenexa High Performance Institute in London, quoted from "CSR — the Business Benefits" on the Qualtrics website.

[9] Gallup Report, a study of 2.5 million manager-led teams: "State of the American Manager: Analytics and Advice for Leaders" report

[10] 15FIVE study reported July 23, 2020 survey of 1000 full-time employees in the US, as reported on PRWeb.

[11] Entrepreneur Magazine, "5 ways to Strengthen Your Bond with Your Team" by Matt Straz.

[12] United States Marine Corp, Marine Corps Training Command B130936 Student Handout.

[13] "Benefits of Collaboration for Teams and Business. Source: Queens University of Charlotte.

[14] Cited from the BIT.AI Blog. Data source Salesforce.

[15] Gusto survey, as cited in BIT.AI.

[16] Gallup poll, cited in Forbes Jan 16, 2019: "10 Timely Statistics About the Connection Between Employee Engagement and Wellness."

17   Behaviors Driving Teaming Success: Dr. Amy Edmondson, Harvard Business Professor.

18   "The Right Culture: Not Just About Employee Satisfaction": Gallup April 12, 2017.

19   SHRM Globoforce Survey, January 2018.

20   Forbes: "Ten Timely Statistics About the Connection Between Employee Engagement and Wellness."

21   Ibid.

22   Report from the Engagement Institute—a joint study by The Conference Board, Sirota-Mercer, Deloitte, ROI, The Culture Works and Consulting LLP.

23   "Beyond Six Sigma" by Dr. Jody Meulaner, Feb 28 2019 Engineering.com

24   Summers, Donna C.S (2011). *Lean Six Sigma: Process Improvement Tools and Techniques*. One Lake St, Upper Saddle River, New Jersey: Prentice Hall. ISBN 978-0-13-512510-6.

25   Official Summary of "Rising to Power, the Journey of Exceptional Executives" by Ron A. Carucci and Eric C. Hansen, Main Idea Press.

26   "Decision Making — Leaders, Stop Avoiding Hard Decisions" — Harvard Business Review citing the study "Rising to Power — The Journey of Exceptional Executives"

27   GALLUP report: "More Harm Than Good: The Truth About Performance Reviews."

28   Ibid

29   Ibid

30   Steve Roesler, from his blog "All Things Workplace".

31   Quoted from Mary Ann Masarech, employee engagement practice leader with BlessingWhite, a division of GP Strategies.

32   Research Report "Forget about engagement; let's talk about great days at work" Blessing White, a Division of GP Strategies.

33   Ibid.

34   Ibid.

35   *Winning*, by Jack Welch, Harper Business ISBN-13 978-0060753948

36   "How Much Time Do We Spend in Meetings?", The Muse, survey from various compiled sources. Found on Muse.com

37   Annual Global 500 report from Brand Finance 2020.

38   Data from Shopify Plus, 2019.

39   Hubspot survey, 2020.

40   Statista data, 2020.

41   Top Box Office Logline Examples, FilmDaily.tv

42   Cited from 11 elevator pitch examples for entrepreneurs." by Amy Saunders; Keap.

43   Based on machine learning and AI analysis of 1 million sales phone call recordings, Gong, 2020 "Nine Secret Elements of Highly Effective Sales Conversations."

44   Hubspot data 2020. Cited from Zety.com

45 Ibid

46 Statista 2020, cited from Zety.com ·

47 "Apex predators in the wild: which mammals are the most dangerous?" Discover Wildlife, BBC. Discoverwildlife.com

48 2.46% to 3.26% is the national sales conversion rate (Statista). 2.86% is the national ecommerce conversion from visitors rate.

49 Ibid.

50 Gong Labs, 2017 data https://www.gong.io/blog/this-is-how-a-bad-quarter-starts-in-sales-as-illustrated-by-data/

51 Listen more" Gong, 2020 "Nine Secret Elements of Highly Effective Sales Conversations."

52 Ibid.

53 *Ultimate Sales Machine*, by Chet Holmes, Chapter 4 Becoming a Brilliant Strategist

54 Ibid.

55 Hubspot survey 2019. https://blog.hubspot.com/sales/sales-process-?_ga=2.14738422.1389194703.1539605304-54427254.1534474280

56 Ibid.

57 Ibid.

58 "The Short Life of Online Sales Leads"—Harvard Business Review. https://hbr.org/2011/03/the-short-life-of-online-sales-leads

59 "Is your Lead Management Leaking? We Tested 433 Companies." Drift.

60 "The Seven best Discovery Call Tips for Sales" Gong Labs.

61 *Strategy Implementation Findings 2020* Bridges Business Consultancy survey.

62 Bridges 2016 Survey "Strategy Implementation"

63 Ibid.

64 Six Disciplines research, 2016.

65 "Erich Ludendorff: Tactical Genius, Strategic Fool" by Williamson Murray, Historynet.

66 Ibid

67 "Many Strategies Fail Because They're Not Actually Strategies" — *Harvard Business Review*, by Freek Vermeulen, professor of strategy and entrepreneurship at London Business School.

68 Cited from Phrases.org.uk

69 Harvard Business Review Sept, 2004: "Why People Follow the Leader: The Power of Transference."

70 University of Scranton research.

71 Ibid.

72 2014 study in *Emotion* magazine.

73 2012 study published in Personality and Individual Differences. Multiple studies on psychological health, notably by Robert A. Emmons, Ph.D. Cited from Forbes Magazine: "7 Scientifically Proven Benefits of Gratitude That Will Motivate You to Give Thanks Year-Round."

74 Ibid.

[75] *Indian Journal of Psychology* https://www.ncbi.nlm.nih.gov/pmc/articles/PMC2802367/)

[76] Quoted from Peak Sports, "The Importance of Visualization in Sports."

[77] Microsoft Data, Jan 22, 2018 reported by Cision.

[78] K-State study (k-state.edu) "How long can a person stay focused?"

[79] Research report: Top 20 Reasons Startups Fail. https://www.cbinsights.com/research/startup-failure-reasons-top/

[80] *Is Pivoting a Last-Ditch Effort or a Sound Business Strategy? Entrepreneur https://www.entrepreneur.com/article/310515*

[81] https://www.psychologytoday.com/ca/blog/flourish-and-thrive/202002/6-powerful-ways-build-new-habits